DSE212
Mapping Psychology

Book **1** Chapters **6-9**

We would like to dedicate this course to the memory of Brenda Smith, Psychology Staff Tutor and member of the course team, who died during the final year of the course's production. She had been a Psychology Staff Tutor since 1995, first in Scotland and then most recently in Ireland, but her close association with the Open University stretches back much further than this. She was an Open University student herself and then later returned to teach and was a tutor who enthused and supported very many students throughout their social science studies. At her funeral one of these students spoke very movingly of her warmth and energy and of the fact that she had really 'made a difference' to their lives. She certainly also made a difference to our DSE212 course team, where her commitment to education for mature students was clear in everything that she said and did, and her immensely hard work influenced many of our plans for the teaching and learning strategy of the course and the content of the texts. She contributed enormously at both a professional and personal level, particularly to the early work of the course team, and we hope that her influence on the course will shine through, helping it in turn to 'make a difference' to the lives of all the students who will study it in the coming years.

DSE212
Mapping Psychology

Book **1** Chapters **6-9**

Edited by Dorothy Miell, Ann Phoenix and Kerry Thomas

This publication forms part of an Open University course DSE212 *Exploring Psychology*. Details of this and other Open University courses can be obtained from the Student Registration and Enquiry Service, The Open University, PO Box 197, Milton Keynes MK7 6BJ, United Kingdom: tel. +44 (0)870 333 4340, email general-enquiries@open.ac.uk

Alternatively, you may visit the Open University website at http://www.open.ac.uk where you can learn more about the wide range of courses and packs offered at all levels by The Open University.

To purchase a selection of Open University course materials visit http://www.ouw.co.uk, or contact Open University Worldwide, Michael Young Building, Walton Hall, Milton Keynes MK7 6AA, United Kingdom for a brochure. tel. +44 (0)1908 858785; fax +44 (0)1908 858787; email ouwenq@open.ac.uk

The Open University
Walton Hall, Milton Keynes
MK7 6AA

First published 2002. Second edition 2007.

Edited and designed by The Open University.

Typeset by Pam Callow, S & P Enterprises (rfod) Ltd.

Printed and bound in the UK by Charlesworth Press, Wakefield.

ISBN 978 0 7492 1628 3

2.1

DSE212 course team: production

Open University staff

Dr Dorothy Miell, Senior Lecturer in Psychology, Faculty of Social Sciences (Course Team Chair)

Dr Paul Anand, Lecturer in Economics, Faculty of Social Sciences

Peter Barnes, Lecturer in Centre for Childhood, Development and Learning, Faculty of Education and Language Studies

Pam Berry, Key Compositor

Dr Nicola Brace, Lecturer in Psychology, Faculty of Social Sciences

Dr Nick Braisby, Lecturer in Psychology, Faculty of Social Sciences

Maurice Brown, Software Designer

Sue Carter, Staff Tutor, Faculty of Social Sciences

Annabel Caulfield, Course Manager, Faculty of Social Sciences

Lydia Chant, Course Manager, Faculty of Social Sciences

Dr Troy Cooper, Staff Tutor, Faculty of Social Sciences

Crystal Cunningham, Researcher, BBC/OU

Shanti Dass, Editor

Sue Dobson, Graphic Artist

Alison Edwards, Editor

Marion Edwards, Software Designer

Jayne Ellery, Production Assistant, BBC/OU

Dr Linda Finlay, Associate Lecturer, Faculty of Social Sciences, co-opted member of course team

Alison Goslin, Designer

Professor Judith Greene, Professor of Psychology (retired), Faculty of Social Sciences

Celia Hart, Picture Researcher

Professor Wendy Hollway, Professor of Psychology, Faculty of Socia Sciences

Silvana Ioannou, Researcher, BBC/OU

Dr Amy Johnston, Lecturer in Behavioural Neuroscience, Faculty of Science

Dr Adam Joinson, Lecturer in Educational Technology, Institute of Educational Technology

Sally Kynan, Research Associate in Psychology

Andrew Law, Executive Producer, BBC/OU

Dr Martin Le Voi, Senior Lecturer in Psychology, Faculty of Social Sciences

Dr Karen Littleton, Senior Lecturer in Centre for Childhood, Development and Learning, Faculty of Education and Language Studies

Dr Bundy Mackintosh, Lecturer in Psychology, Faculty of Social Sciences

Marie Morris, Course Secretary

Dr Peter Naish, Lecturer in Psychology, Faculty of Social Sciences

Daniel Nettle, Lecturer in Biological Psychology, Departments of Biological Sciences and Psychology

John Oates, Senior Lecturer in Centre for Childhood, Development and Learning, Faculty of Education and Language Studies

Michael Peet, Producer, BBC/OU

Dr Ann Phoenix, Senior Lecturer in Psychology, Faculty of Social Sciences

Dr Graham Pike, Lecturer in Psychology, Faculty of Social Sciences

Dr Ilona Roth, Senior Lecturer in Psychology, Faculty of Social Sciences

Brenda Smith, Staff Tutor, Faculty of Social Sciences

Dr Richard Stevens, Senior Lecturer in Psychology, Faculty of Social Sciences

Colin Thomas, Lead Software Designer

Dr Kerry Thomas, Senior Lecturer in Psychology, Faculty of Social Sciences

Dr Frederick Toates, Reader in Psychobiology, Faculty of ScienceJenny Walker, Production Director, BBC/OU

Dr Helen Westcott, Lecturer in Psychology, Faculty of Social Sciences

Dr Clare Wood, Lecturer in Centre for Childhood, Development and Learning, Faculty of Education and Language Studies

Christopher Wooldridge, Editor

External authors and critical readers

Dr Koula Asimakopoulou, Tutor Panel

Debbie Balchin, Tutor Panel

Dr Peter Banister, Head of Psychology and Speech Pathology Department, Manchester Metropolitan University

Clive Barrett, Tutor Panel

Dr Kevin Buchanan, Senior Lecturer in Psychology, University College, Northampton

Dr Richard Cains, Tutor Panel

Professor Stephen Clift, Tutor Panel

Linda Corlett, Associate Lecturer, Faculty of Social Sciences

Victoria Culpin, Tutor Panel

Dr Tim Dalgleish, Research Clinical Psychologist, Brain Sciences Unit, Cambridge

Dr Graham Edgar, Tutor Panel, Research Scientist, BAE SYSTEMS

Patricia Fisher, Equal Opportunities critical reader

David Goddard, Tutor Panel

Dr Dan Goodley, Lecturer in Inclusive Education, University of Sheffield

Victoria Green, Student Panel

Dr Mary Hanley, Senior Lecturer in Psychology, University College, Northampton

Dr Jarrod Hollis, Associate Lecturer, Faculty of Social Sciences

Rob Jarman, Tutor Panel

Dr Hélène Joffe, Lecturer in Psychology, University College London

Dr Helen Kaye, Associate Lecturer, Faculty of Social Sciences

Professor Matt Lambon-Ralph, Professor of Cognitive Neuroscience, University of Manchester

Rebecca Lawthom, Senior Lecturer in Psychology, Manchester Metropolitan University

Kim Lock, Student Panel

Patricia Matthews, Tutor Panel

Dr Elizabeth Ockleford, Tutor Panel

Penelope Quest, Student Panel

Susan Ram, Student Panel

Dr Alex Richardson, Senior Research Fellow in Psychology and Neuroscience, Imperial College of Medicine, London, also Research Affiliate, University Laboratory of Physiology, Oxford

Dr Carol Sweeney, Tutor Panel

Dr Annette Thomson, Associate Lecturer, Faculty of Social Sciences

Dr Stella Tickle, Tutor Panel

Carol Tindall, Senior Lecturer in Psychology, Manchester Metropolitan University

Jane Tobbell, Senior Lecturer in Psychology, Manchester Metropolitan University

Martin Treacy, Associate Lecturer, Faculty of Social Sciences

Professor Aldert Vrij, Professor in Applied Social Psychology, University of Portsmouth

External assessors

Professor Martin Conway, Professor of Psychology, Durham University

Professor Anne Woollet, Professor of Psychology, University of East London

DSE212 course team: update

Open University staff

Dr Nicola Brace, Senior Lecturer in Psychology, Faculty of Social Sciences (Course Team Chair)

Lesley Adams, Course Manager, Faculty of Social Sciences

Melanie Bayley, Media Project Manager, LTS Media

Dr Esther Burkitt, Lecturer in Developmental Psychology, Centre for Childhood, Development and Learning, Faculty of Education and Language Studies

Dr Jovan Byford, Lecturer in Psychology, Faculty of Social Sciences

Sue Carter, Staff Tutor, Faculty of Social Sciences

Lisa Collender, Assistant Print Buyer

Lene Connolly, Print Buyer

Dr Troy Cooper, Staff Tutor, Faculty of Social Sciences

Karen Hagan, Staff Tutor, Faculty of Social Sciences

Paul Hillery, Graphics Media Developer, LTS

Dr Martin Le Voi, Senior Lecturer in Psychology, Faculty of Social Sciences

Dr Helen Lucey, Lecturer in Psychology, Faculty of Social Sciences

Jo Mack, Sound and Vision Producer, LTS

Margaret McManus, Media Assistant (Rights and Picture Research), LTS Media

Professor Dorothy Miell, Professor of Psychology, Faculty of Social Sciences

Marie Morris, Course Secretary, Faculty of Social Sciences

Dr Johanna Motzkau, Lecturer in Psychology, Faculty of Social Sciences

John O'Dwyer, Media Project Manager, LTS Media

Professor Ann Phoenix, Professor of Social and Developmental Psychology, Faculty of Social Sciences

Dr Graham Pike, Senior Lecturer in Psychology, Faculty of Social Sciences

Alvaro Roberts, Media Assistant, LTS Media

Dr Kathy Robinson, Lecturer in Psychology, Faculty of Social Sciences

Dr Lynne Rogers, Lecturer in Psychology, Faculty of Social Sciences

Dr Ilona Roth, Senior Lecturer in Psychology, Faculty of Science

Emma Sadera, Editor, LTS Media

Dr Jim Turner, Lecturer in Psychology, Faculty of Social Sciences

Howie Twiner, Graphics Media Developer, LTS Media

Dr Helen Westcott, Senior Lecturer in Psychology, Faculty of Social Sciences

Christopher Wooldridge, Editor

External authors and critical readers

Elizabeth Barnes, Associate Lecturer, Faculty of Social Sciences

Dr Susan Cave, Associate Lecturer, Faculty of Social Sciences

Dr Helen Clegg, Lecturer in Psychology, University of Northampton

Linda Corlett, Academic Consultant, Faculty of Social Sciences

Dr Tom Dickins, Principal Lecturer in Psychology, University of East London

Dr Graham Edgar, Senior Lecturer in Psychology, University of Gloucestershire

Dr Linda Green, Associate Lecturer, Faculty of Social Sciences

Dr Brenda K. Todd, Lecturer in Psychology, City University

Julia Willerton, Associate Lecturer, Faculty of Social Sciences, co-opted member of course team

External assessor

Dr Judi Ellis, Head of School, University of Reading

Contents

Perception and attention

Graham Edgar

Contents

Aims

This chapter aims to:

- outline the processes of perception and attention
- show how perceptual processes relate to sensation – the registration of information by the sensory organs
- discuss the role of attention in mediating between sensation and perception
- describe the methods used to study perception and attention
- consider how processes of perception and attention are affected by personal, social and cultural factors
- discuss some of the issues that arise when perception and attention are studied in a laboratory setting rather than in the complex environments in which perception and attention usually operate.

1 Introduction

Our senses are constantly bombarded with a vast amount of information: several senses will be receiving information simultaneously and some continuously. There is therefore a huge amount of information available to us, but what happens to it once it has been sensed? In thinking about this question it is important to draw a distinction between sensation and perception.

The term **sensation** refers to how stimuli in the outside world are detected by our senses. The term **perception** refers to what happens to information after it has been detected by the senses. Perception is the processing and modification of sensory information by the internal cognitive processes of the individual, and the end result of that processing. This is an interactive process because, although sensory information provides a crucial input to our cognitive processes, our cognitive processes also influence our sensory systems. This complex interaction is a fundamental feature of perception.

In this chapter we shall explore the way in which one particular cognitive process, that of **attention**, influences what we perceive. Attention is a selection process that operates between what is sensed and what is perceived.

Sensation
The initial detection, by our senses, of stimuli in the world.

Perception
The end result of the processing and modification of sensory information by the internal cognitive processes of the individual.

Attention
A selection process that operates between what is sensed and what is perceived.

A great deal of sensation is concerned with physiological structures and physiological processes. The aim of this chapter is to move beyond the physiology of these sensory structures and detection processes in order to provide an insight into aspects of perception and attention that fall within the remit of cognitive psychology.

Empirical research in cognitive psychology gathered pace following the Second World War. In Chapter 3 and its Commentary, you learned that, although the cognitive psychology tradition began very early in the history of psychology, it was pushed aside for a while by the dominance of the behaviourist tradition, which in its most extreme form denied the existence of cognitive processes. The return of interest in cognitive psychology stemmed, at least initially, from attempts to solve practical problems identified during the Second World War; for instance, pilots attempting to monitor information from a number of sources, or ground staff attempting to guide aircraft into congested aerodromes. This particular strand of cognitive psychology is the **information processing approach**. 'Information' was defined in Chapter 3 as something that is received via the senses, further processed or transformed, and then used to guide action and behaviour. The idea of information and its processing has clear parallels with what has been introduced in this chapter so far: the idea of sensation, attention and perception as related processes.

Information processing approach
An approach that likens cognitive processes (attention, perception, etc.) to the workings of a computer: moving, storing and transforming information.

In Chapter 3, you read that cognitive psychology uses machine metaphors to further its understanding of what goes on 'in the head'. It was suggested that important parallels can be seen between the way that people and machines deal with information despite their obvious differences. The early use of this kind of metaphor, such as the idea of flow charts of 'information processing', coincided with technological advances in telecommunications. Quite soon, the metaphor became that of the computer, with all its complexities. Cognitive psychology is continually exploiting technical advances in computing and mathematics to further psychological understandings of information processing.

By considering the human mind as an information processing system, it is possible for cognitive psychology to treat the mind rather like a computer and to examine how information is gathered, stored and manipulated. One of the appeals of this approach is that it permits research and theorizing to continue even when there are only limited techniques for studying the functioning of the human brain directly. As brain-imaging techniques develop, researchers are increasingly able to study directly how our brains work, an area of study referred to as **neuroscience**. As a result, there has been a significant development in research into perception and attention due to an increasing integration of cognitive psychology with neuroscience to create what is called **cognitive neuroscience**. This integration allows cognitive theories describing how information is processed by the mind to be linked to explanations of the physical functioning of the brain.

This chapter will attempt to cover the full range of approaches described above and will take a similar starting point to that taken by the early cognitive psychologists: the study of practical problems. These examples will help to give an understanding of what the difference is between sensation and perception, and how attention can be seen as a mediating stage between the two. They will also emphasize that perception and attention are not just 'dry' theoretical constructs but are central to psychological explanations of complex behaviour in everyday contexts, and that research on perception and attention can be applied to help solve practical problems in everyday life.

Neuroscience
A field of study that considers the workings of the brain.

Cognitive neuroscience
A field of study that considers the neural mechanisms underlying cognitive processes.

1.1 What is the difference between sensation and perception?

What differentiates sensation from perception? To try and unravel this, let us start with a demonstration. Look at the picture in Figure 6.1.

What do you 'see'? You see a pattern of light and dark patches. This is the *sensation* that the picture gives rise to. Some people will also immediately 'see' more than just light and dark blobs – they will see the image of a cow. Some people may not see the cow immediately – theyt will perceive only a pattern of light and dark blobs. Thus different people may *perceive* the same image in different ways. The sensation is approximately the same for everybody but the perception can be very different.

It may be that, even if you did not recognize the picture immediately, as soon as you were told it was a cow, you recognized it as such. The picture has not changed, but you now have a little more *knowledge* about it. If you still cannot see the cow, have a look at Figure 6.10 at the end of this chapter, which should increase your knowledge still further, then look back to the picture in Figure 6.1. Now can you see the cow? If you can,

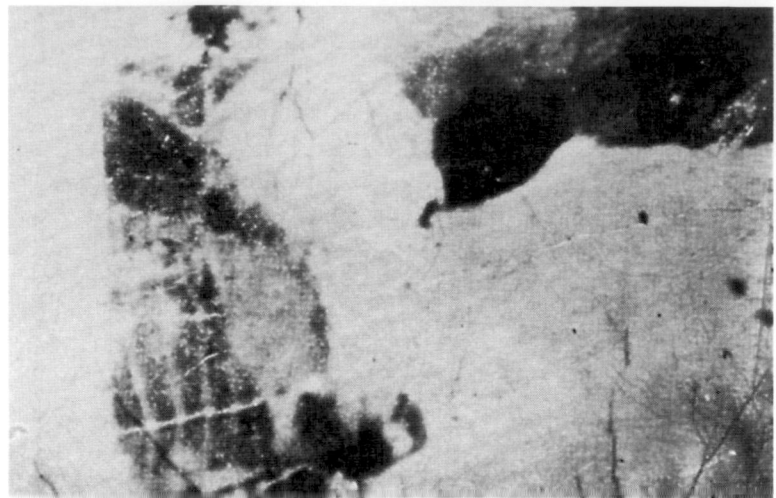

Figure 6.1   What do you see? (Source: Dallenbach, 1951)

but could not before, your *perception* has altered as a result of the extra knowledge you gained from the second picture; from now on you will always see the cow if you are shown this picture again. The sensation, however, will still be the same.

This example is, of course, based on *visual* perception. The same processes apply equally well, however, to the other senses. For instance, consider a sound that you hear for the first time, such as the warning 'boing' on a new computer. The first time you hear it, it is just a 'boing'. After hearing it a few times, your perception is likely to have changed, engendering feelings of dread as you realize that the 'boing' indicates that your machine has just crashed without saving the assignment on which you have spent the last four hours. As with seeing the cow, the sensation remains the same but the perception can change markedly.

There is an implicit assumption in the preceding discussion that you are *consciously aware* of what you perceive, whereas you may not be consciously aware of all that you sense. **Conscious perception** is the conscious awareness of some aspect(s) of the environment as a result of the integration of filtered sensory information with stored knowledge. This does not mean, however, that people only use sensory information of which they are consciously aware. As we shall consider in Section 2.5, some sensory information can be processed *automatically* below the level of conscious awareness. This is called **unconscious perception** and information perceived at this level may still influence how we react. In this chapter, however, the term 'perception' will be used to refer to conscious perception.

Conscious perception
The conscious awareness of some aspect(s) of the environment as a result of the integration of filtered sensory information with stored knowledge.

Unconscious perception
The result of sensory information processed *automatically* below the level of conscious awareness but still capable of influencing how we react and behave.

One of the big differences between sensation and perception is that perception is influenced by the knowledge that an individual already has about the world as a result of experience. Thus the information coming in from the senses, often called **bottom-up information**, is interpreted in the light of stored knowledge, often called **top-down information**, to arrive at a perception of what is present in the outside world and what it means.

1.2 Perceiving the world

Imagine something that you do almost every day. Maybe driving to work, walking to the shops, or even just your routine for getting up in the morning. Think about aspects of the task. For instance, if you are thinking of your journey to work, consider the landmarks you pass, roads that you take, etc. You can probably remember the journey quite well. For example, you drive down the road, turn left by the corner shop, go over the traffic lights, and so on. Now think of a specific instance of that journey, maybe the second time you made that journey last week. Is your recollection of that specific journey different from your 'general' recollection? Can you remember any details specific to that *particular* journey? How many red cars did you see? How many times did you hear a dog bark? You may (or may not) be surprised at how little of a specific journey you can remember. Have you ever arrived at your destination and realized that you have very little recollection of the journey?

From this bit of introspection you may have the idea that perhaps there are two possible representations of your regular journey that you have stored. There is the 'general knowledge' of that journey that is built up over many repetitions – and there are also the specific details that make up a representation of a particular journey. These reflect two different aspects of memory. The general knowledge of the journey is what is usually referred to as 'semantic memory' and the specific details of a *particular* journey would be held in 'episodic memory'. These two concepts will not be considered further in this chapter but will be formally defined and discussed in Chapter 8.

Bottom-up information
Information about the world that flows 'up' from the senses.

Top-down information
Information flowing 'down' from stored knowledge which can influence the interpretation of sensory information.

Notice that, in the above passage, you were asked to introspect *about your personal experience – to search your memory for general journeys, and for a specific journey. This introspecting task provided you with data of the kind we have called 'inner experience' (see Section 2.2 of the* Introduction to this book *– 'A brief look at different kinds of data') and is a good illustration of the use of introspection as a method in psychology. What you experienced was predictable because many people have been asked to do this before – with roughly the same outcome. That is, that their semantic memory of their daily journey would be good, but their episodic memory would be poor. In the study of perception and attention this kind of introspecting and reporting has been used quite often.*

The important question that arises from the demonstration is 'why do you remember so little of a particular journey?' One possibility may be that you simply do not 'take in' a lot of the details of your journey. In other words, you are not consciously aware of some stimuli that impinge on you as you go on your journey. But why not? You were, hopefully, looking around you as you drove to work. Your eyes would have been registering patterns of light and movement, your ears would have been picking up sounds. If you have missed things, you would probably say that you were not 'paying attention' to them. As mentioned above, this introduces a crucial concept, that of attention, which is an essential process operating between what we sense and what we perceive.

Summary Section 1

- When our senses detect stimuli in the world, this gives rise to sensation.
- Conscious perception is the end result of the integration of information from our senses with stored knowledge.
- Information flowing 'up' from the senses is referred to as 'bottom up'. Information flowing 'down' from stored knowledge is referred to as 'top down'.
- Not all perception is conscious, but unconscious perception can still have an effect on our behaviour.
- Much of what we sense we do not consciously perceive as it is filtered out by another cognitive process, attention.

2   **What is attention?**

It seems reasonable to start with one of the earliest written definitions of attention, provided by William James (1890): 'Everyone knows what attention is. It is the taking possession by the mind in clear and vivid form of one out of what seem several stimulus objects or trains of thought.'

What did James mean by the mind 'taking possession' of one stimulus object or train of thought? Without wishing to delve into the precise nature of the mind it is worth elaborating on the idea of attention as a process of *selection*. We could perhaps amend James' original definition a little to something like: 'Attention is the *process* by which cognitive processing resources are allocated.'

The crucial aspect of these definitions is that they emphasize that the individual is selecting only *some* of the information available, with the implication that the non-selected information is not 'attended to'. This raises the possibility that you do not consciously perceive all of the stimuli that you look at. The senses respond to stimuli in the world, receptors are activated, neurons fire – but somewhere between those senses and your conscious awareness of the stimuli, the information goes astray. If, in the previous section, you struggled to remember your particular journey or task, you may have been wondering whether it is really possible that you could have taken so little information in. Could you have been 'paying attention' to so little?

Change blindness

The following rather elegant experiment provides a nice demonstration of how little we sometimes take in as we go about our daily lives. Simons and Levin (1998) conducted a study to illustrate a phenomenon referred to as 'change blindness'. Their study was an attempt to replicate, in an everyday setting, the findings from a number of laboratory experiments that suggest that people fail to detect changes to photographs under some conditions.

6.1 A study of change blindness (Simons and Levin, 1998)

The study was conducted on the campus of Cornell University and involved a researcher carrying a map and approaching a pedestrian to ask for directions to a nearby building (picture a). Ten to fifteen seconds after the initial approach, two other researchers, who are carrying a door, rudely passed between them (picture b). The researcher, who had initially been asking for directions, took over carrying one end of the door and moved away, leaving one of the original door-carriers in his place, who then produced his own copy of the map and continued to ask directions (picture c). The pedestrian was now talking to a completely different person from the one that had originally approached him/her. Despite the fact that the two researchers differed in height (by about 5cm), clothing, and tone of voice, only about half of the pedestrians noticed the change.

(a) (b) (c) (d)

Switching the researcher (Source: Simons and Levin, 1998)

This study is an excellent example of how little of the available information we take in as we go about our daily lives. We will return to it later in the chapter when we have considered other aspects of attention.

In a modification of this study, researchers manipulated the 'social group' of the enquirer – with the researchers this time dressed as construction workers (assumed to be a different social group from the people that were approached for directions). It has been suggested that people tend to focus attention on the *individual* features of a person from a similar social group – but on the general *group* features of a person from a different group (e.g. Rothbart and John, 1985). Thus, in the Simons and Levin study, this would lead to a prediction that the pedestrians should be less likely to detect the change in the 'construction workers' – and this was indeed the case. This study gives a fascinating insight into the interaction of perception, attention and social identity that you met in Chapter 1. It also shows how studies can be used to investigate quite complex phenomena that involve social cues and motivations. The experimental approach to social and motivational factors in perception is explored in Chapter 7.

The Simons and Levin study provides a striking example of how much information we may *not* take in as we go about our daily lives. This leads to an important question for psychologists studying this area – why do we take in so little, or, in other words, why do we not just take in and process everything?

The answer is simple: we *cannot* process everything, we just do not have the brainpower to do it. There is arguably an infinite amount of information in the outside world that we could take in, and our brains (even if very intricate) are only a finite size. Thus, the argument goes, our brains are limited in terms of how much they can take in, process, and store.

2.1 Limited capacity theories of attention

The idea that the amount of information that we can attend to is limited is embodied in a theory put forward by Kahneman (1973), which suggests that within the brain there is some sort of **limited-capacity central processor**. This processor is responsible for analysing incoming information and integrating it with information already held in memory. Unfortunately, as the processor is of limited capacity, some information cannot be processed – and this is the reason why you may be unaware of so much that is happening around you.

One interesting issue is whether the capacity of the processor always remains the same. Can it always cope with the same amount of information coming in? Kahneman suggests that arousal may influence

Limited-capacity central processor
A hypothetical construct used to explain why it is not possible to process all incoming information simultaneously.

the capacity of the processor: the higher the level of arousal the more information can be taken in and processed.

So how do cognitive psychologists design empirical studies to test hypotheses that address complex cognitive processes such as those discussed above? How do they test competing theories? The solution is to use a *simplified* version of the processes, a version that can be brought into the psychological laboratory. Providing the simple version is simple enough, and involves only a very limited number of the many variables that may be operating in everyday cognitive processing, and these variables can be controlled, then the requirements of the experimental method can be met (see the Featured Method Box: Experiments I in Chapter 3).

However, there is a key difference between the behaviourists' use of experiments, as illustrated in Chapter 3, and the way that cognitive psychologists approach experimentation. Cognitive psychologists use experiments to make inferences about 'what is going on in the head'. Thus the dependent variable will be a behaviour of some kind that can be measured in an objective fashion, and the overall design of the experiment will be such that clear inferences can be made about the nature of cognitive processes. A number of such experiments can be classified under the general heading of **dual-task studies** and examples of these studies are described in Box 6.2.

Dual-task studies
Studies that look at how different *pairs* of tasks interact when a participant attempts to perform both tasks of the pair at the same time.

6.2 FEATURED METHOD

Experiments II: Laboratory experiments designed to permit inferences about cognitive processes

Dual-task studies of attention

In dual-task studies, cognitive psychologists try to understand the process by which limited attentional resources are allocated. In everyday life, we cannot attend to everything as there are just too many things going on at once. Consider driving. You are required to attend to the state of the car. Is this car running correctly? Do you need to switch the lights on? You need to attend to numerous other things in the world around you. Is that cyclist going to come out of that side road? Why has the car in front braked? It is difficult for a psychologist to try to work out all the processes that are going on although, as we shall see later in the chapter, some very useful studies have been carried out in realistic settings.

However, it *is* possible to study attentional processes in the laboratory. In the example described here the burden of variables is reduced to just two: the participants are asked to do just two things at the same time: hence the name, dual-task studies. In the laboratory the psychologist can pair *different types of tasks* together; it is this pairing of *types of* tasks that is the experimental manipulation.

It is possible then to see whether certain tasks interfere with each other, and whether it is possible to do some things together at the same time without a problem. Thus, the cognitive psychologist has created in the laboratory a simplified and controllable version of everyday complexity.

To see how this works, let us consider one of the earliest of the dual-task studies. Posner and Boies (1971) asked participants to do two things at once:

1   One task was a letter-matching task. A warning signal was followed by visual presentation of a letter. After an interval of half a second, another letter was presented and participants were asked to judge whether the letters were the same, and to indicate this by pressing a button with their *right* hand as quickly as possible. How quickly the participants responded was recorded.

2   The other task, to be performed simultaneously, was to listen for the presentation of an auditory tone, which could be presented at different times during the visual task, and respond when they heard it by pressing a button with their *left* hand.

Posner and Boies found that if the auditory tone sounded *at the same time* as a letter was presented then the time taken for the participants to make a response was slower than if the auditory tone sounded in between presentation of the letters. This suggests that participants did not have sufficient resources to process and make a response to the two things (the letter and the tone) simultaneously, providing support for the notion of a limited pool of resources. In this experiment the dependent variable was the participants' **response time**, a variable that is commonly used in psychological experiments.

Response time
A measure of how quickly a participant can make a response to a certain stimulus.

The usefulness of the dual-task method is illustrated by a later study that just changed one feature of the original Posner and Boies study and obtained a completely different result (McLeod, 1977). McLeod simply changed the required response to the auditory tone from pressing a button to saying 'bip'. With this small change McLeod found that even if the tone sounded at the same time as the letter was presented, reaction time was *not* slowed. Thus, if the types of response required for the two tasks are separated (from two button presses to one button press and saying 'bip') the interference disappears. This suggests that the resource limitation was in making the *response* to the stimuli, and that if the modality of one of the responses is changed then there is no interference. The implication is that there is a separate pool of resources available to make manual (button-pressing) responses which is independent of the resources available for making vocal ('bip') responses.

From a methodological point of view, these two studies illustrate that different variations of the same basic task can help to clarify the underlying interacting cognitive processes – in this case, how resources are allocated.

According to Kahneman's theory, if somebody is trying to do several things at once, and if the tasks are competing for a common pool of resources, there should be some interference between them. However, there have been numerous studies, such as the McLeod study described in Featured Method Box 6.2, that have demonstrated that it is possible to do two or more tasks at the same time without any mutual interference. This implies that either one or more of the tasks is not drawing on the central processor at all (a possibility that will be considered later) or that each task is accessing a *separate* pool of resources. This idea has been embodied in **multiple-resource theories of attention** (Navon and Gopher, 1979; Wickens, 1992), which suggest that different pools of resources are available for different types of tasks.

Multiple-resource theories of attention Theories that suggest that different pools of resources are available for different types of tasks as opposed to all tasks drawing on a single central pool of resources.

The model of multiple resources available for different tasks is appealing, but it is difficult to establish just how these resource pools are divided and allocated. For instance, is there a different pool of resources available for processing each of the senses? Or maybe there are separate resources for certain types of information (e.g. language, whether written or spoken). It is still not clear whether there is also a necessity for a single 'higher' pool of resources to integrate the processing allocated to the 'lower' pools. This raises the intriguing possibility that Kahneman's and the multiple-resource theories are simply describing different levels of the system, not different systems. This is an issue that is, as yet, unresolved.

Within cognitive psychology, physical metaphors for cognitive processes are common. You have already met the machine metaphor 'limited-capacity central processor', 'resource allocation', 'pools of resources', and you will meet plenty more. Without these physical metaphors it would be difficult to imagine *how a process is implemented in the brain (although, as we shall see, this is getting easier with the use of brain imaging techniques), so the process is conceptualized with the help of a metaphor. But, because these 'physical' metaphors are so seductive (they certainly do make it much easier to think about processes 'in the mind') and so often commonly referred to, they tend to take on a life of their own as if they* really *exist as physical entities.*

2.2 Reducing incoming information - the attentional spotlight

Whether there are one or many pools of resources available to process incoming information, most theories appear to agree that we can only handle a limited amount of sensory information coming in. Thus, cognitive psychologists often regard attention as acting like a filter, filtering out information coming in through the senses so that the higher cortical centres of the brain are not overwhelmed by more information than they can cope with.

One approach that explains how incoming information might be filtered likens attention to a 'spotlight' (Posner, 1980). This **attentional spotlight** illuminates only a small part of the **visual field** (i.e. only a small proportion of everything that is registered by the eyes) and any items that lie within that spotlight receive priority for processing. Any information lying outside the 'beam' of the attentional spotlight receives far less processing – and so saves on valuable resources. A version of this theory suggests that the analogy of attention as a 'zoom lens' might be more appropriate (Eriksen and Murphy, 1987). Here it is suggested that attention can be focused tightly on a narrow area, or broadened to cover a wider area; so you can either put a lot of effort into processing a small area, or spread that effort at a lower 'concentration' over a larger area.

Attentional spotlight
A metaphor for allocation of attention. Whatever falls within the attentional spotlight receives relatively more processing.

Visual field
The area of the environment that could potentially be seen by an individual at any one moment.

Activity 6.1

See if you can move your attentional spotlight. Try this: fixate on (stare at without moving your eyes) a certain point on this page. Now try to see something else 'out of the corner of your eye'. Don't allow your eyes to move, just try to 'concentrate' upon the next word along, then the one beyond that. Perhaps bring your finger close to the point you are fixating on and then gradually move your finger further away, concentrating on the finger but keeping your eyes still and fixated on the original point. While you are trying these exercises you must keep your eyes still, it is only your attentional spotlight that is moving. Now try playing with the zoom. Fixate on a single letter on this page. Concentrate on it as hard as you can, try and see as much detail as possible. Follow the shape of the letter and try and ignore the letters around it. This should focus the spotlight. Now, while still looking at the same letter, try to zoom out: concentrate on everything around you, the rest of the page, the table and the walls. You should become aware of a far wider range of things as your spotlight zooms out.

The attentional spotlight works for hearing as well as vision. When listening to a piece of music that is being played by a number of instruments, we can listen to the music as a whole (spotlight zoomed out), or pick out one particular instrument and follow it (spotlight zoomed in).

Are we still aware of the rest of the music, or does it just disappear? We shall consider what happens to the sensory information outside the spotlight (the information of which you are not consciously aware) later in the chapter.

All of this suggests that you have *control* of your spotlight of attention. You can move it around at will, you can zoom in and out, and you can decide what you want to attend to. This is what is meant by 'paying attention', but is usually referred to in psychology as **selective attention**. This is assumed to be a conscious cognitive process over which we have control and, as such, it also involves *higher* (more consciously controlled) cognitive processes such as expectancy: you are likely to move your attention to a place where you expect something of interest to appear.

Selective attention
A conscious cognitive process controlling allocation of attention, over which we have control and involving cognitive processes such as expectancy

2.3 Voluntary versus involuntary shifts of attention

There are, however, aspects of attention over which we appear to have little, or no control. For instance, Lavie (1995) has suggested that overall perceptual load (the amount of perceptual information available to be processed and over which we do not have direct control) may also influence the size of the spotlight. This effect is evident in driving when perceptual load is high and is known as **attentional tunnelling** (Engel, 1971). This suggests one way in which you may not be aware of all that is happening about you when you are driving. Your attention is 'tunnelled' onto a relatively narrow region, and anything happening outside that region is likely to receive little or no processing (Lavie's experiment is described later in Box 6.3). This process essentially affects the size of the attentional spotlight, but there is also some evidence to suggest that we may not have complete control over *where* the spotlight is directed. When attention is drawn in this way it is usually referred to as **stimulus-induced shifts of attention**. The crucial aspect of stimulus-induced attention is that it is *involuntary* – you do not consciously decide to direct attention to a particular stimulus, it just happens. For instance, a loud noise or a sudden movement might act to draw attention. Anything that *suddenly* appears is likely to provide a strong draw to attention. This, of course, makes sense from an evolutionary perspective: if something suddenly appears you need to allocate processing resources to it as quickly as possible to establish whether or not it is likely to be dangerous, or worth eating.

Think now about what influences attention in different situations. In the case of voluntary attention it is *internal* factors that are controlling

Attentional tunnelling
Occurs when attention is 'tunnelled' onto a relatively narrow region, and anything happening outside that region is likely to receive little or no processing.

Stimulus-induced shifts of attention
Shifts of attention over which we have *no* conscious control and which are driven by something in the environment.

attention; you decide where the attention is going to go. In involuntary attention it is some aspect of the outside world that draws attention; you cannot stop it; the influence is *external*. Posner (1980) referred to the internal, voluntary, control of attention as an **endogenous system** and the effect of external stimuli in attracting attention as making up an **exogenous system.**

What internal factors might influence attention? Perhaps motivational factors such as hunger and anxiety might influence allocation of attention. Could these interact with external features? A bar of chocolate might attract your attention more easily if you are hungry. But remember that many of these influences and processes are operating below the level of consciousness. What does this imply about how our perceptions, interpretations, and behaviours are guided?

From the preceding discussions it is clear that only a proportion of all the vast amount of information impinging on our senses, gets through to consciousness. What happens to the rest of the information? A number of theories have addressed the problem and tried to work out where the filtering is occurring. The ideas put forward suggest that somewhere in the system there is a 'bottleneck' limiting the amount of information that can be processed. Where the theories differ is largely on the issue of *where* the bottleneck occurs in the system and *what happens to* information that fails to get through this bottleneck, and it is to this we turn next.

2.4 Bottleneck theories of attention

The spotlight theory already considered suggests you may reduce incoming information by attending only to a specific area. The following theory, which predates the spotlight theory, suggests that maybe you can filter information according to what *type* it is, i.e. that information can be filtered at the level of our senses. This theory takes us back to some of the earliest studies of attention and, as mentioned in Section 1, to the beginnings of the information processing strand of cognitive psychology as a discipline. These studies were motivated by problems identified during the Second World War and led on to the pioneering work of Donald Broadbent (1954) on auditory attention.

Broadbent (1954, 1971) suggested a **bottleneck theory of attention** – that there must be some 'bottleneck' in the attentional system, and that only a small amount of the available sensory information will pass through this bottleneck. The reason you *need* a bottleneck is evident if you

Endogenous system
The direction of responses (for example, the allocation of attention) by internal processes (motivation, intentions, etc).

Exogenous system
The direction of responses (for example, the allocation of attention) by external factors (salient stimuli, etc).

Bottleneck theory of attention
Theory that suggests a 'bottleneck' in the attentional system such that only a small amount of the available sensory information can pass through.

subscribe to Kahneman's notion that you only have limited resources for processing information. If that is the case, then at some point the amount of information in the system must be reduced, and this is where the bottleneck is likely to be. Broadbent's contribution was to suggest that this bottleneck operates very *early* in the system – filtering out sensory information on the basis of simple physical characteristics (e.g. location of sound, pitch, etc.) so that most of the incoming sensory information receives no conscious processing at all.

Broadbent tested these theories using what he termed a *split-span procedure*. This involved participants being asked to recall a series of digits, which is a conventional way of measuring memory span. However, in Broadbent's task, the digits were presented simultaneously, in pairs – with one digit being presented via head phones to one ear, and the second digit presented simultaneously via head phones to the other ear. So, for instance, the digits 3, 2, and 8 might be presented to one ear, while the digits 9, 4, and 7 were presented to the other. The participants could recall these digits in one of two ways. They could either recall all the numbers from one ear and *then* all the numbers from the other (in which case they might respond 3, 2, 8, 9, 4, 7), or they could recall the numbers by the pairs in which they were presented (in which case they might respond 3,9, 2,4, 8,7). Broadbent discovered that participants found it easier to recall all the numbers from one ear then all the numbers from the other. Recalling by pairs, which involves recalling a number from one ear and then 'switching' to the other ear, was more difficult. This fits in with Broadbent's theory that information was selected on the basis of physical characteristics, in this case the ear to which it was presented (location). Gathering information from a single location is assumed to be inherently easier than continually switching between locations.

The split-span procedure of Broadbent could be manipulated to see which characteristics of a stimulus could be used to filter out information. For instance, participants could be asked to report all the items said in a particular tone of voice – another physical characteristic. Manipulations of this kind suggest that it *is* possible to filter incoming information on the basis of simple physical characteristics.

Although these studies do suggest that incoming information can be filtered on the basis of simple physical characteristics, they do beg a number of questions. Filtering information *only* on the basis of physical characteristics would suggest that you know nothing about the *meaning* of the information. How do you decide, therefore, what information to filter out *if* you know nothing about the rest of it? How do you decide it is time to switch attention to something else if all you know about is the small amount of information you have already selected?

Early or late selection?

The questions generated by these studies started a protracted and ongoing debate about whether selection of material for further processing occurs 'early' or 'late'. Early selection implies that material is selected on the basis of 'low level' physical features and only this information is processed (as Broadbent would suggest). Late selection, in its purest form, would suggest that all information is processed to the level of meaning – and only then do we select what to respond to, on the basis of the meaning.

There is certainly plenty of evidence to suggest that most information is processed at least to some extent. For instance, Treisman (1960) found that people would switch attention if unattended information was *meaningful* to *them* in the current situation. For example, if you were at a party and somebody in a conversation in which you were not involved mentioned your name, you might well switch attention to monitor that conversation; this is known as the 'cocktail party effect'. Treisman's early work suggested that all information was processed to a limited extent, but there have been other approaches (e.g. Deutsch and Deutsch, 1963) that assume that there are *no* resource limitations on processing (unlike Kahneman's proposals). In this view, all material can be processed and the appropriate response to the information is based on *all* incoming information. This represents the opposite extreme to the early selection approach of Broadbent.

So which view is right? There has been a considerable amount of work concerning whether selection is early or late, and (as with so much in psychology) the answer is 'it depends'. For instance, Treisman (1993) and Lavie (1995) believe that the perceptual load (i.e. the amount of information available to the senses) of a task will determine whether the filter will be early or late. Lavie's experiment is described in Box 6.3.

6.3 *Is the filter early or late?*

Lavie (1995) used a modification of a paradigm developed by Eriksen and Eriksen (1974) to study the effects of perceptual load on the filtering of material. In the original Eriksen and Eriksen task, participants had to make a response as quickly as possible (response time was the dependent variable that was measured) to a target letter embedded in the middle of a row of five. If the target letter was drawn from one pre-defined set of letters the participants would have to move a lever to the left; if the target letter was from a different set then the participant would have to move a lever to the right. For instance, participants might be told that if the central letter was an L, K or H they should move the lever to the left; if the central letter was a P or B they should move the lever to the right. Participants might thus be presented with BBLBB and would have to move the lever to the left ignoring the flanking letters, placed there as 'distractors'. Eriksen and Eriksen found that the flanking letters *could* influence the response time to the central letter, even though the participants were supposed to be ignoring them. If the central and flanking letters came from the *same* set (requiring the same response) then response times were faster than if the flanking letters came from a set different from the central target letter. This is called the *flanker compatibility effect.* Essentially, even though participants are trying to ignore the distracting flanking letters, they *can* affect response time; slowing it down if the flanking letters require a different response from the central target.

Lavie modified the experiment described above by changing the *number* of letters in the target set. In the example above there are three letters in the target set. Lavie manipulated the number of letters in the target set from one (low perceptual load) to six (high perceptual load), and found that the interference effects from flanking distractors was significant only in the *low* load condition. Lavie explained this result by suggesting that, if perceptual load is high, then the filter will operate early (filtering out the flanking distractors), but when perceptual load is low the filter will operate later (allowing the distractors to be processed and thus, potentially, cause interference). The early/late selection debate is thus another example of attentional processes being influenced by the *situation* in which they occur. Note the similarity here with the spotlight metaphor. Early filtering looks rather like having the spotlight zoomed in; late filtering like having the spotlight zoomed out. The Lavie experiment just described has been discussed previously (Section 2.3) as an example of a change in the size of the attentional spotlight.

2.5 Automatic and controlled processing

So far, the discussion has focused on the resources available for *conscious* processing of information. The implicit assumption has been that all tasks and processes require a call on processing resources to a greater or lesser extent, and that the amount of information we can take in and process is limited by our available resources. These processes fall under the general heading of **controlled processes**. However, a series of studies, conducted by Schneider and Shiffrin (Schneider and Shiffrin, 1977; Shiffrin and Schneider, 1977), suggested that there may be other attentional processes that operate in a way qualitatively different from controlled processes.

A series of experiments led Schneider and Shiffrin to make a distinction between controlled processes that make heavy demands on processing resources and what they termed **automatic processes**, that were assumed to make no demands on attentional resources, i.e. not to draw on attentional capacity or processing resources and occur without

Controlled processes
Those mental processes over which we can exert conscious control.

Automatic processes
Those mental processes that cannot be consciously controlled.

conscious awareness. This division of attentional processing into automatic and controlled processes has led to the development of what are called **two-process theories**.

Looking back over what we have so far, it is interesting to consider why we need automatic processes. What do we gain from having things done 'automatically'? The obvious answer is that automatic processes, precisely because they *are* automatic, require less of our precious mental 'resources' to operate. This, in itself, would make them very valuable as we can get some things done while directing our limited resources elsewhere.

A classic phenomenon that demonstrates some of the *costs* associated with automatic processing is known as the *Stroop effect* (Stroop, 1935). This is a simple yet elegant demonstration of an interaction between automatic and controlled processes. In a Stroop-type experiment, the participant is presented with a list of words written in different coloured inks. In one condition the words are colour names (red, green, blue, etc.) – and the colour name and the colour of the ink in which it is printed never correspond (the Stroop condition). In the other condition the words are printed in the same colour inks as in the Stroop condition, but the words are colour-neutral (e.g. rat, grand, bolt, etc.). The participant's task is to name the *ink colour* of each word in the list as quickly as possible. In the colour-neutral words condition, this is quite easy to do. But in the Stroop condition, there is considerable interference from the colour name – people tend to find it difficult to avoid responding with the colour that the word describes rather than the colour of the ink in which it is written.

> **Two-process theories**
> These theories suggest that automatic and controlled processes operate simultaneously, the balance between the two depending upon the situation.

Activity 6.2

The Stroop effect described in the text is a visual one, but the same effect can be demonstrated in other modalities. An obvious example is the old trick of trying to 'put somebody off' when they are counting by saying different numbers from the ones that they are currently saying. If they could only ignore what you are saying, then there would be no problem, but they automatically register the numbers you are saying, and this interferes with their counting. Using this effect it is possible to demonstrate an auditory Stroop effect, similar to the visual one. First, you need to persuade four people to help you. Position them in front of you, behind you, and one to each side. Now, ask them (only one at a time) to call out either 'left', 'right', 'back' or 'front' – but not the call corresponding to their position with respect to you. So, the person in front of you will call, left, right, or behind; the person to your left will say right, front or behind – and so on. Your job is, as each person speaks, to name the *position* of that person with respect to you. You should find this task difficult, because you will automatically register what they are saying – and this should interfere with your calling of their position.

Of course, you need something to compare this task with (a control condition) to make sure that it really is the calling of position words such as 'left', 'right' etc. that is giving you problems (and not just that the task is difficult anyway). So, try the task again, but this time get the people to call out words that are not 'position' words – such as 'cow', 'pig', etc. (or even ask them to make up nonsense words like 'fub'). You should now find the task much easier, suggesting that it is the *type* of word that gives a Stroop effect (i.e. the meaning of the word matters).

Comment

The Stroop effect demonstrates at least two interesting effects: first, that an automatic process (reading) can interfere with a controlled process (naming the ink colour) and, second, that automatic processes can be influenced by individual strategies. For instance, it has been found that the strategy of focusing attention on the initial letter of each word reduces the influence of the automatic reading of the words and so reduces the overall Stroop effect. This suggests that automatic processes are not 'free' processes that require no cognitive resources. They may compete with other (controlled) processes for resources and they can be influenced (or at least prevented from 'cutting in') by conscious strategies.

The Stroop effect demonstrates nicely the downside of automatic processes that we discussed earlier. They can be used to get things done with a minimal draw on our resources *but*, under some circumstances, they *can* interfere with controlled processes, and we cannot switch them off.

At the beginning of this section we considered the development of two-process theories of attention: automatic processing being one of the processes, controlled processing the other and we considered that controlled processing requires conscious control. The distinction, however, is not really this straightforward. For instance, reading may be an automatic process, but it is *learned*, which implies that at some point before it was learned it was not an automatic process. So, if (as this suggests) controlled and automatic processes are on a continuum (rather than dichotomous), then what level of conscious awareness is required before a process is considered to be controlled? And, can we learn to change the amount of control we exert over attention? Perhaps we can increase or decrease the level of control depending on the external situation and our internal motivation? Gopher (1993) suggests that attentional control is a *skill* that can be learned and modified, at least to some extent. Certainly, the ability of people to use a strategy of focusing attention on the initial letter to overcome the Stroop effect suggests that this may be the case.

We have spent a lot of time considering how attention is allocated and controlled. An obvious question, therefore, is to ask *what* is doing the controlling? Is there any evidence that some part of the brain is responsible for this control? This is where the contribution of neuroscience to cognitive psychology is invaluable.

2.6 Exploring the links between brain and cognition

As discussed in the introduction to this chapter, the difficulty of measuring what really goes on inside the living human brain has meant that cognitive psychology has, in the past, tended to treat the brain and the processes that occur within it as being contained in an impenetrable black box. More recently, however, a number of functional brain-imaging techniques have been developed that allow the activity of different regions of the brain to be monitored in alert participants while they perform various tasks. An example of one study that has used brain-imaging techniques to study the Stroop effect is given in Box 6.4.

6.4 What does the Stroop task do to the brain?

A number of studies have used functional brain imaging techniques to study the areas of the brain that are active when performing a Stroop task. Two areas of prefrontal cortex that tend to be active when participants are asked to perform two tasks at once (as in the dual task studies described earlier) have been identified. These areas are referred to as the dorsolateral prefrontal cortex (DLPFC) and the anterior cingulate cortex (ACC). Don't worry too much about the names. It is only important to be aware that these are two distinct regions, either (or both) of which may show increased activity if participants attempt to do two things at once. MacDonald *et al.* (2000) hypothesized (based on previous research) that these two regions carry out different functions. Specifically, the hypothesis was that the DLPFC is responsible for maintaining the attentional demands of the task (i.e. ensuring that attention is allocated appropriately), whereas the ACC is more involved in an 'overseeing' role. The ACC could, for instance, be active in monitoring for the occurrence of performance errors or the presence of response conflict such as that which occurs in the Stroop effect when the participant is trying to name an ink colour but automatically reading word names at the same time.

To test their hypothesis, MacDonald *et al.* made a small but significant change to the standard Stroop task and used a technique known as functional magnetic resonance imaging (fMRI) to record activity in the DLPFC and the ACC. The

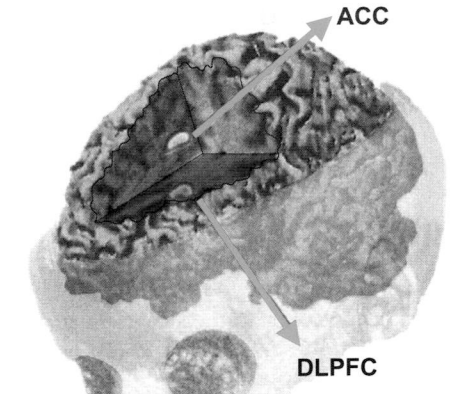

Figure 6.2 The positions of the dorsolateral prefrontal cortex and the anterior cingulate cortex

Note: This scan is a three dimensional image of a brain with a triangular section of the brain removed to reveal internal structures. The pale, shaded area at the bottom of the brain is the surrounding skull. The eye sockets can be seen at the lower left-hand side of the scan.

change they made was that, before each Stroop trial, the participant was given one of two instructions:

(a) To name the ink colour in which the word was written (the standard Stroop task).

(b) To read the word (a more automatic response).

While doing the task, increased activity was observed within the DLPFC when the instruction was to name the colour, but *not* when the instruction was to read the word. Thus, the DLPFC was not active when the task was an automatic one (reading the word) but *was* active when the task was a controlled one (trying to name the ink colour). Also, participants who showed the greatest increase in activation in the DLPFC also showed the smallest Stroop interference effect, consistent with more effective attentional control. This suggests (and only suggests) that the DLPFC may be the area of the brain that does the controlling of controlled attentional processes.

In contrast to the different activation in the DLPFC, *no* change in activity related to the type of task was found in the ACC. However, those participants who showed the largest Stroop effect, also showed slightly greater activation of the ACC. This is consistent with the proposed ACC function of monitoring and evaluating errors.

Functional brain imaging studies, such as the one described in Box 6.4, are invaluable in helping to explain how proposed cognitive processes such as automatic and controlled attention can be implemented in the brain. These techniques have allowed for great advances in understanding of the area but the results need to be interpreted with care. These imaging studies essentially use a correlational technique: seeing which parts of the brain are active at the same time as a particular task is performed. If a particular part of the brain is always active when a certain task is performed, then it seems highly likely that that part of the brain is involved in the task. What it does not easily tell you is how *it might be involved.*

While neuroscience looks at *activity* in different regions of the brain and attempts to deduce what that part of the brain is doing when it is active, **cognitive neuropsychology** looks at what happens when a region of the brain *stops* working as a result of brain damage or other kinds of brain lesion. (You encountered cognitive neuropsychology in Chapter 4 and will come across it again in Chapter 8).

A cognitive neuropsychological approach can be illustrated with Oliver Sacks' account of 'Dr P.', a distinguished musician, who was suffering a

Cognitive neuropsychology
Attempts to gain insight into cognitive processes by studying the effects of brain trauma (lesion, disease, etc).

range of perceptual problems as a result of some form of brain damage – the precise cause was never established by Sacks. This study was published as *The Man who Mistook his Wife for a Hat* (Sacks, 1985). By looking at the different problems experienced by Dr P. it is possible to gain an insight into the underlying workings of his brain. For instance, consider the interaction of sensory information and prior knowledge in the creation of a conscious perception. If gathering sensory information and linking that information with stored knowledge are discrete parts of the process of perception and occur in discrete parts of the brain then it should, in theory, be possible to have one process without the other. This is indeed what Sacks found.

A simple 'test' that Sacks presented to Dr P. was to give him a glove and ask him what it was. Dr P. examined it closely and finally described it as, "A continuous surface, infolded on itself. It appears to have [hesitating] five outpouchings...". Even when pressed, Dr P. could not identify the glove and could only suggest that its function might be, "... a change purse, for example, for coins of five sizes." Plainly, the sensory aspects of the glove were clear to Dr P. – the description was a good one. Unfortunately, Dr P. was unable to link this with the knowledge of what a glove looks like. It is worth noting that he *was* able to make use of some kinds of stored knowledge: he was able to use language very well and even brought in knowledge of a 'change purse'. But while he was able to sense something it was impossible for him to link this to the appropriate knowledge. This inability to recognize common objects despite normal sensation is referred to as **agnosia**. Thus this suggests that the sensing of information and the linking of that sensory information to stored knowledge must be handled by different parts of the brain, as it is possible to lose one without the other. Can this type of selective loss be found with any of the other processes discussed in this chapter?

Is the process of recovering stored knowledge and the allocation of attention handled by different areas of the brain? Sacks conducted a rather elegant test suggesting that this may be the case by asking Dr P. to imagine entering a local square from the North side and describe the buildings he passed. Note, this is done from memory, so there is no fresh sensory input necessary for this task. Dr P. described all of the buildings that he would pass on his right – but none of those on his left. Sacks then asked Dr P. to repeat the task, but to imagine entering from the *South* side. Again, Dr P. mentioned only those buildings on the right, even though these were the ones he had ignored previously. Thus, the knowledge was there, but he appeared to be only attending to one side.

This is referred to as **unilateral spatial neglect**. Dr P. was drawing information from memory, but individuals with this condition, even if they have a full range of sensory information coming in, will still ignore items

Agnosia
The inability to recognise objects despite normal sensory input.

Unilateral spatial neglect
A tendency to ignore one side of the visual field or one side of an object – despite normal sensory input.

on one particular side. For instance, patients with this condition, if asked to draw a clock face, will tend either to omit all the numbers from one side, or to try and cram all twelve numbers onto one side of the clock face (see Figure 6.3).

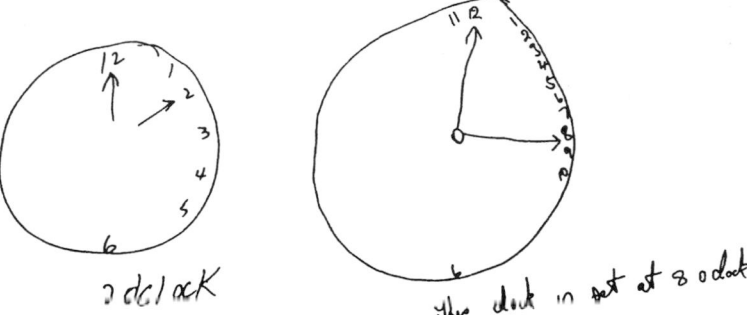

Figure 6.3   Two examples of clock faces drawn by patients with unilateral spatial neglect (Source: Halligan and Marshall, 1993)

So, what do these studies of deficits contribute to our understanding of cognitive processes? They suggest that the different processes already discussed in this chapter must be represented, at least to some extent, in different parts of the brain – as one process can apparently fail, leaving others intact.

We will now move on from attention to consider what happens to information after it has passed through the attentional filter. How can we explain how *perception* operates? The next section considers some contrasting theories that attempt to explain this issue.

Summary   Section 2

- A large amount of what our senses pick up, we do not perceive.
- The reason that we do not perceive everything we sense may be because we have only limited processing resources to handle incoming sensory information.
- Attention is the process by which cognitive resources are allocated.
- Sensory information to be processed may be selected by something analogous to a spotlight, illuminating areas that are to receive preferential processing.
- Control of the attentional 'spotlight' can either be internal (controlled by goals and intentions) or external (drawn by salient stimuli).
- As resources are limited, at some point in the system incoming information must be reduced to a manageable level, leading to a

bottleneck, which might occur either early (at the sensory end of the system) or late (at the response end).

- Not all processing of incoming stimuli requires conscious control. Some can be done automatically below the level of conscious awareness.
- Cognitive neuroscience (the study of the functioning of the human brain) allows us to deduce which areas of the brain are involved in different aspects of attention.
- Cognitive neuropsychology is a part of cognitive neuroscience that attempts to infer how cognitive processes operate by studying individuals who have suffered some sort of trauma (disease or lesion) to the brain.

3   Theories of perception

3.1   Gregory's 'constructivist' theory of perception

The discussion in this chapter so far has explored the notion that perception is a process of taking in information from our senses, filtering it using attentional processes, and integrating what is left with what we already know. The **constructivist theory of perception** put forward by Richard Gregory (1966) provides an explanatory framework for perception that reconciles these elements into a coherent theory. Gregory's theory is referred to as 'constructivist' because it is based on the idea that the sensory information that forms the basis of perception is incomplete. This is either because we do not register all the information in the first place, or we do register it with our senses but do not attend to it. Gregory suggests that it is necessary to *build* our perception of the world from *incomplete* information. To do this we use what we already *know* about the world to interpret the sensory information coming in, and to 'make sense' of it.

Gregory's theories are concerned primarily with visual perception, although the basic approach would apply equally well to the other senses. The essence of Gregory's theory is that, in trying to perceive something, we form a series of **perceptual hypotheses**. People use the incomplete sensory information coming in and, combining that with what they know, form a hypothesis of what it is they are perceiving. Returning to the cow at the start of the chapter, what you sense is a pattern of black

Constructivist theory of perception
The notion that perception is 'built' from incomplete sensory data with the aid of stored knowledge.

Perceptual hypotheses
Stages in an iterative process of combining incomplete sensory information with stored knowledge to arrive at a hypothesis (best guess) of what the individual is perceiving.

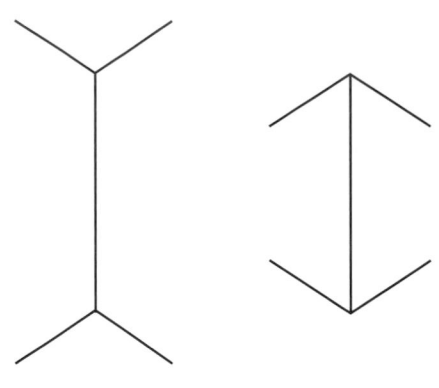

Figure 6.4   The Müller-Lyer illusion. Although the two vertical lines are identical in length, the one on the left typically *looks* longer.

Size constancy
The awareness that the actual size of a stimulus remains constant despite changes in the size of the retinal image (e.g. when the stimulus moves away).

and white blobs. If you look at the picture at the end of the chapter, you can see that the pattern is associated with a 'mooing' noise. Thus the most plausible hypothesis is that what you are looking at is a picture of a cow, because you *know* that cows go 'moo'. If you did not know this fact then that particular cue would be far less useful in guiding your perception of the picture.

Gregory's theory is especially good at explaining why we see visual illusions. For instance, consider the Müller-Lyer illusion, as shown in Figure 6.4.

Gregory suggests that, although the Müller-Lyer figure is just a series of simple lines, we *interpret* the figure in terms of our experience and knowledge of the world. A plausible hypothesis is that there are two three-dimensional figures representing corners, as shown in Figure 6.5.

There is still another stage to go through to explain the illusion. The next step is to assume that people see the receding corner (on the left) as being further away. This corner is further away but the image of the line on your retina is the *same size* as the apparently closer line in the right figure. The only way this could happen in the real world is if the left-hand line was longer; so you *perceive* the line as longer (even though the lines registered by your eyes are the same length). This is an example of what is called **size constancy** and is the reason why, as people move away from us, we just see a person of constant size moving further away, and not a shrinking person.

Gregory assumes that our knowledge of the world influences the way in which we perceive the Müller-Lyer illusion. One implication of this is that people with different backgrounds and experiences might perceive the illusion differently. Segall *et al.* (1963) tested people from a number of different cultures and found that those least susceptible to the illusion were the Bete people,

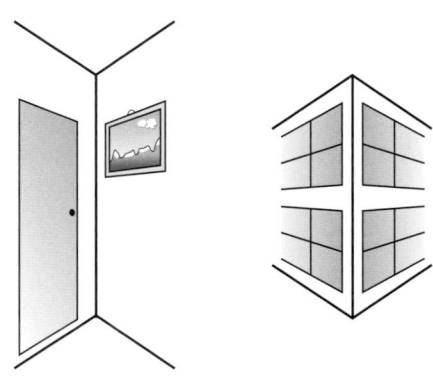

Figure 6.5   Gregory suggests that we interpret the Müller-Lyer figures as two corners: one coming towards us and the other receding.

who live in a dense jungle environment with relatively few corners. Thus the work of Segall *et al.* provides support for Gregory's theory.

Activity 6.3

The Müller-Lyer and similar illusions may also work as a *haptic* illusion – via the sense of touch (Révész, 1934; Over, 1968). Try getting some drinking straws and stick them down on some card in the shape of the Müller-Lyer illusion. Now try running your hands over the illusion with your eyes closed. You should still experience the illusion.

Comment

It is difficult to understand how Gregory's theory can explain the Müller-Lyer illusion working as a haptic illusion (although the theory can be modified to accommodate the haptic illusion by suggesting that you *visualise* the illusion as you are feeling it). Some other modifications of the Müller-Lyer illusion that still work are even more difficult for Gregory's theory to explain. For instance see Figure 6.6 below.

The illusion still works but it is difficult to see how the figure could be interpreted as corners. There are numerous explanations for illusions such as the Müller-Lyer, apart from the perceptual hypotheses of Gregory's theory. For example, Day (1989) suggested that we see the illusion as a result of **perceptual compromise**. This theory suggests that we judge the length of the lines as a compromise between the actual length of the line and the overall figure of which it is part. Therefore, the figure on the left being longer overall, the line at its centre is also seen as longer. This is a simple explanation and everything that is needed to explain the illusion is there in the stimulus; there is no need to postulate any particular role for stored knowledge and experience. This fits nicely with Gibson's theory of 'direct perception' which we shall consider in Section 3.2.

Perceptual compromise
The influence of the whole of a figure on attempts to make judgements about any part of it.

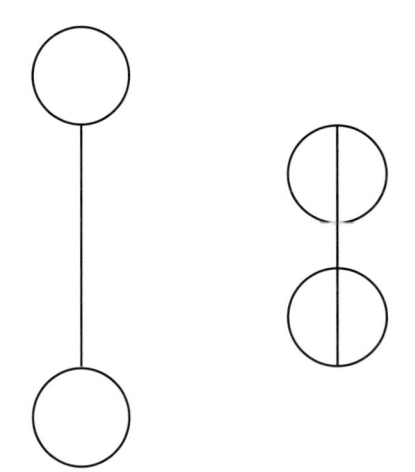

Figure 6.6   Modified Müller-Lyer figure (after Delboeuf, 1892)

So, while Gregory's theory is appealing in that it provides an explanatory framework suggesting how we integrate bottom-up information (from our senses) with top-down information (our knowledge), it does not appear to provide a complete explanation of perception. It has been argued that Gregory's theory underestimates the richness of sensory information and that it also struggles to explain how we can keep forming and resolving perceptual hypotheses in a dynamic, ever-changing world. This aspect of perception is perhaps better dealt with by another theory of perception that will be considered next.

3.2 Gibson's theory of direct perception

Gibson's (1950) theory provides an interesting contrast with Gregory's in that it considers that incoming sensory information is far from impoverished (as Gregory would suggest) but is, in fact, rich in information, leading to **direct perception**. As a result of this, Gibson's theory of perception is very different from that of Gregory, in that Gibson suggests that everything that is needed for perception is there already in the sensory information. Gibson's theory suggests that we perceive the world 'as a whole' rather than breaking it down into a series of discrete objects. Perceiving something is never done in isolation, but as part of a wider context, and Gibson's theories also emphasise the *dynamic* nature of perception. We do not perceive a sequence of static images, but a dynamic ever-changing scene with aspects of the environment being seen from different perspectives as we (and they) move about. Thus, there is far more information available to us in a dynamic scene than in a static 'snapshot' of the world. Illusions, so easily explained by Gregory's theory, are in Gibson's theory essentially artefacts: a result of removing people from a 'natural' environment and moving them into the 'artificial' world of the laboratory. Day's explanation of the Müller-Lyer illusion, involving perceptual compromise, is a good example of an explanation that does not require input from stored knowledge – everything is there in the stimulus. The problem is, many visual illusions and images do often seem to rely on stored knowledge to be perceived (such as the cow figure right at the start of the chapter) and, although Gibson might regard them as artefacts, they *do* occur.

Direct perception
Perception without the need for integration with stored knowledge.

As suggested by Bruce *et al.* (1996), however, one area in which Gibson's theories do seem quite plausible is that of instinctive, visually-guided behaviour. For instance, consider a frog attempting to snare a fly with its tongue. All it needs to do is to sense a small (fly-sized) flying object and to use that sensory information to guide the tongue to catch it. It does not need to 'know' anything about flies or to form any hypotheses, it can just sense and react, which is likely to be much faster, and therefore more effective, than considering a series of hypotheses, recognizing a fly, and then trying to catch it.

There is no need for the theories of Gregory and Gibson to be mutually exclusive. It is possible that they are describing different aspects of the same process. Also, of course, the theories of Gregory and Gibson are not the only theories of visual perception. There are many others, and the reason that these two have been discussed in this chapter is that they represent extremes in terms of the role they see for stored knowledge in perception, which is central to Gregory's theory and superfluous to Gibson's.

One aspect of perception that neither Gregory nor Gibson really addresses is how does it *feel* to perceive things? What is our inner *experience* of things in the outside world? This is the domain of another approach in psychology, distinct from cognitive psychology and with strong philosophical connections, referred to as phenomenological psychology.

3.3 Phenomenological approaches to perception

Phenomenologists reject the notion that the world as it appears – either through our senses or as an interaction of sensory input and cognitive processes – is sufficient to explain perception fully. Instead, they seek to understand our experience and consciousness of what it is we are perceiving, i.e. **phenomenological experience**. They believe that what we perceive is a complex product of who we are (our past history), our current understanding and the present context. While Gregory's theory is more concerned with *how you come to recognize something*, phenomenology concentrates on *what the experience of perception is*, what it feels like, what it means to you.

Phenomenological experience
An individual's unique experience of perception of the world.

The founder of the phenomenological tradition was a German philosopher–mathematician called Edmund Husserl. For Husserl (1931) our understanding of the world lay in the fundamental relationship he called *intentionality*. As used by phenomenologists, intentionality describes the action of the mind reaching out to the stimuli that make up the world and interpreting them in terms of our own personal, meaningful experience. Subsequently phenomenologists have taken Husserl's theories of consciousness in different directions, focusing, in particular, on lived experience (for instance, what it is like to experience an illness), although here we will concentrate on the topic of perception.

Consider our conscious experience, for instance, of how we perceive a simple three-dimensional object like a cube. At any one time we can only see the cube from one angle or perspective. However, our perception is dynamic and we do not only experience the one side. Instead, we 'see' sides that are hidden (including the inside) and we perceive something more, something that relates to the 'identity' of the cube: we have a sense of the cube as something more than simply that which we see. As the context changes and as we turn the cube around or use it in different ways, so our perception changes.

A good example of how phenomenologists think perceptions change depending on one's own lived experience is the contrast between how a toddler and a gambler might see a 'cube'. A toddler, playing with building blocks, is likely to experience the cubes through taste and feel. The gambler who rolls a dice experiences an adrenal rush, a vision of wealth, a sporting challenge. While the child may perceive the block as something to build with, the gambler is probably conscious only of the top face of the dice cube, where numbers equate with success or failure. In these ways, perception is complex, a product of context and meanings. To understand perception, phenomenologists say, we need to focus on our consciousness, experience and the intentional relationship with the object concerned. In a way, phenomenologists are claiming that we see things not as *they* are, but as *we* are

Thus phenomenologists emphasise that the way we attend to objects affects what we perceive and that our consciousness of an object is a product of our histories and experience. These points return us to the start of the chapter where we considered the image of the cow and how your experience affected your perception of it – particularly if you did not see it as a cow at first. Now consider Figure 6.7, another extremely well known 'illusion' where there is more than one way of seeing something.

This is known as a reversible figure because it can be seen as either a light vase or two dark faces looking towards each other. You can therefore perceive the picture as two different things, despite the fact that the sensory information does not change. The pattern of activation on the retina is the same, it is the perception that changes. A key concept here is the notion of **figure** or **ground**. If you see the vase then you are perceiving the vase as the figure and the faces just make up the ground (background). If you see the faces, then the figure and ground have been reversed. Phenomenologists explain this reversible figure effect by suggesting that all aspects of perception have a *directional* focus, in which individuals are seen to be directing their attention onto something. Thus the figure/ground illusion is an example of our ability to direct our attention in a particular way. In this example we have

Figure
Reference to the object of interest in a scene, as opposed to the 'ground'.

Ground
Reference to the background, made up of all parts of the scene (apart from the figure), and against which the figure is set.

Figure 6.7   A reversible figure (Source: adapted from the original illusion by E. Rubin, 1915)

another role for attention (apart from filtering sensory information) in perceiving the world. While the sensation remains the same, the way in which we attend affects what we perceive – another example of the complex interaction between these two processes.

The example above of figure and ground is a visual one, but you have already encountered an auditory version in this chapter. An attempt to move your attentional spotlight as you are listening to music (Section 2.2) could be considered to be an auditory version of a reversible figure. Attend to one instrument and that becomes the foreground and all others become the background; attend to one of the 'background' instruments and figure and ground change.

3.4 A challenge to the attentional spotlight

Earlier in the chapter we talked about altering the position of the attentional spotlight and its size, but could you consciously focus your attentional spotlight on the vase shape and avoid perceiving the faces? Alternatively, could you split your attentional spotlight to cover the two face shapes – and not cover the vase in the middle?

This brings us to an alternative conception of how we allocate attention to things. Rather than attention being allocated to an *area* or *space* as the spotlight theory would suggest, it can be allocated to an *object*. This would certainly fit with Husserl's phenomenological approach of striving to understand and interpret *things* in the physical world. There is evidence that, at least under some circumstances, attention can be allocated to objects rather than areas of space around us. First of all it is worth thinking about how you define a *single* object.

If items are grouped close together (proximity), then they are more likely to be a part of the same object. Also, things that move together at the same speed and in the same direction (common movement) are likely to be parts of the same object. It is not difficult to think of a common example of this. If you see something moving behind some railings or in the undergrowth, only parts of the object will be visible. You can, however, infer that it is one object if all the sections you can see move together and, from a practical point of view, you can gauge how big it is. The importance of defining what constitutes an object, and the principles by which this might be achieved, are the domain of another branch of psychology, Gestalt psychology (literally translated from German as 'shape' or 'form'). **Gestalt psychology** has had an impact on social psychology as well as on studies of perception, and suggests that we use our own knowledge of the properties that link component parts of a single object (grouping, proximity, common motion etc) to allow us to identify and

Gestalt psychology
A branch of psychology that emphasises the importance of identifying whole objects within a scene as an essential part of perception.

interpret objects. For Gestalt psychologists, the whole *is* more than the sum of the parts.

Both the phenomenological and Gestalt approaches to perception suggest that at least one of the goals of perception may be to define and interpret objects (i.e. to define objects in terms of what we already know). As already mentioned, there is some evidence to suggest that attention can be allocated to an object (rather than to a region of space). For instance, Driver and Bayliss (1989) demonstrated that attention could be directed to items that were grouped by common movement even though they were not spatially contiguous – as would be required if attention were simply allocated to regions of space like a spotlight.

Whether attention is allocated to a region of space or to a particular object is still open to debate As usual in psychology, the answer is almost certainly that it is neither wholly one or the other, but a bit of both. Which process applies will probably depend upon the precise situation. For instance, if you are sitting in a completely dark room and expecting something to appear in front of you, then it makes sense to allocate attention to an area of space, as there would be no objects to allocate attention to. On the other hand, if you are trying to track a moving object, then it is likely to be easier to allocate attention to the object, rather than to a constantly changing region of space.

Before moving on, let us once more review what we have so far. To perceive something consciously, it appears that we take the vast array of sensory information at our disposal, filter it using our attentional processes, and combine it with knowledge that we already hold (according to Gregory anyway). One implication of this is that there should be a strong interaction between attention and perception. There is plenty of evidence from the cognitive psychology that we have considered so far suggesting that this is the case.

Throughout this chapter you have already encountered metaphors such as bottlenecks and filters. This is because cognitive psychology is attempting to deal with the working of the brain and mind, something that is very difficult to conceptualise without the use of metaphors and has, in the past, been extremely difficult to study directly. The brain imaging (fMRI) studies that we considered earlier are an exciting development in that they allow us to detect which regions of the brain are active at any particular time. In the next section we will go still further down into the workings of the brain to see how the interaction of attention and perception may occur at a *neuronal* level.

3.5 Brain mechanisms of perception and attention

In Section 2.6 we considered some *areas* of the brain that may be involved in the process of attention. Now we move on to consider how attention might directly affect perception, and how this could be implemented at a neuronal level in the brain. How could the attentional processes we have been discussing (such as attention to a particular object or area of space) be implemented? Some interesting work that has a bearing on this has been conducted by Maunsell and McAdams (2000) and is described in Box 6.5.

6.5 *Attention affecting perception*

Throughout this chapter we have been considering the interaction of attention and perception, and from the discussions in this chapter there appears to be plenty of evidence to suggest that such interactions do occur. Cognitive neuroscience is beginning to provide direct evidence (at a lower level of analysis) for how these interactions may occur in the brain. In Section 2.6 we looked at studies of brain imaging picking up activity in different *regions* of the brain. The study that will be discussed here looks at the responses of *individual neurons* in the brain using single unit recording techniques such as those described in Featured Methods Box 4.1 in Chapter 4.

Maunsell and McAdams (2000) examined how changes in attention affect the responses of individual neurons in the visual cortex of monkeys. Certain neurons in the visual cortex are 'tuned' to respond when a monkey looks at a pattern of lines of a particular orientation. Each individual neuron of this type will have a 'preferred' orientation that it will respond to. For instance, certain neurons will respond maximally to a vertical pattern, whereas others will respond maximally to a horizontal pattern. Although these neurons 'prefer' a certain orientation, they will also respond, to a lesser extent, to patterns that lie close to this orientation. Other factors can also influence the response of these neurons, for example, the contrast of the pattern. Maunsell and McAdams measured neuronal responses when a monkey was attending to a pattern of a certain orientation (examples of the sort of patterns used are shown in Figure 6.8) and compared the responses with those obtained when the monkey was *not* attending to that pattern.

What they found was that *directing attention* to a particular stimulus was just like turning up the contrast of the pattern. The neuron did not respond to different orientations or to more orientations, but just responded *more vigorously* to the orientations it was already tuned to. This could be compared to twiddling the contrast control on a television. The contrast changes, but the picture remains the same. Thus, focusing attention on a pattern (a change in a cognitive process) and increasing the contrast of the pattern (a change in the stimulus) can have a similar effect on the response of a neuron.

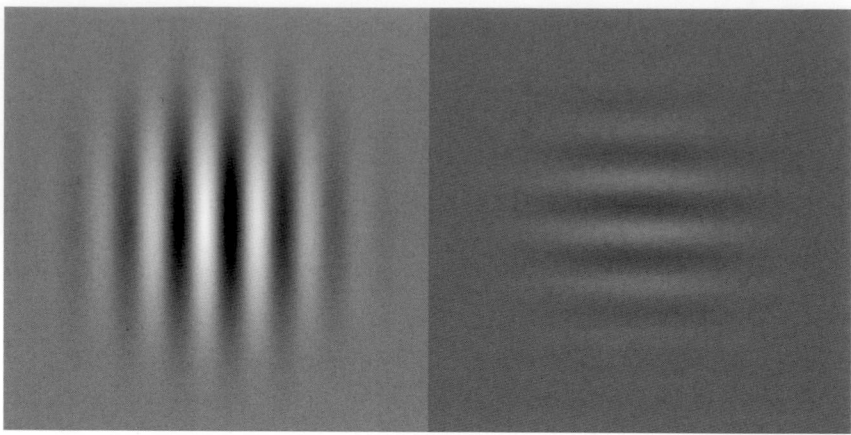

Figure 6.8   Stimulus patterns of the sort used by Maunsell and McAdams (2000)

The pattern on the left is vertically oriented and of high contrast; the pattern on the right is horizontally oriented and of low contrast.

The results of the Maunsell and McAdams study suggest that attention can influence neurons in exactly the same way as changing information from the senses does. Thus, as far as the neuron in the visual cortex is concerned, input coming 'up' from the senses and 'down' from cognitive processes (like attention) all have the same effect. Cognitive neuroscience has therefore provided an example of how attention might act at a neuronal level. Before getting too carried away, it is important to bear in mind that this study was conducted using very simple stimuli, and there is much work still to be done before neuroscience can explain how you came to arrive at work without realizing how you got there. But it *is* a good start.

We have considered how the processes of attention and perception might operate, and looked to see how the brain might implement these processes, and the interactions between them. Now we will finish this chapter as we began, considering whether the processes we have covered can explain behaviour in situations outside the laboratory. This is the 'acid test' for any theory. Theorizing is all very well, but can the theories explain things that happen in the everyday world?

Summary Section 3

- Gregory's constructivist theory of perception suggests that the sensory information we receive is incomplete and that our perception of the world results from a series of perceptual hypotheses generated by the interaction of sensory information with stored knowledge.
- Gibson's theory of direct perception suggests that there is sufficient information in the sensory input to interpret the world, without needing to appeal to stored knowledge.
- The phenomenological approach to perception concentrates on the effect that our experience and interaction with the world has on our perception.
- The Gestalt approach considers that our knowledge makes a perceptual object more than the sum of its parts.
- It is possible that attention can be allocated to an object rather than, or as well as, a region of space.
- Single unit recordings of neurons in the visual cortex of monkeys suggest a possible mechanism by which attention and perception may interact at a neuronal level.

4   Cognitive processes in the everyday world

Earlier in the chapter we considered how little information you may take in while going on a routine journey. Having reviewed a number of the processes involved in attention and perception, we can go back to the example of driving. We can consider how the processes we have explored might explain why we can perform a task such as driving and yet have so little recollection of it; and we can think about what the consequences of perceiving so little might be.

4.1 'Looked but failed to see' accidents

The problem with working on 'automatic', as may be the case with a regular journey, is that you may come to 'see what you expect to see' or, conversely and more importantly, 'you do not see what you do not expect to see'. This is typified by a class of road accident referred to as 'looked but failed to see' (LBFS). The term was first coined by Sabey and

Staughton (1975) and refers to occasions when drivers have driven into something and claimed subsequently that they simply 'did not see it'. Accident reports suggest that these accidents are particularly common at road junctions and that cyclists and motorcyclists are more likely to be the victims than other car drivers. Much of the research in this area has concentrated, in the terms used in this chapter, on a failure of sensation, suggesting LBFS accidents are a failure on the part of an individual to *detect* relatively small targets such as motorcycles – i.e. they are simply not conspicuous enough.

Lack of conspicuity is almost certainly a factor in many of these kinds of accident. But later research (e.g. Cole and Hughes, 1984) suggests that the **sensory conspicuity**, that is, the intrinsic properties of an object that are likely to be registered by the senses such as shape, colour, brightness, may not always be enough to lead to detection and *conscious* perception of that object. Cole and Hughes suggested that **attention conspicuity** is an important factor, that is, how likely an object is to draw attention to itself. This can be influenced by the factors that we have already discussed that may affect attention, such as the expectations of the individual. Thus, if you are expecting to encounter a motorcyclist you are more likely to perceive one. This sounds self-evident, but it is easier to appreciate the problem by considering the reverse case: if motorists are *not* expecting to encounter a motorcyclist, then they may fail to perceive one no matter how 'visible' they are. It is important therefore to make a distinction between sensory conspicuity and attention (or cognitive) conspicuity (Wulf *et al.*, 1989).

The implication of this is that motorists might drive into something that has high sensory conspicuity at least in part because they do not expect it to be there. How can this everyday practical problem be researched?

4.2 Researching complex practical problems

A series of studies by Langham (1999) and his co-workers (Langham *et al.*, 1998, 2002) suggests that such accidents do occur, as demonstrated by incidents involving police cars (that are *designed* to have high sensory conspicuity) that were attempting to block off a lane on a road.

Langham *et al.* investigated the phenomenon that stationary police cars, fitted with a full range of sensory conspicuity enhancers (reflective and retro-reflective materials, flashing lights, etc.), such as the car in Figure 6.9, are sometimes hit by drivers who subsequently claim that they did not see them. Note that the LBFS accidents described earlier are the result of a failure of **visual search**. At a junction, individuals are looking for any traffic crossing that junction in a fairly short time interval. The kind of problem investigated by Langham *et al.* involves a different task. It still involves a

Sensory conspicuity
The likelihood that an object will be detected based on its intrinsic properties registered by the senses, such as shape, colour, brightness.

Attention conspicuity
The likelihood that an object will draw attention to itself.

Visual search
The task of picking out a particular target item from a number of irrelevant (distractor) items.

Figure 6.9 Spot the police car. Some people do not

failure to perceive a conspicuous object, but the task is a **vigilance** task – keeping a look out for dangerous objects over a long time period, a drive down a motorway as opposed to the time spent to cross a junction.

Langham *et al.* (1998) approached this practical problem by using two rather different methods in a complementary way. First, they conducted a survey to identify some of the factors involved in LBFS accidents and then used this information to design a series of experiments to investigate some of these factors.

To obtain the survey data, Langham *et al.* requested that the Institute of Traffic Investigation organise a nationwide campaign to solicit certain information from police forces about accidents involving police vehicles, in an attempt to identify some of the factors important in LBFS accidents. Advertisements were also placed at police conferences and in the journal 'Impact'. From this approach they obtained useable details of 29 vehicle accidents from twelve UK police forces that satisfied the following criteria:

1   The police vehicle involved in the accident was fitted with conspicuity enhancers (see Figure 6.9, above).

Vigilance
The task of monitoring over a period of time for the appearance of a target item.

2   The accident involved an actual collision with the police vehicle, police officer, or associated equipment.

3   The accident report referred to the driver claiming s/he did not see the police vehicle in time.

4   The accident was caused by someone with a valid driving licence.

5   No plausible explanation other than a late detection error could be given for the accident.

6   The accident was attended by a police officer other than the one involved in the accident.

Where possible, the same details were obtained about all these accidents including such things as location of accident, police vehicle orientation, lighting, weather conditions, etc. The survey identified a number of interesting aspects of LBFS accidents with police vehicles including:

• There were more accidents when the police vehicle was parked 'in line' (stopped in a lane and facing in the same direction as the prevailing traffic) than when it was parked 'echelon' (parked across a lane 'side-on' to the direction of traffic).

• Deployment of warning signs and cones did not guarantee detection.

• Although the accidents occur on motorways and dual carriageways, 62 per cent of the accidents examined appeared to be within 15 km of the drivers' homes.

• Only one of the drivers was under 25 years old, thus novice drivers are likely to be under-represented in the sample.

It is worth now stepping back to consider these LBFS accidents in the context of the processes discussed so far in this chapter.

Activity 6.4

Can you explain some of the factors behind these accidents? Can you explain how somebody can drive into something as conspicuous (at least at a sensory level) as a police car without, apparently, even seeing it? Think back to the routine journey we were considering right at the start of the chapter, and indulge in a little speculation as to what attentional processes are involved (or not involved as the case may be) and whether these processes could explain a LBFS accident.

Comment

Driving on a dual carriageway is a familiar task – and may be a familiar part of a regular journey, especially if it is near home. Thus a lot of the processing of the task may be automatic, with most resources directed internally – thinking about other things. It is also extremely rare, on journeys of this kind, for there to be a stationary car parked in one of the lanes; therefore it is not expected. Also, from past driving experience in general, motorists expect any vehicles they see on the road to be moving. Even if they do detect (at the sensory level) the police car, previous driving experience and expectations may lead motorists to *perceive* it as moving. And, this is a greater problem if the police car is parked 'in line', as this would be the correct orientation for a *moving* car. If it is parked 'echelon' then previous driving experience would suggest that this is not the usual orientation for a moving car.

Previous experience seems to play a crucial part in these accidents. The results of the survey mentioned above (although based on a relatively small number of cases) do generate some predictions that can be tested experimentally, in a laboratory, and this is the approach that Langham *et al.* (2002) took. Among other things, they investigated the role of previous driving experience in LBFS accidents involving police cars. The specific hypothesis that Langham *et al.* (2002) tested was that drivers with less driving experience (who appear to be under-represented in the survey described above) would be less influenced by the orientation of the stationary car, as they would be less inclined to assume that all cars are moving. A series of video clips, which had been filmed from a moving car in a controlled situation, were shown to two groups of drivers – experienced and inexperienced. The drivers were asked to identify potential hazards. In only one of the video clips was there a stationary police car: parked either in-line or echelon. Experienced drivers recognized the echelon-parked police car as a hazard faster than the in-line one. Inexperienced drivers took about the same amount of time to detect the hazard whatever the parking orientation of the police car. These findings can be taken as support for the hypothesis that experienced drivers take longer to perceive the in-line police car as stationary, because their driving experience will tend to suggest that a car in this orientation on a dual carriageway is moving.

6.6 FEATURED METHOD

Experiments III: Combining methods to bring complex cognitive phenomena into the laboratory

In the discussion above you have seen that it is possible to study everyday phenomena that relate to complex and interacting cognitive processes. Langham *et al.* took a practical problem – a particular kind of road traffic accident – that was thought to be related to attentional processes and began to study the operation of these cognitive processes by means of a survey of LBFS accidents, highlighting some of the possible contributory factors. Once these possible factors were isolated, they could be expressed as hypotheses about the causes of LBFS accidents and these hypotheses could be tested in a laboratory.

So in Langham *et al.*'s research, the next step involved designing a controlled experiment to test the hypothesis in the laboratory using standardized stimulus materials (video clips), and a behavioural test as the dependent variable – the time taken to identify a hazard. Strictly, this was a quasi-experiment because the experimenters did not manipulate the independent variable. They did not manipulate the participants' driving experience but instead recruited participants who already could be classed as experienced or inexperienced. The findings of the experiment supported the hypothesis about prior knowledge and expectations influencing the drivers' attentional processes in a way that might, in everyday life, make them less safe on the roads.

Langham *et al.*, however, are fastidious in pointing out the difficulties of studying everyday problems in a laboratory setting. Although the laboratory studies allow a greater degree of *control* of the situation, there are many differences between the lab and the outside world. This issue is known as *ecological validity*. Can the findings achieved in the laboratory setting be said to be equally valid in the outside world?

Possible differences inherent in the laboratory setting as compared with everyday life, are emphasized by another study of drivers approaching an intersection. Ebbesen *et al.* (1977) examined how drivers decide whether it is safe to cross an intersection when a car is approaching. They looked at this problem both *on the road* and in a driving simulator (which, as the name suggests, is designed to mimic driving 'on the road' as closely as possible in the laboratory). In the laboratory, it appeared that the drivers were basing their decisions about whether or not to cross on a complex estimation of the distance and velocity of the approaching cars. The participants driving on the simulator made errors on 9 per cent of trials. In a real situation however, drivers appeared to use a much simpler measure (time to contact of the oncoming car, which does not require distance and velocity to be mentally computed separately) to judge whether to cross. These drivers made no errors. This study, which produced clearly different results in the two settings, suggests that there may be problems with trying to replicate a situation from everyday life in the laboratory - even when a simulator is used.

But does this imply that only studies conducted in the everyday world are valid? Studies in the everyday world certainly have difficulties of their own. Two obvious problems already mentioned are the number of variables acting at the same time and the lack of control of those variables. You may get a result, but not be able to work out what caused it because so many different variables may contribute to the overall result. You do not have sufficient control of the situation to vary only one variable at a time as you might like to do in a true experiment.

This suggests that you cannot be sure that the results you obtain in everyday life are any more valid than those obtained in the laboratory. For instance, consider the finding that, when driving *on the road*, drivers made no errors when judging whether to cross a junction. These are real drivers, driving on real roads, and not making any errors. This raises the question of whether the finding can be *generalized* to suggest that drivers *never* make any errors in such situations, which seems unlikely.

Consider the accident reports discussed earlier on LBFS accidents. These drew data from reports of road accidents and suggest that a lot of these occurred with drivers failing to 'see' other road-users at junctions at all, let alone deciding whether there was time to cross. Also accident statistics suggest that drivers *do* make mistakes at junctions – and bad enough ones to lead to accidents. Thus, although the Ebbesen *et al.* study was carefully conducted, it still does not seem to give the complete picture. From the discussion above it appears that there was an unusually low error rate in the everyday world observations (none!) and an unusually high rate in the simulator studies. Imagine what would happen if drivers made an error at a junction on nine per cent of their journeys. This suggests that both types of study have their problems. For instance the low error rate in the real world studies may have been due to a number of factors such as:

- The drivers drove as they normally would but the sample was too small to pick up any errors. Ebbesen *et al.* observed over 2,000 drivers, but this is still only a tiny fraction of road-users.

- The drivers may have suspected they were being observed and therefore changed their behaviour, perhaps driving more carefully. Ebbesen *et al.* took great care to try and make the observations unobtrusive, but there is always the possibility that the drivers noticed something out of the ordinary (although, from the previous discussion, it is surprising what drivers do not notice!).

On the other hand, the unusually high error rate in the simulator may have been due to other factors such as:

- The cues provided by the simulator may not be as good as those available in the real world for judging the speed and distance of oncoming cars, thus making the task more difficult. That is, the simulator is not a completely accurate portrayal of a driving task.

- No matter how realistic a **simulation** is, drivers will *know that it is only a simulation*; if they crash they will not get hurt. Therefore the risks of being hurt are really non-existent and this may well affect their driving behaviour, leading them to make more mistakes in the simulator.

Simulation
The attempt to mimic, as closely as possible in a controlled setting, a real-world situation.

This discussion of methods and the fundamental and unavoidable experiential difference between driving-on-a-real-road and driving-in-a-simulator also illustrates that perception is not just limited to the perception of objects in the environment. Individuals may also use information gathered from the environment, together with stored knowledge, to make quite complex and abstract judgements about the

Perceived risk
The level of risk that an individual *believes* they are exposed to.

Risk homeostasis
The modification of behaviour to maintain perceived risk at a constant level.

whole situation they are in. As discussed above, they may well assess the level of risk that they are exposed to in any particular situation (particularly one such as driving). Thus, drivers may judge the **perceived risk** of the actual situation they are in and this may have an influence on how they behave in that situation. Perceptions of this kind are explored in more detail in Chapter 7.

This is related to another phenomenon that is referred to as **risk homeostasis** (Wilde, 1982). You have already encountered the notion of homeostasis in Chapter 4 in relation to maintaining the body in an optimal state. Risk homeostasis is a similar notion, but suggests that individuals like to operate at a constant level of perceived risk. Risk homeostasis applied to driving suggests that drivers make a judgement of risk from moment to moment based on their perception of the situation they are in and their perception of their ability to cope with it, and change their behaviour accordingly. The implications of risk homeostasis are interesting: give somebody a bigger, safer, car and they will drive more dangerously. From your experience do you think this is the case?

Summary Section 4

- Failure of attention may be implicated in 'looked but failed to see' (LBFS) accidents.
- It is possible to bring certain features of complex, everyday world phenomena into the laboratory in simplified form for experimental study.
- There are problems with attempting to apply results found in the laboratory to the everyday world. People may not behave the same way in the laboratory as they would outside, so the ecological validity of a laboratory study is an important issue.
- Studies conducted in the 'real world' are not without problems. They are more difficult to control and the results may be difficult to interpret.
- Risk homeostasis suggests that individuals' perceptions of risk may influence their behaviour.

5 Final thought

The studies described in this chapter illustrate how difficult it is to study psychological processes, either in the laboratory or in everyday life. For this reason, psychologists tend to adopt a range of approaches. The results of any one study are unlikely ever to be completely conclusive, but must be interpreted in the light of findings from other studies.

The phenomenological approach describes the mind reaching out to stimuli in the world and interpreting them in terms of our own personal experience. This embodies a crucial paradox for the study and understanding of such processes as perception and attention: The *totality* of any situation, including its *meaning* for the individual concerned (at that moment), will have a crucial effect on the way in which perception and attention operate. Thus the very fact that the study is done in a laboratory or in the outside world will inevitably affect the as-experienced nature of the stimuli impinging on the individual. In the laboratory, the psychologist does have some control over the *physical* nature of stimuli that the participant is exposed to. But different individuals may *experience* these same stimuli in different ways. This is part of a wider issue: in any situation, experimental or otherwise, the psychologist has little or no control over how an individual's prior knowledge and experience will influence processes such as attention and perception.

Perception involves a lot more than just recognizing objects in the world, or identifying sounds. Our experience, knowledge, biases and prejudices, and the meaning of the situations in which they are encountered will all influence perception and attention: which gives some idea of how complex the processes are and how problematic it can be to study them. The best a psychologist can do is to try to measure or at least estimate these factors and take them into account. For instance, if the psychologist believes that a particular type of experience (such as the ability to drive) is important to a study, then they may try to control for that experience, for example only selecting participants that have the same level of driving experience.

The material discussed in this chapter was chosen not only to give you an overview of how the processes of perception and attention operate, but also to illustrate how basic psychological methods and new techniques can be used to enhance our knowledge of these processes. This chapter demonstrates some of the problems inherent in the study of cognitive psychology and also how different techniques (such as cognitive psychology, cognitive neuropsychology and neuroscience) can be combined to give a clearer picture of what is going on.

It also attempts to show how results gained in the laboratory can be applied in the everyday world but how difficult it can be to do this. Trying to solve practical problems was really the starting point for modern cognitive psychology and so it is good to try and bring things full circle and look at how the knowledge we have gained over the years can be applied.

Finally, this chapter should have demonstrated that, although we know a lot about how perception and attention operate and interact, there is still plenty left to find out.

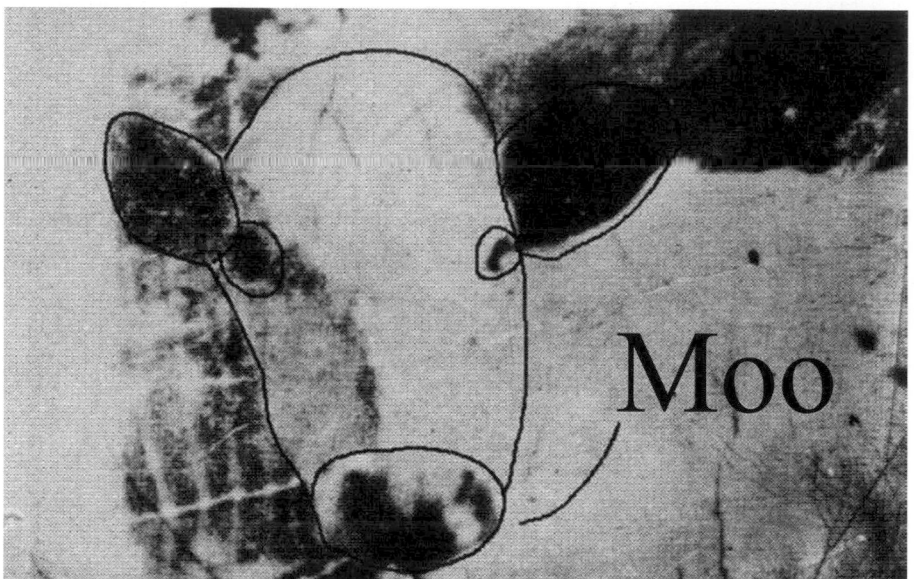

Figure 6.10 Now do you 'see' the cow from Figure 6.1?

Further reading

General texts on cognitive psychology: these two texts cover similar material and provide more detailed coverage of the areas described in this chapter. The style of both books is open and approachable, making them fairly easy to read.
Gross, R. and McIlveen, R. (1997) *Cognitive Psychology*, London, Hodder & Stoughton Educational.

Groome, D. and Dewart, H. (1999) *An Introduction to Cognitive Psychology and Disorders*, London, Taylor and Francis.

Specialized text on attention: this book provides an in-depth coverage of attention in far greater depth than this chapter.
Styles, E.A. (1997) *The Psychology of Attention*, Hove, Psychology Press Ltd.

Specialized text on perception: this is the equivalent reference for perception to the Styles one given above for attention. This text covers aspects of perception mentioned in this chapter in considerably more depth, and also looks at a number of areas that are not considered at all in the chapter due to lack of space.
Bruce, V. and Green, P.R. (1996) *Visual Perception, Physiology, Psychology, and Ecology*, 3rd edition, Hove, Psychology Press.

Background reading on cognitive neuropsychology: this well-known book is a fascinating and easily accessible account of cognitive neuropsychology in action.
Sacks, O. (1986) *The Man Who Mistook His Wife For A Hat*, London, Macmillan. Originally published 1985, Gerald Duckworth and Co.

References

Broadbent, D.E. (1954) 'The role of auditory localisation and attention in memory span', *Journal of Experimental Psychology*, vol.47, pp.191–96.

Broadbent, D.E. (1971) *Decision and Stress*, London, Academic Press.

Bruce, V., Green, P.R. and Georgeson, M.A. (1996) *Visual Perception, Physiology, Psychology, and Ecology*, Hove, Psychology Press (3rd edn).

Cole, B.L. and Hughes, P.K (1984) 'A field trial of attention and search conspicuity', *Human Factors*, vol.26, no.3, pp.299–313.

Dallenbach, K.M. (1951) 'A puzzle-picture with a new principle of concealment', *American Journal of Psychology*, vol.64, pp.431–3.

Day, R.H. (1989) 'Natural and artificial cues, perceptual compromise and the basis of veridical and illusory perception', in Vickers, D. and Smith, P.L. (eds) *Human Information Processing: Measures and Mechanisms*, Amsterdam, Elsevier, pp.107–9.

Delboeuf, J.L.R. (1892) 'Sur une nouvelle illusion d'optique', *Bulletin de L'Académie Royale de Belgique*, vol.24, pp.545–58.

Deutsch, J.A. and Deutsch, D. (1963) 'Attention, some theoretical considerations', *Psychological Review*, vol.70, pp.80–90.

Driver, J. and Bayliss, G.C. (1989) 'Movement and visual attention: The spotlight metaphor breaks down', *Journal of Experimental Psychology: Human Perception and Performance*, vol.15, pp.448–56.

Ebbesen, E.B., Parker, S. and Konečni, V.J. (1977) 'Laboratory and field analyses of decisions involving risk', *Journal of Experimental Psychology: Human Perception and Performance*, vol.3, pp.576–89.

Engel, F.L. (1971) 'Visual conspicuity, directed attention and retinal locus', *Vision Research*, vol.11, pp.563–76.

Eriksen, B.A. and Eriksen, C.W. (1974) 'Effects of noise letters upon the identification of a target in a non-search task', *Perception and Psychophysics*, vol.16, pp.143–9.

Eriksen, C.W. and Murphy T.D. (1987) 'Movement of attentional focus across the visual field: a critical look at the evidence', *Perception and Psychophysics*, vol.42, pp.299–305.

Gibson, J.J. (1950) *The Perception of the Visual World*, Boston, Houghton Mifflin.

Gopher, D. (1993) 'The skill of attentional control: acquisition and execution of attentional strategies', in Kornblum, S. and Meyer, D.E. (eds) *Attention and Performance XIV: Synergies in Experimental Psychology, Artificial Intelligence and Cognitive Neuroscience*, Cambridge, MA, MIT Press.

Gregory, R.L (1966) *Eye and Brain*, London, Weidenfeld and Nicholson.

Halligan, P.W. and Marshall, J.C. (1993) 'The History and Clinical Presentation of Neglect', in Robertson, I.H. and Marshall, J.C. (eds) *Unilateral Neglect: Clinical and Experimental Studies*, Hove, UK, LEA.

Husserl, E. (1931) *Ideas: General Introduction to Pure Phenomenology* (vol.1) New York, Macmillan.

James, W. (1890) *The Principles of Psychology*, New York, H. Holt and Company.

Kahneman, D. (1973) *Attention and Effort*, Englewood Cliffs, New Jersey, Prentice-Hall.

Langham, M.P. (1999) *An Investigation of the Role of Vehicle Conspicuity in the 'Looked but Failed to See' Error in Driving*, unpublished PhD, University of Sussex, Brighton.

Langham, M.P., Hole, G., Edwards, J. and O'Neil, C. (1998) *Can the 'Looked but Failed to See' Error Involve Highly Conspicuous Police Patrol Cars? Evidence from Accident Reports and Laboratory Studies*, First Engineering Psychology Conference, British Psychological Society Special Interest Group, University of Southampton.

Langham, M., Hole, G., Edwards, J., and O'Neil, C. (2002) 'An analysis of "looked but failed to see" accidents involving parked police cars', *Ergonomics*, vol.45, no.3, pp.167–85.

Lavie, N. (1995) 'Perceptual load as a necessary condition for selective attention', *Journal of Experimental Psychology: Human Perception and Performance*, vol.21, no.3, pp.451–68.

MacDonald, A.W., III, Cohen, J.O., Stenger, V.A. and Carter, C.S. (2000) 'Dissociating the role of the dorsolateral prefrontal and anterior cingulate cortex in cognitive control', *Science*, vol.288, pp.1835–8.

Maunsell, J.H.R. and McAdams, C.J. (2000) 'Effects of attention on neuronal response properties in visual cerebral cortex', in Gazzaniga, M.S. (ed.) *The*

New Cognitive Neurosciences, Cambridge, Massachusetts, The MIT Press, pp.315–24.

Navon, D. and Gopher, D. (1979) 'On the economy of the human processing system', *Psychological Review*, vol.86, pp.214–55.

McLeod, P.D. (1977) 'A dual task response modality effect: Support for multi-processor models of attention', *Quarterly Journal of Experimental Psychology*, vol.29, pp.83–9.

Over, R. (1968) 'Explanations of geometrical illusions', *Psychological Bulletin*, vol.70, pp.545–62.

Posner, M. (1980) 'Orienting of attention', *Quarterly Journal of Experimental Psychology: Human Experimental Psychology*, vol.32, pp.3–25.

Posner, M.I. and Boies, S.J. (1971) 'Components of attention', *Psychological Review*, vol.78, pp.391–408.

Révész, G. (1934) 'System der optischen und haptischen Raumtäuschungen Z', *Psychol,* vol.131, pp.296–375.

Rothbart, M. and John, O.P. (1985) 'Social categorization and behavioral episodes: A cognitive analysis of the effects of intergroup contact', *Journal of Social Issues*, vol.41, pp.81–104.

Rubin, E. (1915) *Synsoplevede Figurer,* Copenhagen, Gyldendalske.

Sabey, B. and Staughton, G.C. (1975) *Interacting roles of road environment, vehicle and road user,* 5th International Conference of the International Association for Accident Traffic Medicine, London, TRRL, Crowthorne, Berkshire.

Sacks, O. (1986) *The Man who Mistook his Wife for a Hat*, London, Macmillan (originally published 1985, Gerald Duckworth).

Schneider, W. and Shiffrin, R.M. (1977) 'Controlled and automatic human information processing: I. Detection, search and attention', *Psychological Review*, vol.84, pp.1–66.

Segall, M.H., Campbell, D.T. and Herskouits, M.J. (1963) 'Cultural differences in the perception of geometrical illusions', *Science*, vol.139, pp.769–71.

Shiffrin, R.M. and Schneider, W. (1977) 'Controlled and automatic human information processing: II. Perceptual learning, automatic attending and a general theory', *Psychological Review*, vol.84, pp.127–90.

Simons, D.J. and Levin, D.T. (1998) 'Failure to detect changes to people during real-world interaction', *Psychonomic Bulletin and Review*, vol.4, p.644.

Stroop, J.R. (1935) 'Studies of interference in serial verbal reactions', *Journal of Experimental Psychology*, vol.18, no.6, pp.643–62.

Treisman, A.M. (1960) 'Contextual cues in selective listening, *Quarterly Journal of Experimental Psychology*, vol.12, pp.242–8.

Treisman, A.M. (1993) 'The perception of features and objects', in Baddeley, A.D. and Weiskrantz, L. (eds) *Attention, Awareness, Selection and Control*, Oxford, Oxford University Press.

Wickens, C.D. (1992) *Engineering Psychology and Human Performance* (2nd edn) New York, Harper Collins.

Wilde, G.J.S. (1982) 'The theory of risk homeostasis: implications for safety and health', *Risk Analysis*, vol.2, no.4, pp.209–25.

Wulf, G., Hancock, P.A. and Rahimi, M. (1989) 'Motorcycle conspicuity – an evaluation and synthesis of influential factors', *Journal of Safety Research*, vol.20, pp.153–76.

■ Commentary 6: Perception and attention

Chapter 6 ('Perception and attention') takes forward the discussion in Chapter 5 of people as biological entities whose psychological processes are necessarily situated in social and cultural contexts.

Theory

1 Psychologists develop theoretical constructs to clarify the issues they study and to build testable theories. In cognitive psychology, theoretical constructs often draw on machine-based and other physical metaphors such as communication channels and computers.

Methods

2 Much of the study of perception and attention is within the experimental cognitive psychology tradition, although methods have been diversified to include neuropsychological and brain-imaging techniques.

3 Behavioural and biological data, analysed from an outsider viewpoint, are central to the study of perceptual processes. But, traditionally, introspection – an insider viewpoint – has always been important as well.

4 The complexity of perception and attention, and their embeddedness in the everyday world, mean that laboratory experiments may compromise ecological validity. Practical applications of cognitive theories have to take this into account.

Themes

5 Even though some of its biological structures are fixed, perception can change, both through experience and also because of moment-to-moment changes in sensory cues.

6 Perception can be thought of as the result of lifelong interactions between *biology* (from genes to the structure of sense organs) and each person's *experience* in their particular environments – a form of the general interplay of nature *and* nurture.

■ Thinking about theory

We spend most of our waking lives *perceiving*, whether visually, aurally or through our other senses (e.g. touch, smell and taste). But, as we have already seen in previous chapters, the apparently most simple and effortless things that we do are often psychologically complicated. So what kinds of starting points do psychologists use as they set about theory building?

Defining and using theoretical constructs

One starting point is to define the *building blocks* with which to work. We have seen that psychologists have made a distinction between sensation, attention and perception. Each of these terms is an everyday word in common usage, but, in the study of perception, they are also *theoretical constructs*. Theoretical constructs permit understandings to be extended and we have seen in the chapter how they are used in theory building and testing. Having three constructs makes it possible for psychologists to propose, and then test, possible *relationships* between them. Sometimes the focus has been on the processes separately and sometimes on the interactions between them. In other cases the focus has been on the cognitive aspects of the process as a whole (usually called perception) which can provide vivid and seemingly immediate experiences of the world. The phenomenological view of perception, in particular, is of one holistic process in the service of what is called the perceiver's *intentionality*.

Theoretical constructs are the elements that are used to build specific theories. For example, Erikson's notion of 'identity crisis' in Chapter 1 is a theoretical construct, as is the idea of 'personality traits' in Chapter 5. None of these theoretical constructs actually exists in the world. They are hypothetical but they provide ways of thinking about aspects of identity and personality. Without the division into the three processes (sensation, attention and perception), psychologists would not have been able to identify what underlies 'change blindness' – produced through our routine filtering of information and failure to *attend* to all the *sensations* we receive. Furthermore, such theoretical constructs can explain how, even when we have the same *sensations* (e.g. of patterns of light and dark entering our eyes from 'bottom-up' information), different people can have different *perceptions* as a result of 'top-down' processes which introduce personal experiences and knowledge into the perceptual process.

The impetus of practical problems and theorists' own interests

Another starting point for building theory is the social and historical context of the time, and the practical problems that emerge in different periods. We have already seen these kinds of influence at work in earlier chapters. For example, in Chapter 5, progress in theorizing personality was driven by the preoccupations with 'genetic inheritance' of people like Galton and Cattell, and the new requirements of education policy and military selection for *measurement* of personality. Similar forces have influenced the development of perception research. For example,

James Gibson's ideas on direct perception came out of his research on improving airline pilots' ability to land safely, and Broadbent's early work on attention also was directed by practical problems such as the attentional overload of air-traffic controllers.

At a more social and cultural level, just as in the case of psychometrics and personality measurement, technological advances have had a particularly important role in research on perception and attention. The particular strand of cognitive psychology that has been concerned with perception and attention uses the information-processing approach which is very much a product of technological changes – advances in telecommunications and computer science. The machine model of the mind became central to cognitive psychology. But, as the author of Chapter 6 has shown very clearly, even newer technological advances have influenced cognitive research. We have seen that brain-imaging techniques enable cognitive psychologists to combine information-processing models and inferences with biology and the brain – the birth of cognitive neuroscience.

The use of metaphor

Chapter 6 has vividly demonstrated how, over many decades, cognitive psychologists have made extensive use of metaphor to facilitate their theorizing and model building. Cognitive psychologists, unlike behaviourists, set out to deal with 'what is in the head'. Behaviour *is* used, but as data from which to make *inferences* about mental processes. This requires a great deal of ingenuity and very clear predictive models so as to be able to choose between competing hypotheses on the basis of empirical findings. But, at the same time, we know that the brain is 'wet-ware' – that is, it is made up of biological tissues and fluids, with chemicals and electrical discharges. It is difficult to span the gap between a brain and cognitive processing: hence the many metaphors that have been used to further thinking and theory building in psychology, and in cognitive psychology in particular. The use of metaphor is very important in psychology. Information processing is itself a metaphor, as is any machine model of the mind – channels, pools of resources, filters and so on.

■ Thinking about methods

In this chapter you have seen how different methods and different kinds of data are used to provide evidence, reflecting the range of processes, perspectives and levels of analysis involved in studying perception. Nevertheless an important part of research into attention and perception has been conducted within the experimental cognitive psychology tradition.

Diversity of data and methods

The psychology of sensation has studied the sense organs and central nervous system, and this biological perspective has relied on biological methods and material data. Increasingly, biological methods, material data and case-study accounts are being used in the form of neuropsychology and in the development of cognitive neuroscience. All these approaches take an outsider viewpoint, although case studies also employ personal accounts of experiences. The insider viewpoint has always played an important role in the study of perception. After all, it is our *experiencing* of perception – of sensation, attention and perception – that is so central to everyday functioning. One of the starting points of empirical psychology was introspection – verbal reports of 'perceiving objects' (in Wundt's laboratory) and William James's reports of his 'streams of consciousness', which included what we would think of as perceptions of what was going on around him. Another early influence on the beginnings of the tradition of cognitive psychology was the philosophy of the phenomenologists for whom an essential feature of perception was how we experience it as a holistic phenomenon embedded in the 'intentionality' of the perceiver. The methods here have often been introspective, relying on people's accounts of their inner experience of the perceptual process. The use of illusions and similar demonstrations like the 'cow picture', the reversing face/vase figure and the Müller-Lyer illusion seen in Chapter 6 provide very important kinds of insider data for the exploration, and ultimately the explanation, of perceptual phenomena.

Perception as part of the experimental cognitive psychology tradition

Research on some aspects of perception and attention has developed within the cognitive psychology perspective and its traditional scientific, outsider viewpoint. However, since we cannot see mental processes, cognitive psychologists have to devise experiments that use behaviour as their data, but go beyond the behaviour to test theories of how cognitive processes like perception work. In order to arrive at testable hypotheses, research on perception has to break down the cognitive processes being studied into manageable parts. As a result, cognitive psychologists interested in perception are concerned with studying processes rather than studying people as a whole (or 'holistically'). This division into manageable parts is an aspect of the simplification that is necessary for controlled laboratory experimentation. But simplification can have unwanted implications for our understanding of the way that perception operates in the everyday world.

Laboratory research and everyday experience

Laboratory studies have allowed psychologists to control variables in order to be able to interpret findings and then generate new hypotheses. But, in order to get a more complete picture of the processes of perception and attention in ordinary life, cognitive psychologists have diversified their methods, sometimes using simulation, and sometimes moving out of the laboratory. This move is important for theory, because cognition in the laboratory, where meaningfulness of the stimuli is controlled, may be inherently different from cognition in ordinary life. It is also important practically, because there are many everyday problems concerning perception and attention that might benefit from relevant research. Sometimes differences between the outside world and a laboratory setting mean that laboratory-based experimental studies have low ecological validity. For example, it has been shown that drivers react in different ways in the laboratory compared with on the road. However, as Graham Edgar points out, 'real-world' experiments raise their own set of difficulties. Neither type of experiment is perfect and good explanations of perception and attention require an interchange between research in the laboratory and studies of ordinary behaviour in everyday life.

Thinking about themes

Is perception fixed or does it change?

Before you started this chapter, you may have assumed that perception is fixed: we see 'what is there' and 'what is there' does not change. Indeed, the biology of perceptual systems is, to some extent, fixed. However, the chapter started with a demonstration of how different people can perceive different things when they attend to the sensations they receive from a series of light and dark patches. For those who did not initially see the 'cow', the chapter demonstrated that our perceptions can change, even when our sensations stay the same. This flexibility of our perceptions is sometimes evident from second to second as our perceptions of figure and ground shift (as, for example, in the two faces/vase ambiguous figure presented in the chapter). And we saw that the perceptions of experienced drivers are likely to differ from those of inexperienced drivers making the same driving judgements. Phenomenological theory and 'top-down' approaches both help to make sense of this perceptual flexibility in terms of the motivations of the perceiver, personal experiences and prior knowledge. We must conclude, therefore, that perception *can* change, even though some of its biological structures are fixed.

The inextricable linking of nature-nurture: biology and experience in environments

One of the themes in the chapter you have just read is that sensation, attention and perception all require both biological structures *and* experience in the world. In earlier chapters and commentaries the term *nature* has referred to biology in some relatively fixed sense, either genetic endowment itself or the biological structures that develop early in life. In other words, nature is understood as the enabling and sometimes constraining influence of 'what is there already'. *Nurture* has referred to the impact of the environment, in its widest sense, on what people (and non-human animals) become. What we are arriving at is an understanding of nature in a more general sense, as the biological structures and processes which in themselves change as life goes on, and nurture as experience of all kinds. The continuous interaction between these two is a lifelong process of change and flexibility. For example, we have seen in Chapter 6 that we are both enabled and limited by the biology of the sense organs and the central nervous system (including the brain). However, *what* we attend to and *what* we perceive (and thereby what we will feel and do) are related to our past and present experiences, our motivations and the social context in which we are perceiving, as well as the properties of the object being perceived.

In the chapter that follows (Chapter 7, 'Perceiving and understanding the social world'), the focus shifts from the perception of the world in general to the perception of people, and of judgements and decisions in the value-laden social world.

Perceiving and understanding the social world

Kevin Buchanan, Paul Anand, Hélène Joffe and Kerry Thomas

Contents

Aims

This chapter aims to:

- illustrate how the experimental method is used in social psychology, in particular in the study of social cognition, and to consider its strengths and weaknesses
- identify the mental structures and processes involved in perceiving and understanding the social world
- present evidence of some of the biases that influence social perception and judgements
- consider explanations for these biases, ranging from possible shortcomings in information processing to the pervasive influence of social experience, motivations and culture
- consider what is meant by the claim that people are not rational in their attributions to others and in their judgements more generally.

1 Introduction

In this chapter we continue with the topic of perception, taking up the story where Chapter 6 ended and asking questions about perception as embedded in the context and flow of everyday lives. How do we perceive complex 'objects', including other people and events? How do we make the judgements and decisions that are necessary, on a moment to moment basis, to inform our behaviour? Does our social experience affect what we 'see' and how we make judgements? This broad topic is known as **social cognition**.

Social cognition
The processing of social knowledge – perceiving, thinking, judging and explaining objects, events, relationships and issues in the social world.

1.1 The origins of the study of social cognition

Cognitive psychology

The study of social cognition began in part from increasing efforts within cognitive psychology to 'understand cognition as it occurs in the ordinary environment and in the context of natural purposeful activity' (Neisser, 1976, p.7). This quotation comes from a book called *Cognition and Reality*, one of those rare, identifiable 'turning points' in the history of psychology. Neisser argued that cognitive psychologists working within the information processing approach should 'pay more attention to the details of the real world in which perceivers and thinkers live and the fine

structure of information which that world makes available to them'
(1976, p.7–8).

Social psychology

While cognitive psychologists began with perception and moved towards
inclusion of the social world, social psychologists began in the social
environment, with perception of 'social objects' such as people, events,
and social issues. The first social psychologists used people's **attitudes**
about other people and social issues so as to understand social behaviour.
What we believe or know and how we think (our cognitions) have also
always been at the centre of theories about how we perceive people. The
roots of the study of social cognition can be traced back to the
contributions of Fritz Heider, an Austrian-born psychologist who moved to
the USA in 1930, about the same time as many European academics of his
generation.

Heider argued that in order to understand social behaviour we must
pay attention to how people perceive and struggle to make sense of their
social worlds, usually in terms of cause and effect (Heider, 1958). In
personality studies (see Chapter 5) and in person perception, psychologists
often regard people as operating like 'intuitive scientists', an idea related to
Heider's term, 'naïve psychology', and also to 'common-sense' theories of
personality. In this view, people are thought to look for regularity and
predictability in the world around them, building models of cause and
effect so as to control their lives. Heider applied these ideas to our
perception of other people and their actions. In a famous study using
cartoons of moving shapes, Heider and Simmel (1944) demonstrated how
we 'go beyond' the information that is given and the compelling nature of
attributions of cause and effect (see Box 7.1). Some still figures of these
animated cartoon shapes are shown in Figure 7.1.

Attitudes
A combination of our
beliefs (cognitions) and
feelings, and thought to
be an influence on our
behaviour.

Attributions
The explanations we
arrive at to account for
the causes of our own
behaviour (and its
outcomes) and other
people's behaviour (and
its outcomes).

7.1 The perception of causality (Heider and Simmel, 1944)

Three groups of participants were shown a simple animated cartoon in which
three geometric shapes – a small circle, a small box and a large box – moved
around a much larger rectangular box, one side of which could open like a door
on a hinge.

One group of participants was simply asked to describe what they saw. A second
group was asked to interpret the movements as the actions of people, and the
third group was asked to do the same as the second, but the movie was run
backwards. There were about forty participants in each group.

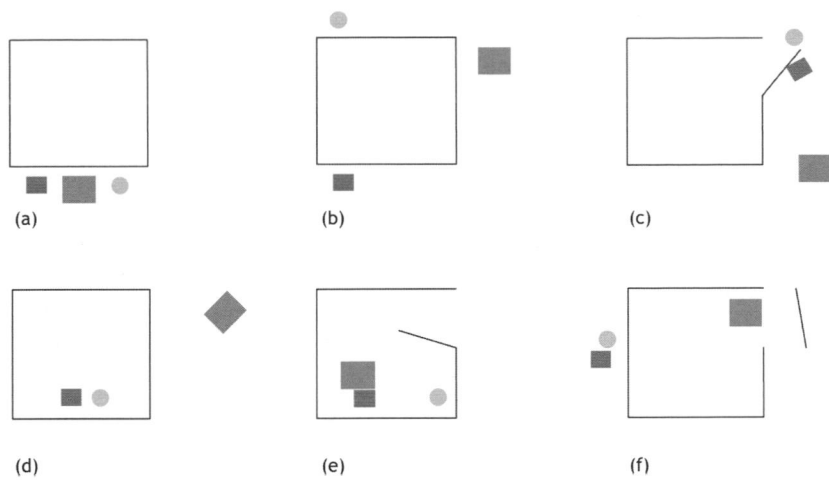

Figure 7.1 A sequence of shots, adapted from the Heider and Simmel (1944) animated cartoon

None of the participants in the second and third groups had any difficulty with the task, and they were more than happy to describe the shapes in human terms and answer questions about their interpretation of what the shapes were 'doing'. Of the 34 participants in the first group, *all but one* also described the movements in terms of human actions – without any prompting whatsoever. Moreover they, like those in the other groups, were all very prone to attribute human characteristics and intentions to the two squares. The geometric shapes were seen as 'fighting', 'chasing', 'attacking' and 'fleeing'. The descriptions were strikingly animistic, almost as if stories were being told. The shapes were described as 'two men in rivalry for a woman', or as a 'family conflict between two parents and a child'. Typically the large square was seen as aggressive or bullying and the smaller square as defiant and heroic. The circle was viewed as timid or fearful.

Although the Heider and Simmel experiment might seem a simplistic starting point, the development of research on social perception and cognition has had enormous practical significance. The findings in this area are relevant to psychologists' understanding of what happens in courtrooms, how responsibility is allocated, all kinds of problem solving, how risks are assessed, and how decisions are made about what levels of risk are acceptable in societies.

This chapter will focus on the way people go about making decisions in the flow and complexity of everyday life. Under such circumstances, information is usually incomplete and/or uncertain and so people cannot always be sure of the grounds on which they are making decisions. We will start in Section 2 by considering how knowledge may be represented in our minds and how this may affect our perceptions. In Section 3 we examine some aspects of how we perceive and understand other people's behaviour. In Section 4 the focus is on processing information to arrive at decisions or make judgements in everyday life. Section 5 gives an account of an applied, cross-cultural research project about how people deal with information about a health risk. The final section reviews the central theme of the chapter: how rational are we when we process information and make decisions?

Experimental social psychology
A perspective that frames its questions about social phenomena so that they can be studied using experimental methods.

Apart from the applied case study in Section 5, the research described in this chapter comes from the psychological perspective of **experimental social psychology**. Research within this perspective means that the topics often have to be simplified and taken out of 'real life' and into the psychologists' laboratory. You saw already, in Chapter 6, how difficult it can be to take research on perception and attention out of the laboratory and into the world of everyday life. Not only does a move into the laboratory necessarily reduce the complexity of what can be studied, it can produce *different results* from those gained outside. This is because the nature of what is being studied in the laboratory is, in some important ways, not the same as what happens in everyday life. You will see in this chapter that questions about ecological validity apply just as much, and possibly more, to research in social cognition than in cognitive psychology more generally.

Summary Section 1

- Heider suggested that people generally operate like naïve psychologists: they try to make sense of the world in terms of regularity, predictability and, particularly, cause and effect.
- In the flow and urgency of everyday life, information processing and decision making is based on incomplete and uncertain information, and often involves 'going beyond' the information available.
- The perspective of experimental social psychology frames questions about social phenomena in such a way as to permit use of experimental methods.

2 Social schemas: how knowledge shapes perception of the social world

You may appreciate already that the move from Chapter 6 to Chapter 7 has introduced more complicated 'objects of perception'. The process of perceiving in the social world goes well beyond an identification of 'what kind of object' is being perceived, and includes trying to understand another person's intentions. Perceiving a cube is likely to be much easier, in terms of what is taken in and categorized, than perceiving, making sense of and deciding what to do when faced with a defendant in a courtroom.

2.1 Schemas in social perception

An important feature of perception, noted in the previous chapter, is that what we perceive is shaped by 'top down information' – our knowledge, expectations and assumptions about the way the world is. Perception of the social world is no different, and this is most clearly illustrated when those expectations and assumptions turn out to be wrong.

A TV commercial some years ago started with a shot of a youth with shaven head, Doc Marten boots and combat trousers, running along the pavement in a city street. Another camera angle reveals him to be running towards a smartly dressed man standing on the pavement some yards away. A third shot shows him pushing the man aside, and a fourth shot pulls out to show there is a wooden pallet of bricks suspended above the man, and that the pallet is tipping and the bricks are about to fall on him. The point being that, before the fourth shot, most viewers will have formed a particular interpretation of what is happening – that the youth is going to physically assault the man. The fourth shot then reveals this interpretation to be mistaken – in fact, the youth is trying to protect the man, not hurt him. These four 'shots' are shown overleaf.

This is an example of how social perception is shaped by our knowledge of how things *usually* happen in the social world. Psychologists have proposed that there are cognitive structures involved in this process. Each structure is called a **schema**. Here the term 'cognitive structure' refers to a particular way in which knowledge or information is organized in memory, and how it is stored, accessed and used in the ongoing processing of information that makes up our waking lives. It is a

Schema
A mental structure containing knowledge relating to a particular kind of object.

A sequence of camera shots that only gradually build up to an 'explanation' of the action

structure of the 'mind', rather than the brain, that may or may not be reflected in actual connections between neurons.

A schema is a structure in which all knowledge relating to a particular object is packaged together. The concept of 'schema' in psychology can be traced back to Bartlett (1932). He used the idea of schema to explain (among other things) the finding that when English people were required to retell a Native American folk tale, the story would change over a series of retellings to become a more recognisably 'English' story (see Chapter 8, Section 3.1).

In social psychology, the objects on which schema are based are 'social objects', and include types of person, types of social situation or activity, social institutions like universities, or even 'social issues' like 'animal rights'. So you see that the word 'object' is being used here in a much broader sense than in the discussion of perception in Chapter 6. In a schema, knowledge is packaged so that each piece of information is linked to the whole. Storing knowledge in this way means that when just a few bits of information are perceived, this can activate the whole structure, enabling us quickly and efficiently to recognize the object. When we see the Doc Marten boots, the shaven head and the combat trousers this information triggers our schema for the social category 'skinhead', thus putting all our knowledge of this social category immediately at our disposal – including, for example, the 'fact' that they are inclined to criminality and violence. Of course, in this case we were mistaken – but the point is that most of the time we are not, and that on the whole **schematic processing** is an effective and efficient way of making sense of social experiences. Social psychologists have identified different types of schema. For example, **person schemas**, containing knowledge about types of people, at the level of personality traits; and **role schemas**, containing knowledge about social roles such as the 'skinhead' schema referred to above. Role schemas contain knowledge about the expectations of behaviour associated with the role (e.g. parents do not leave their young children unattended). **Event schemas,** also known as **scripts**, contain knowledge about social situations or social activities. We have scripts for going to the cinema, eating out in a restaurant, and so on. Scripts like this enable us to participate successfully in these activities, and also enable us to recognize them when we encounter them.

Schemas are clearly *generalized* representations of objects. We do not expect or experience all parents or all visits to the cinema to be exactly the same. Schemas contain knowledge of the general characteristics of the object, but also leave room for variation in specific instances. The formation of schemas can be seen as involving the abstraction of common features from many specific instances over time.

Another important characteristic of schemas is that the knowledge represented in schemas is *shared* knowledge. We do not have our own unique implicit personality theories, or scripts or stereotypes. Social schemas are not just social in the sense that they relate to social objects - they are social in the sense that we share them with other people and they would not be effective otherwise.

2.2 Some costs and benefits of schematic processing

Why does our cognitive system use schematic processing? To answer this question, you should recall the notion of a *limited capacity processor,* discussed in Chapter 6. Cognitive psychologists argue that, at any moment of our waking lives, we simply do not have the cognitive capacity to attend to all the information available to us through our senses. So we have developed ways of filtering out what isn't important, and selecting what is. Schemas can be seen as a part of this filtering process.

Schemas help *simplify* the enormous complexity of the world we encounter through our senses. Once activated, a schema tells us what to attend to, and what information about the object is relevant for our understanding. For example, when we meet a person for the first time, we don't have to treat everything about them as having equal informational

Schematic processing
An efficient, but sometimes constraining, way of processing information based on pre-existing schemas.

Person schema
A mental structure that contains knowledge about types of people at the level of personality traits.

Role schema
A mental structure that contains knowledge about social roles and social groups.

Event schema/script
A mental structure that contains knowledge about social situations and activities.

value – we can quickly categorize them in terms of a schema, and apply an interpretative framework that tells us what is relevant and what isn't. As they work to cut down on irrelevant information, schemas also provide us with additional information that *is* relevant. This information tells us what to expect, and thus schemas also make the world more predictable.

This information processing efficiency, however, does not come without costs. One obvious cost, as shown by the examples given earlier, is that our assumptions can sometimes be wrong. There are, however, more serious and pervasive problems than this. Schematic processing may produce biases or distortions in perception that are difficult to overcome. And schemas tend to be *self-confirming*. If we interpret what we see in light of our expectations, then we see what we expect to see. These problems of distortion and self-confirmation are illustrated by a social psychological experiment carried out by Darley and Gross (see Box 7.2).

7.2   The self-confirming nature of schemas (Darley and Gross, 1983)

Darley and Gross (1983) carried out an experiment that demonstrates the way in which the assumptions embodied in schemas influence our interpretation of social information, so that what we see ends up confirming those assumptions. They showed US college students a videotape introducing a young girl called Hannah. This character was a fictional person played by an actress. Two versions of the tape were used. In one version, Hannah was portrayed as of 'high socio-economic status', living with professional parents in a wealthy suburban area. In the other version, she was portrayed as of 'lower socio-economic status', living with her working-class parents in a run-down urban area.

Participants were shown one or the other of these 'introduction' videotapes. Some participants were also shown another videotape of Hannah answering questions in an oral exam, with the examiner stating after each response whether it was right or wrong. The pattern of right and wrong answers varied in such a way that it was not obvious whether Hannah was doing well or badly in the exam.

The participants who watched *only* the introduction video were asked to judge Hannah's academic ability on the basis of this information. Irrespective of the version of the introduction videotape they watched, they rated her as being of average ability. That is, her socioeconomic status (and any stereotypical assumptions that might be triggered by it) appeared to have no influence on the judgement. The participants who saw the exam video as well as the introduction video were also asked to make a judgement of Hannah's ability, but here the judgement was based on both videos. In this case, their judgements showed evidence of the influence of stereotypes. Those who saw the exam plus the 'high socioeconomic status' video judged Hannah to have higher ability, and as getting significantly more right answers than those who watched the exam plus the 'lower socioeconomic status' video.

It seems, then, that participants interpreted the same information differently according to their expectations. More importantly, it shows that this information ended up confirming their expectations. In the 'lower socioeconomic status' condition, participants saw 'evidence' in the exam performance that confirmed their assumption that people from poorer backgrounds have lower academic ability.

The basic cognitive process involved in schematic processing is categorisation, a topic that was introduced in Chapter 3, Section 3. The very nature of categories affects how they might be used in thinking and reasoning. Things belonging to a category are put there on the basis that they are more similar to other things that are included within the category, and that all the things in the category are collectively quite different from all the things excluded from the category. So when we think in categories, the very process itself results in us exaggerating the similarities *within* categories and the differences *between* different categories. The Darley and Gross study shows that this process can result in rich children being judged as more similar to each other (as high in academic ability) than less well off children (judged to be low in academic ability). And that this can happen even though there is a large overlap of academic ability between most children of both categories. So we might make important judgements about a particular child's academic ability because of his or her category membership *before* we know anything about that particular individual's academic ability.

It was this kind of 'distortion' of perception that was the basis of the research on social identity and intergroup relations carried out by Tajfel and his colleagues that you met in Chapter 1. Tajfel argued that we perceive a person to be more like a typical category member than they actually are because we overgeneralize and apply a **stereotype**. The word stereotype (from the idea of a printer's template) has been appropriated for psychological use precisely because it represents the way that social perceivers produce an identical image each time they encounter a member of the social group to whom the stereotype applies. The insight that schema theory offers is that this overgeneralization is an *inevitable consequence* of a basic cognitive process.

Stereotype
A mental representation of a person as more like a 'typical' member of a social category than the person actually is. Seen as an inevitable consequence of the basic cognitive process of overgeneralization.

2.3 Developing schema theory further

You might think that schema theory leaves little in the way of choice or control, implying that our perceptions, interpretations and judgements are *determined* by the way our cognitive system works. Because our cognitive system is designed to minimize processing demands, we see things in terms of our assumptions and expectations, and we seem to have no choice in the matter. This view of the social perceiver is sometimes referred to as the **cognitive miser model**, because it portrays us as being very 'mean' with our processing capacity, only spending what we absolutely have to. While this is clearly true to some extent and some of the time, it does seem rather to overstate the case. There may be many occasions when we make judgements based purely on stereotypical assumptions, but there are also occasions when we are able to go beyond these assumptions, and when our perception is not entirely determined by them.

Recent work in social cognition has tried to accommodate this point, shifting the balance of control more towards the perceiver, and away from the workings of the cognitive system itself. This, in turn, has brought the issue of motivation into the picture in that people take control of their cognitive processes *when motivated to do so*, that is, when it helps them to achieve their goals or meet their needs. (This seems to be the same idea as that of moving between automatic and controlled attention that was discussed in Chapter 6, Section 2.5). When making judgements about another person, sometimes people will seek out information that is *not* consistent with the relevant schema, rather than apply the schema unthinkingly. A study by Ruscher *et al.* (2000), described in Box 7.3, shows that when we are dependent on another person as well as ourselves for the achievement of a particular goal, our impression of that person is likely to involve more than the mere registering of 'schema-congruent' information. Instead, we take account of other, '*schema-incongruent*' information. When it matters, and we need to be more certain of the accuracy of our social judgements, then we are not slaves to our expectations and assumptions, but are able to go beyond them.

Cognitive miser model
A view of the social perceiver as someone who uses as little processing capacity as possible and thus is limited to seeing things in terms of assumptions and expectations.

7.3 Cognitive strategies and motivational relevance (Ruscher et al., 2000)

Ruscher *et al.* (2000) were interested in how impressions of a target person might vary as a function of the target's 'motivational relevance' to the person forming the impression. 'Motivational relevance' here means the extent to which the target is relevant to the achievement of a goal that is important to the social perceiver. When a person is motivationally relevant in this way, we might expect that the perceiver would be more interested in getting an accurate impression of that person, rather than simply relying on a stereotypical judgement. This is what the researchers set out to test. They told student participants they were to take part in a study of 'workplace relations', and that this would involve them being paired with a local person from outside their university to work on a task. The task was to involve completing a crossword puzzle testing both local knowledge and knowledge of the university. In fact, the task and the local person were fictitious, and were invented for the purposes of the experiment. Each student was presented with nine cards describing attributes of the person they would be working with, and were asked to form an impression of that person. They read the cards one at a time. The first card implied the person was an alcoholic, and of the remaining eight, four described attributes congruent with the category 'alcoholic' (e.g. compulsive, forgetful) and four were non-congruent (e.g. cautious, motivated). After reading the cards, participants were asked to report their impression of their prospective partner. They did all this under different conditions, only two of which need concern us here. In an 'interdependent' condition they were told the pair who performed best would get $20; and in an 'independent' condition they were told the best student expert would get $10, and the best local expert would get $10.

The researchers measured the *amount of attention* participants gave to the information on the cards by recording the time it took them to read each card. As well as this, the reported impressions were analysed to obtain measures of *complexity* and *bias* (how negative they were). It was predicted that, compared with students in the independent condition, students in the interdependent condition would *spend more time* reading the schema-incongruent cards, and would also form a *less biased* and *more complex* impression of the target person (more complex because they attempted to integrate both congruent and incongruent information). The basis for this prediction was that the 'interdependent' students would be motivated to form a more accurate impression, because the reward depended on their partner's performance as well as their own. The results of the study confirmed these predictions. The authors concluded that motivational relevance does indeed play a part in social perception, leading perceivers to form impressions that are not simply based on stereotypical characteristics, but that incorporate other characteristics not predicted by the stereotype.

Motivated tactician
A model of the social perceiver as having multiple cognitive strategies to choose from, based on goals, motives and needs.

This kind of evidence calls into question the adequacy of the cognitive miser model, and its emphasis on cognitive efficiency. Clearly efficiency is an important factor in that we avoid doing any more processing than we need to do. However, the point is that it is our *needs* that determine what we do – we select the cognitive strategy best suited to meeting those needs. In light of this, Fiske and Taylor suggest that a better model of the social perceiver is the **motivated tactician**, described as 'a fully engaged thinker who has multiple cognitive strategies available and chooses among them based on goals, motives and needs' (1991, p.13). Here, the emphasis shifts from efficiency to motivation: the impression we form of another person will depend on their motivational relevance to us.

A further implication of this model is that it gives us a more detailed picture of the *automatic* aspects of social perception. The description of schematic processing presented in earlier sections portrays it as an automatic process, happening without any conscious control on our part. If we bring motivation into the picture, however, things become a little more complicated. The issue may be to what extent there are levels of **automaticity** in the cognitive processes by which we make decisions under moderate degrees of uncertainty. Fiske and Taylor (1991) offer descriptions of these different levels. For example, the purest form of automatic processing is referred to as 'preconscious automaticity', which they describe as unintentional, involuntary, effortless, autonomous and outside of the perceiver's awareness. One example of this is when 'stereotypes are instantly activated by physical attributes' (p.272), such as the skinhead haircut and Doc Marten boots seen from across the street. This level of automaticity can be contrasted with the kind of processing used by Ruscher *et al.*'s 'interdependent' participants, which Fiske and Taylor refer to as goal-dependent automaticity. Although in some respects this is automatic, in that the perceiver lacks awareness of the process and is not consciously intending to engage in it, it is not *fully* automatic. On some level at least, the perceiver is choosing to make more cognitive effort than in other circumstances, and thus there is some evidence of intentional control.

Automaticity
The idea of schematic processing as an automatic process, happening without any awareness or conscious control on our part.

Billig (1987), a social psychologist who does *not* work within the experimental social psychology perspective (although he used to), has argued that 'social thinking' (thinking about people and events) involves more than the ability sometimes to escape the dictates of an otherwise automated cognitive system. He argues that thinking involves an 'internal movement' between different viewpoints, rather than simply taking one view (our schema) and maybe adding a bit of supplementary information when we absolutely need to. Just as we argue and debate with each other in making sense of the social world, so, Billig maintains, we debate with ourselves as part of the same process. The TV ad mentioned earlier was advertising a newspaper, and advocated seeking all 'points of view', urging potential readers to get the full picture. Schema theory needs to develop further to address the fact that, in making sense of the social world, we are easily and routinely able to see more than one side of the argument.

Summary Section 2

- The 'top-down' influence on social perception and cognition is shaped by expectations of how things usually happen in the social world. The cognitive structures involved are known as schemas.
- Schemas are generalized representations and the knowledge they encode is shared knowledge.
- Schemas help simplify the world. They cut down on irrelevant information and provide additional information. But they can introduce distortions and are self-confirming.
- Schematic processing is largely automatic and below conscious awareness. Nevertheless it can be influenced by motivational states and intentions.

3 Attribution theories: 'common-sense' explanations of behaviour

In this section the focus moves to how people make sense of both other people's behaviour and their own. Attribution theories aim to describe and explain the processes involved in attributing causes to people's behaviour, asking questions like *what information* do people use when making judgements about causes? And *how is that information processed?*

3.1 Attribution and 'common-sense' psychology

Let's return to the example involving the 'skinhead' youth used in Section 2.1. To keep things simple, let's just take the shot of him running along the city street (the first shot). As a bystander observing this behaviour, you are likely to attribute a cause to it. You might assume that he is behaving the way he is because he is either escaping justice, or is chasing someone with aggressive intent. *Or* you may think his behaviour is primarily a result of being very late for an appointment, or seeing his bus about to draw away from the kerb. From the point of view of attribution theory we would want to know: which cause did you choose as most likely out of this range of causes? Why did you choose it? And what information led you to make this choice?

Heider argued that when we make judgements about people's actions we look for causes. And we look for causes 'within the person' (called **internal/dispositional causes**) or causes 'in the environment' (**external/ situational causes**). You may recognize this distinction between disposition and situation: it was discussed in Chapter 5. We might explain the behaviour of the youth running along the street as being due to something internal such as aggressive intent or as due to something external – the missed appointment, or the departing bus. Heider argued that *all* attributions of causality could be understood in terms of these two sets of factors and saw them as representing a *dimension* of causality: The more we attribute a person's behaviour to their inner disposition, the less we attribute it to the external situation they are in. This dimension has been incorporated into later theories of attribution such as the **locus of causality**.

3.2 Theories of attributional reasoning

A number of theories have been developed to examine the process by which we attribute people's behaviour (including our own) to internal and external causes. Jones and Davis (1965) concluded that, wherever possible, we explain *other people's* behaviour in terms of internal causes because internal attributions are more useful. An external attribution tells us only how the person acts in the present situation whereas an internal attribution tells us something about the person, and thus tells us how they might act in other situations as well, so having greater predictive value. This idea also implies that we are often more concerned to make sense of the person than simply to explain the behaviour.

Harold Kelley (1967) developed a detailed account of how we use information in causal reasoning, often known as the **covariation model**. This theory proposes that we use information from previous behavioural events to help make sense of the one we are currently attending to. He suggests that we consider how behaviours and situations vary together, or *covary* or correlate. In doing this, he suggests, we behave very much like a scientist, systematically assessing how different variables change in relation to one another, as a way of determining causal relationships. Kelley's portrayal of us as 'intuitive scientists' echoes Heider's earlier point about 'naïve psychology'; the difference is that Kelley begins to specify the kinds of procedures and data that the naïve psychologist might use.

Internal/dispositional causes
Factors that motivate behaviour and that are located 'within' the actor (e.g. personality, mood, ability).

External/situational causes
Factors that motivate behaviour and that are located in the actor's environment.

Locus of causality
The location of the cause of behaviour (internal or external), or the location of the cause of outcomes of behaviour like success or failure.

Covariation model
This model proposes that we make sense of current behaviour by considering information, from past and present, relating to its consistency, distinctiveness and consensus.

Kelley proposes that we assess covariation by considering and weighing information relating to three variables: consistency, distinctiveness and consensus. The theory is generally illustrated by starting with a one sentence description of a behavioural event to be explained – for example: 'Derek is late for work'. The three variables listed above can be mapped onto three components of the behavioural event, these being the *actor*, the *action* and the *situation* (after Brown, 1986).

In assessing the variable 'consistency', we look at how the action varies when we hold the other two variables, 'the actor' and 'the situation', constant. That is, we ask the question 'Is Derek always late for work?' If the answer is yes, there is high consistency; if no, then consistency is low.

In assessing distinctiveness, we look at how the action varies when we hold the actor constant but vary the situation. In relation to our example, the question here would be something like 'Is Derek late for other things?' If no, there is high distinctiveness (because the action is distinctive to this particular situation); if yes, distinctiveness is low.

In assessing consensus, we vary the actor while holding the action and situation constant, asking 'Are other people late for work?' If yes, consensus is high; if no, it is low.

As you can see from Table 7.1, we would then use the 'values' of these three variables to assess whether the cause is internal or external. If consensus and distinctiveness were low, and consistency was high, we would locate the cause internally, in the person; if the values for consensus and distinctiveness were high, we would locate the cause externally, in the situation.

Table 7.1 **The relationship between levels of three kinds of social information and causal attributions**

Consensus	Consistency	Distinctiveness	
Do other actors do this action in this situation?	Does actor always do this action in this situation?	Does actor do this action in other situations?	Cause attributed
No = low consensus	Yes = high consistency	Yes = low distinctiveness	Internal
Yes = high consensus	Yes = high consistency	No = high distinctiveness	External

A major virtue of Kelley's theory is that it offers precise and testable predictions about how different levels of CCD information (consensus, consistency, distinctiveness information) should lead to different attributions of cause, and a great deal of social psychological research has been done using the experimental method, to test these predictions. In such studies, participants are usually asked to read a short description of a behavioural event called a **vignette** that contains various levels of CCD information. They are then asked to assign an internal or external cause to the event. The use of experiments based on vignettes to test social psychological theories in the laboratory is discussed in Featured Method Box 7.4.

Vignette
A short description of a person, event or behaviour, used in an experimental setting, which permits control over the amount and nature of information provided to participants.

7.4 FEATURED METHOD

Using vignettes in experimental social psychology

When carrying out experimental research in social psychology, we often want to get data on how people respond to or make sense of social situations. In order to do this, while retaining experimental control, researchers have developed various strategies to bring the situation into the laboratory; one such strategy is to use vignettes. A vignette is a short description of an event, situation or behaviour. An example of a study using vignettes is McArthur's (1972) work testing Kelley's covariation model of attribution. She used vignettes containing brief descriptions of 16 different behavioural events, such as 'Sue is afraid of the dog', or 'Ralph trips over Joan's feet while dancing'. In different conditions of the experiment, these descriptions were combined with different levels and types of CCD information. So, for example, in one condition each participant would be presented with the following vignette:

> *Sue is afraid of the dog.*
>
> *Sue is afraid of most dogs.*
>
> *Few people are afraid of this dog.*

while a participant in another condition would get:

> *Sue is afraid of the dog.*
>
> *Sue is often afraid of this dog.*
>
> *Sue is not afraid of most dogs.*
>
> *Many people are afraid of this dog.*

McArthur wanted to test the effect of these different types and levels of information on the nature of the causal attributions made by participants, so each vignette was accompanied by written questions eliciting these attributions. For example, in the case of the above examples, participants were asked 'Why is Sue afraid of the dog?' and had to choose from response options such as 'Something about Sue' or 'Something about the dog'.

As you can see, the use of vignettes means that participants in the same condition are presented with exactly the same 'social situation'. It also gives the researcher precise control over the independent variable (in this case, the level of CCD information). This kind of control would obviously not be possible if we were studying responses to a real-life situation. Vignettes are also convenient and easy to use, and make it possible to gather data from large numbers of participants, which, in turn, makes it more likely that the sample represents the population from which it is drawn.

One disadvantage of vignettes is that they have low ecological validity, in that reading a vignette in the laboratory is clearly quite different from observing an event or behaviour in the course of everyday life. On the other hand, the *experimental* study of some phenomena simply would not be possible without their use. This is true in the case of McArthur's study above, and is also true of other vignette-based studies, for example those studying attributions of responsibility for stranger and 'date rape' (e.g. Bell *et al.*, 1994).

Generally, social experimental studies based on vignettes show that people use CCD information in the ways predicted by the theory. Other research, however, has called into question some assumptions of Kelley's theory. In particular, there is evidence that attribution theories overstate the 'rationality' of people's causal reasoning.

3.3 Rationality in making decisions about the causes of behaviour

There is now a large body of evidence showing that our judgements about the causes of behaviour are often not completely 'rational'. Sometimes these departures from 'rationality' are referred to as biases, sometimes as errors. However, the term 'error' implies that we attribute the *wrong* cause, whereas in real life the right cause is often not obvious, or even identifiable. For this reason, 'bias' would seem to be the more appropriate term.

Some of the biases involve a difference between the way we explain others' behaviour and the way we explain our own. For example, when explaining the behaviour of other people we tend to favour internal rather than external attributions, a tendency referred to as the **fundamental attribution error** (FAE). However, this tendency disappears when explaining our *own* behaviour – instead, we tend to favour external attributions, a phenomenon referred to as the **actor/observer effect**. So, observing Derek coming in late to work, I would tend to assume that he is not a punctual person, or at least hasn't made sufficient effort to ensure he

Fundamental attribution error
The tendency, when explaining the behaviour of other people, to favour internal rather than external attributions.

Actor/observer effect
The tendency to favour external attributions for our *own* behaviour, while favouring internal explanations for others' behaviour.

gets in on time. But if it was me in the same situation, doing the same thing, I would be more likely to explain my behaviour in terms of the unfortunate chain of events that morning that led to my being late. However, it is important not to overstate the difference here. Evidence shows that actors do still see internal causes as important for their own behaviour, but tend to attach more weight to external causes, and vice versa for observers of others' behaviour. A classic study providing evidence of these biases is described in Box 7.5.

7.5   The actor/observer effect (Storms, 1973)

Storms (1973) designed an experiment to investigate the nature and causes of the actor/observer effect. The study involved groups of four participants, all strangers to each other, seated round a table. Two were given the role of 'actors', and were asked to have a 'getting acquainted conversation', and two took the role of 'observers', each being asked to observe one of the actors while they were conversing. Two video cameras were set up in view of the participants, each videotaping one of the actors during this conversation.

In the experimental condition, when the conversation ended, the participants were told that the videotape of one of the actors was faulty. All four were then asked to watch the tape of the other actor, and complete a questionnaire that asked them to rate the actor's behaviour in terms of dispositional and situational causes. Note that in this condition, the actor who was on the tape was one of the participants observing his/her *own* behaviour.

The control condition was exactly the same except for the fact that participants were told that *both* tapes were faulty, and their ratings were based on the observations of the behaviour of the actors during the actual conversation, rather than being based on a video-recording of one of them.

Statistical analysis of the findings showed that, on the whole, actors tended to favour situational explanations of their behaviour, whereas observers tended to favour dispositional explanations of the same behaviour, thus providing evidence of the fundamental attribution error (FAE). However, the main interest in this study was the way in which the actor on the tape explained his/her own behaviour, compared with the explanations of actors who did *not* observe themselves on tape. Storms found that the explanations of the actor observing himself/herself moved more into line with those of the observers, demonstrating the actor/observer effect (AOE). Storms' evidence supports a perceptual explanation of the FAE and AOE, because a change in *perceptual perspective* led to a change in *causal explanations*.

Other empirical evidence of biases suggests that people simply don't take sufficient account of some of the information available to them. Why should this be? One likely explanation is based on the notion of **perceptual salience**. In his explanation of the FAE, Heider sums this notion up nicely with the phrase 'behaviour engulfs the field': for the observer, the actor is the most salient aspect of the perceptual field and so attracts our attention and then tends to figure more prominently in our explanations of behaviour. Notice that this also explains the actor's bias in the Storms (1973) experiment. For the actor, it is the situation that has perceptual salience – thus he/she is more likely to see the causes of his/her behaviour in the situation rather than as being internal. You may recall that, in Chapter 6, similar explanations were given for objects in the perceptual field in terms of attentional processes of figure and ground.

Perceptual salience
One aspect of the perceptual field is particularly significant for the perceiver, and thus attracts more attention than other aspects.

Miller (1984) compared middle-class US participants with middle-class Indian Hindus, testing adults and children of ages 8, 11 and 15 years old from both cultures. While US adults showed FAE – a bias towards dispositional attributions in explaining others' behaviour, Indian Hindus showed the reverse, favouring situational causes. Attributional preference (whether dispositional or situational) increased with age, with the 8 year-olds in the two groups showing no preference, and the data from the 11 and 15 year olds showing increasing divergence in line with the preference shown by the adult sample from their culture. Evidence like this suggests that FAE maybe a product of culture or ideology, influencing perceptual salience. Western culture is characterized by individualism, with action and motivation assumed to emanate from the individual. This can be contrasted with less individualistic cultures, where the social group takes precedence over the individual, and thus behaviour might tend to be explained by causes lying outside the individual.

As well as FAE, and these actor/observer differences, psychologists have identified a **self-serving bias**. There is some evidence that people have a tendency to attribute their successes to internal causes, and their failures to external causes. If we get a poor mark for an assignment, we might account for this in terms of the difficulty of the assignment, or the fact that we didn't have enough time to do it properly. If we get a good mark, we might explain it in terms of the hard work we put in. An empirical demonstration of this tendency is described in Featured Method Box 7.6 (Lau and Russell, 1980).

Self-serving bias
An information processing bias which serves the perceiver's interests in some way, for example the tendency to attribute one's success to internal causes and failure to external causes.

7.6 FEATURED METHOD

Content analysis in an experimental study

Content analysis
A procedure used to represent qualitative data (i.e. language and its meaning) in quantitative (numerical) form.

In the study, 'Attribution in the sports pages', Lau and Russell (1980) used 'stimulus material' taken from media reports, rather than constructing vignettes. The data collected were qualitative and consisted of relevant themes contained in newspaper articles. The method used is called **content analysis** and is a procedure used to *quantify* (i.e. represent numerically) qualitative (linguistic) data.

The process of quantification is crucially important to experimental research. Testing relationships between variables requires numerical measures of those variables, so that statistical analyses can be carried out. This is relatively straightforward when the variable being measured is response time, or the number of words recalled from a presented list. Variables that are expressed through written or spoken language are not so readily quantifiable. However, they can be measured by assigning units of linguistic data (sentences, for example) to one of a number of 'meaningful' categories, resulting in a frequency count for each category. This process of categorisation is known as coding. The entire process, from deciding what codes to use, doing the coding itself, to the subsequent statistical analysis, is known as content analysis.

Lau and Russell predicted that baseball and football players and managers would explain the outcome of games differently according to whether they had been won or lost, and thus show evidence of a self-serving bias in attributional reasoning. To test this prediction, they analysed newspaper articles covering 33 major sporting events, and extracted a total of 594 explanations from 107 articles. The explanations were then coded in terms of locus of causality – that is, whether they attributed the outcome to internal or external causes. Here are some examples:

Piniella has done it all – This was a Yankees team manager referring to the performance of their star player after a win. It was coded as internal because it refers to something about the Yankee as a player.

I think we've hit the ball alright. But I think we're unlucky – This was from a member of the losing Dodgers team after the same game. It was coded as external because it attributes losing to bad luck, which is a cause external to the player/ team.

Content analysis, although aiming eventually for a degree of quantification, involves meanings and interpretation. Therefore there is a risk that it will reflect the coder's own subjective biases. To deal with this, more than one coder is used, with the aim of establishing high levels of agreement between them. The level of agreement can be measured using correlation, giving an index of inter-rater reliability. Lau and Russell used two coders (themselves) who agreed on 88 per cent of the explanations. Another way of increasing objectivity and reliability was to have each explanation copied from the newspaper onto a card, so that coding would not be influenced by information contained in the text surrounding the explanation. Coders also need to have some strategy for dealing with disagreements. In Lau and Russell's study, disagreements were discussed by coders, and if agreement was not reached within one minute, the explanation was discarded from the study. This led to agreement on 96 per cent of the explanations.

An important advantage of content analysis is that it opens up the possibility of using 'real life' data, as in Lau and Russell's study, while at the same time retaining the advantages of quantification and a degree of experimental control. In doing this, it promises greater ecological validity than studies based solely on materials and situations manufactured by researchers.

In this study it was found that there was a greater tendency to attribute wins to internal factors (e.g. the team played well) than to external factors (e.g. the opposing team played badly), but that internal attributions were made more often than external attributions for both wins and losses. This finding differs from other studies, which have shown a preference for *external* explanations of failure. Lau and Russell argue that the discrepancy in the findings of their study compared with other studies is due to norms relating to the real-life context of the study. They claim that 'the typical (often called the base-rate) attribution for sports performance in general is internal' (p.36). In this situation, the self-serving bias worked to shift the base-rate, rather than reverse the mode of attribution.

Several explanations have been suggested for this self-serving bias. One is that it should be thought of as a **cognitive bias**, based on what we *expect* to happen. That is, we expect to succeed because we are making an effort to succeed, so when we do succeed we naturally assume it is due to that effort rather than to external factors. Conversely, because we fail *despite* our efforts, we tend to attribute failure to situational factors. Another possible explanation is that the self-serving bias is a **motivational bias** – driven by a need to enhance our self-esteem, or to present ourselves in the best possible light. This could also be an example of a need to feel in control and the centre of successful action – success comes from within and failures are not our fault.

It has been found that people with high self-esteem tend to make more self-serving attributions than people with low self-esteem (e.g. Shrauger, 1975). This could be interpreted as showing that self-serving attributions *cause* an increase in self-esteem, thus supporting the motivational explanation. However, the direction of causation is not clear here – it could be that the high self-esteem is causing the self-serving attributions rather than the other way round. In which case, we could argue that the evidence supports a *cognitive* explanation, since someone with higher self-

Cognitive bias
An information processing bias that is thought to be caused by the way the cognitive system works.

Motivational bias
An information processing bias that is thought to be caused by the perceiver's goals or needs.

esteem is more likely to *expect* to succeed. Given these difficulties, it is perhaps not surprising that research has so far failed to distinguish reliably between cognitive and motivational explanations of self-serving biases.

Another important issue to consider when evaluating attribution theory is the assumption that people are concerned to find *causal* explanations for behaviour in the same way that a scientist might. Is this really what people going about their everyday business do when they try to explain behaviour? To illustrate this problem, imagine you are Derek's boss and you observe him turning up for work late. You ask him 'Why are you late?' and he replies 'I just couldn't be bothered to get up when the alarm went off'. This is certainly a plausible *causal* explanation, and may well be true, but as Derek's boss that was not the question you were asking him. The 'why' question you asked was not about a causal explanation, but was asking Derek to account for his being late in the context of his responsibility as an employee to be at work on time. What you want is an account that gives a reason for a breakdown in 'social order', and that might re-establish that order (by acknowledging the transgression, offering an apology, or providing an acceptable excuse). As Derek has failed to do this, even though he has offered a reasonably good causal account, he will probably be in trouble with you as his boss.

We can see then that people do not explain behaviour 'in a vacuum', as a scientific exercise. Another related issue is that attribution theories portray people as simply receiving and interpreting information. What this misses is that people are just as likely to be *providers* of this information in the context of particular purposes (like getting themselves off the hook when they arrive late for work). If attribution theory claims to be a *social* psychological theory, it needs be able to encompass and explain these 'real life' aspects of causal attribution.

Summary Section 3

- Attribution theories propose that people distinguish between internal/dispositional factors and external/situational factors in their attempts to understand the causes of behaviour.
- Kelley's covariation model proposes that when we try to attribute causes to people's behaviour, three variables are considered – consensus, consistency and distinctiveness.
- Experimental social psychologists often use vignettes as stimulus material in studies of attribution.

- When explaining the behaviour of others we tend to favour internal rather than external attributions – the fundamental attribution error (FAE).
- When explaining our own behaviour we tend to favour external attributions – the actor/observer effect (AOE).
- People have a tendency to attribute their successes to internal causes and their failures to external causes. This is an example of a self-serving bias.
- Our concern with 'why' people do things sometimes reflects a concern with social accountability rather than a need to find causal explanations.

4   Do we process information accurately when making judgements?

Whether you are buying a car, voting for a politician or assessing some risk to your health, you are making a judgement. People often confess to having a poor memory, but rarely do we hear people say that their judgement is poor. But just how good are we at making judgements? In this section, we examine this question by drawing on a psychological literature that reveals, and attempts to explain, some of the mechanisms and problems associated with decision making (Kahnemann and Tversky, 1973).

4.1 Judgemental biases

We have already seen that a great deal of our information processing happens below awareness and in a hurry. And when we make judgements and decisions in our everyday worlds, the information available to us is never complete. So how good are we at assembling and making use of all the information that is available to us?

Activity 7.1

Try this activity yourself and/or you could ask a friend to do it. Try to answer the following questions, then compare your answers with the ones found in the comment:

1   Which is the more likely form of death in the US: murder or suicide?

2   If 10 friends want to divide up into groups:

    (i)   How many different subgroups comprising two people can be formed?

    (ii) How many different subgroups comprising eight people can be formed?

▼ *Comment*

In North America, survey evidence suggests that people believe murder is more common than suicide, although statistically suicide is nearly 50 per cent more prevalent. If we think about how murder and suicide are reported in the press, then it's not too difficult to see that people may be able to recall more examples of murder than of suicide. The relative accessibility of instances of murder and suicide is consistent with a substantial number of North Americans giving the wrong answer. Did you give the wrong answer?

   The answer to the second question is that it is possible to form 45 subgroups of two people and 45 subgroups of eight people from a group of 10. But in studies using this question the participants' median estimate for the number of two-person subgroups is 70, whereas the median estimate for the number of eight-person subgroups is 20. So in the first case they overestimate and in the second they underestimate. What did you do? A possible explanation of why we do this is discussed below.

Availability heuristic
Refers to the practice of making judgements on the basis of examples or instances that are accessible to the cognitive system/ decision-maker. Examples may come to mind more easily if they are more memorable or easier to construct.

The two examples in Activity 7.1 illustrate a commonly found bias that follows from the rule of thumb in information processing called the **availability heuristic**. In both examples, the mental ability to *generate examples* seems to be important.

   In the 'cause of death' question the coverage of murder compared with suicide in various media helps bring more examples to mind. Perhaps there is a motivational element at play too: because we might think that murder is more serious than suicide there is a greater drive to search for examples of murder. And any reports on murders we might have come across in the media may well have had more perceptual salience and been more memorable. In this case, the use of the availability heuristic combined with patterns of media coverage leads people to make judgements that are systematically incorrect, i.e. biased.

   When it comes to the question about groups, the source of bias seems to be more purely cognitive than motivational. If one imagines 10 people in a line, it is possible to form five groups immediately just by pairing individuals together. On the other hand, forming different groups of eight requires greater effort. It is easy to *imagine* one group of eight and not too difficult to construct two further groups made by substituting the excluded individuals. But after three groups, things seem to become more involved. Constructing groups of eight seems to require more creativity to determine what they are, and more memory to keep track of and count them as we generate them. So perhaps the ease with which examples can be imagined determines the *availability* of instances as we think, and ultimately our judgements about their relative frequency.

In another study, which explored how we sometimes fail to use information, Kahneman and Tversky (1973) presented participants with very short vignettes, explaining that these vignettes had been selected *at random* from person descriptions of engineers and lawyers. Here is an example:

> *Dick is a 30 year-old man. He is married with no children. A man of high ability and high motivation, he promises to be quite successful in his field. He is well liked by his colleagues.*

You can see that the description does not tell you much about the chances of Dick being a lawyer or an engineer, indeed it was designed to be uninformative with respect to profession. In one experimental condition, the participants were told that this description was of a person drawn randomly from a room containing 70 per cent lawyers. In the second experimental condition participants were told the personality description was of a person drawn randomly from a room containing 30 per cent lawyers. The participants were asked to give the probability that Dick was a lawyer. In both experimental conditions, the participants said that the probability of Dick being a lawyer was 50 per cent. They seemed to have understood that the description was uninformative about Dick's profession, but failed to use a crucial piece of information that they *had* been given: they had been told the underlying proportion of lawyers present in the room.

This is an example of what has come to be known as the **representativeness heuristic**. It seems that because the vignette about Dick could equally well describe either a lawyer or an engineer, the judgement that people give ignores the information given to them about the prior probabilities, in the case of the first experimental condition, the 70 per cent likelihood of Dick being a lawyer. Again we have an example of a judgemental mechanism that, under certain conditions, leads people to make systematic errors.

Representativeness heuristic
Refers to a tendency to make categorisations according to whether an item is representative of the category to which it might belong.

In this particular case, the bias could be explained by perceptual salience. The actor, Dick, is the most salient part of the perceptual field and attracts attention – increasing the weighting of the personality vignette and displacing the information about baseline probabilities.

How good are we at judging *what* we know? People who find themselves on TV quiz shows are often asked how confident they are about getting the next question right. If you have a choice between taking your winnings, or risking all and going on to the next question, then it clearly matters not only *what* you know, but also how good you are at assessing the quality of your knowledge. The extent to which a person knows about the accuracy of their judgements is referred to as **calibration**. And this kind of calibration is clearly important in many everyday situations during which judgements and decisions have to made. Whether you are deciding which course to study next or what job to go for, how successful you think you will be is a vital part of making the decision that is right for you.

Calibration
The extent to which a person knows about the accuracy of their own judgements.

Activity 7.2   (Optional)

This is quite a long activity but, if you have time, you could do it using yourself as the respondent and/or you could ask a friend to try it out.

The exercise is adapted from Wright (1984). Below you will find 20 questions: for each question start by first indicating which of the two options you think is the right answer. Then indicate how *confident* you are that your answer is right. In judging your confidence use assessments of 0.5, 0.6, 0.7, 0.8, 0.9 and 1.0. So if you say you are 0.5 confident that means you think there is a 50:50 chance of you being right, and likewise up to 1, which means you are certain. These are, in effect, probability judgements.

1. Which is nearer London?	New York ...... Moscow	**Confidence** ......
2. Where are the Atlas Mountains?	Europe ...... Africa	**Confidence** ......
3. When did China join the UN?	1972 ...... 1971	**Confidence** ......
4. Which legs do cows use first when getting up from the ground?	Hind legs ...... Front legs	**Confidence** ......
5. Which is the smallest country in South America?	Ecuador ...... Uruguay	**Confidence** ......
6. Where was Frank Sinatra born?	Sicily ...... USA	**Confidence** ......
7. Which is longer?	Panama Canal ...... Suez Canal	**Confidence** ......
8. Which was 'discovered' first?	Theory of Relativity ...... Aspirin	**Confidence** ......

9. Which tropic is north of the equator?	Capricorn ...... Cancer	**Confidence ......**
10. When was the modern Olympic games started?	19th C ...... 20th C	**Confidence ......**
11. Which is heavier?	Carbon Dioxide ...... Air	**Confidence ......**
12. Which camel has two humps?	Bactrian ...... Arabian	**Confidence ......**
13. What is the capital of New Zealand?	Auckland ...... Wellington	**Confidence ......**
14. Who launched the first satellite?	United States ...... USSR	**Confidence ......**
15. Which country produces more natural rubber?	Brazil ...... Malaya	**Confidence ......**
16. Which does Japan produce more of (by weight)?	Wheat ...... Rice	**Confidence ......**
17. Which was formed first?	South-East Asia Treaty Organisation ...... North Atlantic Treaty Organisation	**Confidence ......**
18. Biennial means ...?	Twice a year ...... Once every two years	**Confidence ......**
19. The average gestation period for elephants is ...?	Over one year ...... Under one year	**Confidence ......**
20. Aladdin's nationality was ...?	Chinese ...... Japanese	**Confidence ......**

Now mark your answers (the correct answers are given at the end of the chapter). Then enter your scores in the table below. For example, if you said you were confident with probability 0.9 in four questions, and you got three right, the row beginning 0.9 below should have the numbers 0.9, 4, 3, 0.75 entered. The results will tell you how well calibrated you are.

Calibration Table

Your confidence level	Number of questions for which you were this confident (1)	Number of correct responses (2)	Proportion of responses correct (2) divided by (1)
0.5			
0.6			
0.7			
0.8			
0.9			
1.0			

Comment

If you found that the numbers in the far right-hand column (proportion of correct responses) were the same as those in the far left-hand column (confidence level), this means you are perfectly calibrated. In other words, you have an accurate view of how good your knowledge is, at least for this task. But more probably, the figures in the far right hand column will tend to be lower than those in the far left hand column indicating that you were correct less often than you thought you would be.

If, in the above exercise, you *were* correct less often than you thought you would be, your results are in keeping with a widespread research finding. Many researchers (e.g. Fischhoff and Lichtenstein, 1977) have found evidence that people in the Western world tend to be *over-confident* about their knowledge. This finding does, however, need to be treated with caution on several grounds. First, a great deal of the research has drawn on university undergraduates as participants; and in the West, education teaches self-confidence. But there is another interesting question to be asked. For those who do display over-confidence, should this be thought of as an error in processing, i.e. an inability to be accurate about the self? Or should we perhaps think of it as a useful motivational mechanism? Overconfident people, with positive self-images (providing they are not wildly inaccurate) may be more effective in many settings, ranging from child-rearing to collaborating with colleagues at work.

Several of the 'biases' we have examined could be said to have survival value – for example, survival in an uncertain but competitive world where speed of processing may be more important than absolute accuracy. We might also consider the possible evolutionary advantage of over-confidence (see Chapter 2). Providing it doesn't threaten survival, we might argue that evolution favours those who undertake and succeed at risky activities (like hunting large and potentially dangerous animals). Those who are overly confident or overly optimistic are more likely to engage in such activities and unless the losses from failure are catastrophic, they will outperform those who are correctly confident (i.e. more cautious).

4.2 Judgements about risk

Risk is not just a feature of hunting wild animals or engaging in dangerous sports – it is an element of everyday life. We constantly make judgements about what to do, what to choose, what to change and how to plan, but always under conditions of uncertainty. However, much as we try to control our worlds and make them predictable, information is always incomplete and our judgements and decisions always carry an element of risk.

Risk assessment and risk management are disciplines in their own right, where risk is estimated using statistical analyses, in as objective a way as possible. Calculations are made of the *probability* (the uncertainty element) of, for example, an accident at a nuclear power plant, and the estimated *cost* (the value element) of an accident. With nuclear energy it is very difficult to estimate the probability of such an accident because the probability is very small and there are few statistics on accidents available. The costing of a nuclear accident is also very difficult since such an accident is not just costly in terms of money but is also profoundly affected by social values. Nevertheless, engineers and scientists do make risk assessments of this kind. Similarly, medical scientists make risk assessments of health hazards like smoking; and the findings are widely publicized and used in health campaigns.

But how do these *expert* conceptualisations of risk relate to risk assessments that we all make in ordinary life, like the driver at the road junction, or the more conscious judgements we make when faced with, say, a decision to change job? How do people generally think about risk? Are they accurate when they judge risk? Does it make any sense to talk about accuracy in this context?

When psychologists study people's perceptions of risk, usually in the hope of understanding their risk-related behaviour, the focus is on people's *beliefs* about risk, which include subjective estimates of the probability of what might happen, and subjective *evaluations* and feelings about the outcomes. Together, these beliefs and feelings constitute people's attitudes to particular risks. Some research has focused on the *content* and *salience* of people's beliefs and feelings about particular risks – such as the risks associated with different energy systems (e.g. Thomas *et al.*, 1980; Thomas, 1981). Another study used factor analysis to find the *common belief dimensions* underlying how people perceive a wide variety of risks, from mountain climbing to exposure to asbestos (Slovic *et al.*, 1980). They found three underlying concerns: dread – a measure of how *involuntary* risk exposure was felt to be; unknown risk – an indication of the unfamiliarity or distance into the future of a hazard; and a third factor, which related primarily to the number of people exposed to a hazard.

So studies of what people believe is *salient* reveal rather different conceptualisations of risk compared with those of experts. And these beliefs are often very different from the information available in the media and educational literature. This has been found to be true for technological risks, where acceptance has become a social and political issue (like genetically modified foods and nuclear energy), and health risks. For example, irrespective of the empirical evidence, some people 'believe' that smoking won't harm *them*; or they re-define the situation and redirect their attention making salient the belief that 'this next cigarette will not give me cancer'. Graham (1987) found that people *know* that smoking leads to lung cancer but smoke because of the positive immediate benefit – the sense of well being. Immediate gain overcomes long-term potential loss. There are clearly factors that affect perception of risk other than the objective probabilities and the magnitude of the negative consequences attached to those probabilities.

4.3   Optimistic bias

Optimistic bias
Occurs when people are more optimistic than objective statistics warrant.

There is evidence that people are more optimistic about risk than the statistics warrant – an **optimistic bias**. For example people imagine, unrealistically, that the future holds few adverse events (Taylor, 1989) and expect such events to strike others, rather than themselves (Weinstein, 1982). Taylor and Brown, in 1994, claimed that, typically, above 95 per cent of the United States population exhibit unrealistic optimism in relation to a wide array of risks, and it is not limited to any particular age, sex, educational or occupational group (although this may have changed).

Psychologists have used questionnaires to study how people judge a vast array of the health and safety risks. For example, Weinstein (1987) asked participants about 32 health and safety risks, such as getting a drinking problem, becoming HIV positive, or getting arthritis. The questions were presented in the following format:

1   Compared to other men/women my age, my chances of getting arthritis in the future are:

   much below average
   below average
   a little below average
   average
   a little above average
   above average
   much above average

2   Compared to other men/women my age, my chances of getting a drinking problem in the future are:

   much below average
   below average
   a little below average
   average
   a little above average
   above average
   much above average

The participants were asked to rate their chances on a seven-point scale ranging from much below to much above average, with average as the mid-point. If they rated their chances as below average, they were construed as optimistic, and if above average, as pessimistic. Note that people were being asked to compare themselves to someone *similar* to themselves. So, the devisors of the scale hoped that a young person thinking about their chances of contracting arthritis, for example, would compare himself or herself to another young person with fairly similar chances. Since most people think their risk is less than average, even though this is mathematically impossible, this finding is regarded as a *biased* perception.

One explanation of optimistic bias could be lack of experience of the problem in the past and difficulty in imagining it or how it might arise in your life. For example, if you have never used what you see as addictive drugs, and know no one who has, you are unlikely to think that you may become a drug addict. This could be an instance of the operation of schema and expectations on the basis of *availability heuristic* and could be seen as a limitation on cognitive processing due to limited experience and/or limited imagination.

Another explanation might be based on *motivational* factors rather than experience or imagination. Perhaps people compare themselves (consciously and/or unconsciously) with others who are at particularly high risk in order to maintain a sense of low personal risk. If you were thinking about your chances of contracting HIV, you might compare yourself with someone whom you regard as highly promiscuous and this may make you feel relatively optimistic. This could be seen as a motivation to feel better, or in psychoanalytic terms, a denial – *a defence against anxiety*. There is some research that supports this view. Taylor and her colleagues have suggested that the more threatening a condition, the greater the optimistic bias evoked. A vivid illustration of this is provided by Taylor *et al.* (1992) who examined the beliefs about AIDS risk in a sample of gay men at risk of HIV infection. The study indicated that the men in the sample who knew they were HIV positive were significantly more optimistic about not developing AIDS than the men who knew they did not have HIV. But this finding is not always supported. Weinstein's results have often pointed in the opposite direction, showing that the more severe an event is felt to be the less optimistic a bias it evokes (e.g. Weinstein, 1987). Therefore, the motivation that underpins optimistic bias is not clear-cut.

There are some other important debates in the optimistic bias literature. For example to what degree does optimistic bias exist in the *population as a whole* (see Myers and Brewin, 1996; Myers and Renolds, 2000) rather than in smaller sections of the population, called 'repressive copers', who feel extremely optimistic and so skew the overall findings? When we talk of 'people' being optimistically biased, and we base this on predominantly Northern American samples, can we then say that people in general, the world over, are optimistic about their risks? To what extent does optimistic bias exist cross-culturally (see Peeters *et al.*, 1997; Kleinhesselink and Rosa, 1991; Heine and Lehman, 1995; Taylor and Armor, 1996)? And how does optimistic bias link to the 'actual' risks faced (see Klein and Radcliffe, 1999)?

Perhaps people appear to be optimistically biased because they have already taken the precautions (such as not smoking) that will lower their likelihood of contracting illnesses such as lung cancer. Another explanation might be about *control*. Could optimistic bias, in part, be an instance of the over-confidence we saw in Section 4.1? Perhaps people overestimate the skills they possess that would allow them to avoid being affected by the risk, believing that they are in control and their particular behaviours – such as eating well or not smoking – mean that they are unlikely to become ill. This could be the same as the self-serving bias – success and good outcomes are seen to come from the self and from effort and as controllable. There is evidence that people do seem to feel more optimistic about those risks where human control can play a role in prevention, and overall it does seem that perceived controllability is a key determinant of the level of optimistic bias. But it has also been found that people tend to see themselves as having control over even those events that are heavily determined by chance (Taylor and Armor, 1996). For example, we know that people feel that they exert control when they throw a dice, even though the outcome of this event is linked to chance. Optimistic bias reflects a general tendency to perceive events as being more under personal control than they actually are (Harris and Middleton, 1994).

You may have noticed that in the course of the chapter, in several different contexts, the discussion has turned to people's concern about being able to control their environments. But notice also that this need to control appears to be so important that people construct versions of the world in which they feel they are in control - even though they are not. For example overconfidence and other self-serving biases. Defensive versions of the world can be advantageous if they permit us to get on with surviving without being hampered by anxiety. This viewpoint is one of the underlying principles of the psychoanalytic perspective – the idea of psychological defences. You will meet this perspective in Chapter 9 and also later in this chapter, in Section 5.

So far in this chapter the questions asked about social cognition have been the kind that can be tested using experimental designs and/or closed-format questionnaires, or questions about beliefs. Such approaches cannot, however, give a picture of how people ordinarily feel about risks. This aspect of social cognition requires a different method, one in which spontaneous meanings and pathways of thought are elicited rather than researchers imposing scales, and questionnaires involving comparisons with others, which all have their particular **demand characteristics**. In the next section we consider the method and findings of a case study (a cross-cultural exploration of ideas about the risks associated with HIV/AIDS) that explores beliefs about risk in an open-ended way, using a non-experimental method.

Demand characteristics
Features of a psychological method that lead people to respond in particular, constrained ways.

Summary Section 4

- People often use particular examples to make judgements about categories. Failure to generate examples may be a cognitive shortcoming – which, in turn, may have a motivational source. Both of these can lead to judgmental biases.
- People use 'rules of thumb' called heuristics to help simplify judgement. Different heuristics, such as availability or

representativeness, can give rise to biases when applied inappropriately.

- People are often overconfident when estimating the extent to which their own judgements will be correct.
- Everyday information processing and decision-making occur under conditions of uncertainty and therefore involve risk.
- People do not generally conceptualise risks in the same way as experts.
- In some situations people tend to be more optimistic about risks than the statistics warrant. This is known as the optimistic bias. It is not clear to what extent this finding of an optimistic bias applies across cultures.
- Optimistic bias has several possible explanations. Among these are the availability heuristic, a defensive motive to 'feel better', overconfidence about personal effectiveness and a desire for control.

5   People's understanding of a health risk: the case of HIV/AIDS

The research discussed in this chapter so far has been drawn from the experimental social psychology perspective. Using a different method, however, can allow different questions to be asked. The study examined in this section explores beliefs about the risk of contracting HIV and developing AIDS in an effort to understand more fully the motivational aspects of biases. Psychologists and those responsible for risk reduction are urgently attempting to understand the apparent 'irrationality' of people's perceptions of health risks. Why do large minorities of lay people continue to take what experts regard as major risks (Douglas, 1994)? An example of this is the continuing practice of unsafe sex in groups of people in which levels of HIV are high. These are people who have a good understanding of HIV-related issues, and who are likely to have been exposed to health education materials intended to change their cognitions (e.g. see Offir *et al.*, 1993).

5.1   An outline of the research method

In this chapter, the focus has been on knowledge, motivations, needs and 'tactics' (see Section 2.3) *belonging to individuals.* The study described here illustrates how attributions, beliefs and narratives about risk reflect *collective* ideas that belong to particular groups and cultures. These are called the **social representations** of risk. Social representations not only contain the specific contents of people's thoughts, but are also important in social life because they both express and protect the *identity* of the groups that subscribe to them.

Social representations
Shared cognitive and linguistic structures that we use to make sense of the social world.

Like schema, social representations can be thought of, in part, as cognitive structures that we use to make sense of the social world. But social representations theory (Moscovici, 1981) emphasises the communication processes through which these shared representations are formed and transformed. Think of them as:

> *... a set of concepts, statements and explanations originating in daily life in the course of inter-individual communications. They are the equivalent in our society of the myths and belief systems in traditional societies; they might even be said to be the contemporary version of common sense.*
> *(Moscovici, 1981, p.181)*

Joffe (1999) conducted an interview-based, cross cultural study of the widespread sense of personal invulnerability expressed by many people faced with risk, in particular towards the risk of HIV/AIDS. She used a social representations approach and the main data were *what people said* about the risks and threat of HIV/AIDS. Lay representations of HIV/AIDS were obtained using semi-structured, depth interviews.

The participants were 60 Britons and South Africans. The sample was chosen in accordance with a matched set of criteria to ensure comparability across cultures and groups. A basic criterion for selection was that respondents were urban, young adults with a high level of education. Half of the respondents were British and half South African. They were drawn from the major urban centres in the two countries: London, Johannesburg and Soweto. The average age in the sample was twenty-three in each country. The majority of the respondents had successfully completed secondary school, with two-thirds (in both countries) being college or university educated. In each of the two countries the sample was composed of white heterosexuals (half were male), black heterosexuals (half were male) and gay men (white and black, a number of whom were HIV positive).

The interviews were designed to elicit each respondent's own ideas concerning the origin and spread of AIDS. Therefore the questions were open and were as non-directive as possible, although there was some structure to the interviews because the intention was to make comparisons between responses. The focus was on the following topics: where HIV/

AIDS originated, how HIV/AIDS spreads, which group(s) are worst affected by AIDS in the respondent's own country, the respondent's personal sense of risk in relation to HIV/AIDS. Each transcribed interview was coded using a computerized system that provides both qualitative and quantitative data (see Featured Method Box 7.6). The program was employed to generate details of the themes and processes evident in the interviews of individuals, subgroups and the total sample.

Since social representations are influenced by 'messages' that circulate in the culture, the researcher also carried out a systematic analysis of the ideas about HIV/AIDS which circulated in the social context to which lay thinkers had been exposed at the time of being interviewed. This included scientific representations obtained from a thematic analysis of the high-impact medical journals, and an analysis of the public health campaigns on AIDS that had been transmitted in the two cultures.

5.2 Some findings of the study

When asked where AIDS originated, most respondents linked it with a continent with which they did *not* identify. Over three quarters of the white respondents, in both the British and South African samples, stated that AIDS originated in Africa, while an even greater proportion of black respondents, in both samples, declared that it originated in the West. Of course, the way in which this finding is presented rests upon the assumption that the white people in the sample, whether British or South African, did not identify with Africa, and, similarly, that the black people did not identify with the West. With few exceptions, the interviews were shot through with evidence of this style of identification. For example, in response to the question concerning how HIV/AIDS spread, a third of both the British and the South African samples answered by distancing their in-group from AIDS, as demonstrated in excerpts from both countries.

> It is like word association, isn't it. I think about AIDS: I think of drug use, I think of decadent stars [celebrities], I think of homosexuals. I very rarely think of heterosexuals when I think about it ...when I think about it ... usually it belongs more to people in the white community ... It is just the way I've been trained I suppose. Because they tend to do more, I don't know. Their sexuality seems more perverse.

(British black heterosexual male)

> In South Africa, we do have immorality but we do have people who stick to their principles: the blacks.

(South African black heterosexual male)

These extracts demonstrate that an interview question about the spread of HIV evoked a blatant denial of the link between these people's in-groups and the spread of HIV. A moralistic judgement concerning 'the other' was also summoned to the respondents' minds by the question – 'immoral' people are linked to the spread of AIDS.

In addition to being linked to foreign continents and to out-groups, AIDS was associated with various 'deviant' practices. Over two-thirds of both the British and South African samples mentioned at least one of the following five factors in association with the origin and spread of HIV: aberrant sexuality (including promiscuity); group rituals (including cannibalism and scientific experimentation); 'Third World' conditions (including a lack of Western medicine and overcrowded living conditions); unhygienic practices; and the practices of uneducated people. Half of this group combined at least two of the five factors, arriving at what the researcher called the 'sin cocktail' – generalizing the extent to which the factors are practised, and linking them to specific groups. The salient point is that these practices were said to occur among those with whom the person talking *did not identify*: while a white respondent may have linked AIDS among black people to promiscuity and wife swapping in Africa, a black respondent might have linked it to promiscuity and scientific experimentation in the West.

When asked direct questions concerning their personal risk, over two thirds of the total sample (excluding those who had HIV or AIDS) stated that their own chances of contracting HIV were below average. Differences between the gay and heterosexual, white and black, male and female groups were not significant. Furthermore, the Britons and South Africans were equally likely to represent their own vulnerability to HIV as below average. This is an instance of the optimistic bias discussed earlier and supports the findings of a number of studies in which groups more at risk of contracting HIV do not show a greater sense of vulnerability to it, when compared with groups less at risk.

5.3 An interpretation of 'irrationality' concerning HIV/AIDS risk

In Joffe's study, the respondents distanced themselves, and their in-group, from the threat of HIV/AIDS and from responsibility and blame: the 'good' (low risk and little blame) was seen as residing in the in-group and the 'bad' (high risk and high blame) in the out-group. This is what Joffe, in her discussion, calls the 'not me' response. It can be thought of as a psychological defence; and it might be the result of a combination of the biases we have seen earlier in this chapter.

Joffe, however, goes beyond the usual idea of psychological defence by moving the explanation from protection of the individual to the group. She suggests, on the basis of the similarity of the content and elaboration of beliefs within identifiable groups, that the defence belongs to the group, and operates to protect the group and the individual's identity as a member of that group.

Joffe's examination of the expert sources of information, such as medical journals in the early years of the potential pandemic, showed that scientists, too, were attributing the origins of AIDS to outgroups, to foreigners, to minorities, and to foreign cultural practices. And these representations were later elaborated and spread in the media. This illustrates how individual minds interact with messages that circulate around them, in forging a 'not me' response to misfortune. You may remember from Chapter 1 that group membership can involve exaggeration of similarities between in-group members and exaggeration of differences from out-group members. It was suggested that this process may originate in the exaggeration of differences between categories and can become fixed in schemas (see Section 2.2 of this present chapter).

Joffe's findings also provide evidence for attribution theories. For example, you may remember Heider's idea that people act like scientists and psychologists (albeit 'naïve' ones) and seek causes, attributing the cause of success and positive events to the self (dispositional attributions) and the cause of failure and negative events to others. And the fundamental attribution error predicts that negative events that befall others are likely to be seen as dispositional (their own fault, they are to blame). So Joffe's findings in this study, using a very different methodology, support the findings of attribution theory and the biases that the information processing approach has identified, although her interpretation is of a very different kind.

Summary Section 5

- A cross-cultural exploration of naturalistic beliefs about HIV/AIDS revealed an optimistic bias. People conceptualize risk in ways that reduce their own risk and their in-group's culpability and locate the risk and blame in outgroups. This has been called the 'not me' response.
- The 'not me' response is a defence that operates at the level of the group rather than the individual. It protects the in-group and protects and expresses social identity.

6   Review: biases and irrationality

In this chapter we have seen that perceiving and understanding the social world has to take account not only of basic cognitive processes but also the *environment in which social cognition takes place*. People have to deal quickly with incomplete information and use it to reach decisions, sometimes consciously, more often unconsciously, in order to act in the world. There are survival pressures on our cognitive processing.

Are there shortcomings in the ways we process information? The answer is probably yes. The research described in this chapter shows that there is evidence of distortions of perception such as overgeneralization within and between categories, and self-confirming schema. There is evidence of systematic biases such as the fundamental attribution error, optimistic bias and failure to use available information. But it is very difficult (and may prove impossible) to disentangle possible failures and biases in cognitive processing from meaningful and functional selection and structuring of information. If the parameters for how we process information are set by culture and motivation rather than logic, does this constitute a shortcoming? After all, self-confirming schema, on the whole, work – even if sometimes we might wish we could change them, or take moral exception to them.

However, when experimental social psychology addresses social cognition, it imports two ideas of what people are like: the information processing approach from cognitive psychology (which likens cognitive processes to the workings of a computer, see Chapter 6 and Chapter 8); and, from social psychology, the idea that people are intuitive scientists seeking 'truths' in a logical and rational way. Both of these sets of assumptions have been incorporated into theories generated by the experimental social psychology approach, such as attribution theory, and the result is a set of expectations about objectively correct and logical ways to perceive the world – a kind of *prescription*. And it could be said that much of what we interpret as distortions or biases in information processing are only seen as 'failures' because of our expectations.

These expectations are not only incorporated into the underlying models of what people are like, they are also built into the experimental methods that are most commonly used in research. The experimental study of social cognition permits only certain kinds of tasks to be performed, certain questions to be asked. This chapter has illustrated the ways in which well-defined aspects of the complex social world can be brought into the laboratory and studied in a controlled way (e.g. by the use of vignettes). The strengths of the experimental social psychology perspective are tightly articulated theories, hypothesis testing and the accumulation of a body of knowledge. You have seen that several of the methods used have 'correct' answers built into their design, providing a baseline against which people's answers can be checked. For example, the risk questionnaires that require a comparison with others have a mathematical notion of correctness built in because ratings of 'below average' are necessarily defined as biased. The activities in Section 4 also had objectively correct answers. But in ordinary life, 'absolute correctness' may not be the goal.

There are other questions that cannot be asked within the experimental approach. For example, we saw in Section 5 that an exploration of *naturalistic* thinking about risk revealed a complex and defensive way of thinking about risky behaviour not at all like the expectations of medical scientists who write health education literature. Human information processing does *not* necessarily follow the rules of logic or mathematics.

There is also the more general issue of the ecological validity of many experimental studies on information processing and social cognition. It has been argued that the sorts of questions and tasks used (for example in calibration and confidence tests) do not adequately reflect the nature of judgmental tasks as people actually encounter them in everyday life. Our cognitive framework might be hardwired to deal with information as it naturally presents itself to us in the environment. In this case, experimental evidence of a bias or distortion might be due to the low ecological validity of the experimental design.

Risk perception also highlights another difficulty in the ways that 'bias' and 'irrationality' in human information processing are conceptualized. Risks *can* be estimated using mathematics and expressed in probability terms, giving an objective (sometimes called 'correct') baseline for judgements. But people do not arrive at the same perceptions and understandings as engineers and health experts, *because they do not start from the same place*. Risks often seem to be encapsulated and attended to in ways that reduce the implications of risky behaviours, probabilities are discounted and utilities interpreted in idiosyncratic ways. So people have their own conceptualisations of risk and they are rational in their own terms – in terms of meanings, cultural processes and the functions that their perceptions serve.

So we might conclude that there are two underlying issues regarding questions of bias and irrationality. First, do we have cognitive shortcomings that make us inefficient? Second, since rationality is a property of machines, mathematics and maximisation, why should we *expect* people to operate in this kind of prescribed way? People survive and prosper by having their own versions of rationality. These versions of rationality may have evolutionary origins, they may relate to short-term goals, such as avoiding anxiety and enhancing a feeling of control; and they are certainly influenced by cultural expectations.

When the focus is on machine-based and logical models of information processing a lot can be gained – but much is missed. For example machines do not talk and debate with each other like people do; they do not have a collective life in the way that people do, participating in organized and orderly social practices, sharing representations and understandings. Evidence of biases draws attention to our inevitably partial perceptual perspective, our needs and motivations, and the influence of culture and ideology. But, these are only limitations if you start with an expectation of rationality as the standard against which to measure thinking and behaviour. We could argue instead that the rationality expected by information processing accounts is simply not appropriate to the contexts and demands of everyday life.

Summary Section 6

- Overall the evidence suggests that the information processing approach to social cognition has shortcomings. But it is difficult to separate such shortcomings from the influence on the selection and processing of information of motives and meanings.
- Cognitive psychology and experimental social psychology tend to prescribe models of the person as thinking in machine-like ways and/or operating like scientists seeking truths in a logical and rational way. The evidence suggests that this is not so.
- The use of experimental methods tends to provide 'correct' answers and, by implication, 'incorrect' answers. But in ordinary life, correctness may not be the goal and may not even exist.
- Experimental studies may construct tasks that are low in ecological validity thus leading to apparent ineffectiveness in information processing.
- Non-experts have their own ways of conceptualising risks and these are rational in their own terms, i.e. in terms of meanings, cultural processes and the functions these understandings serve for individuals and groups.
- The rationality expected – or prescribed – by information processing accounts may not be appropriate to the contexts and demands of everyday life.

Answers to Calibration Questions in Activity 7.2

(1) New York. (2) Africa. (3) 1971. (4) Front Legs. (5) Uruguay. (6) USA.
(7) Suez Canal. (8) Aspirin. (9) Cancer. (10) 19th C. (11) Carbon Dioxide.
(12) Bactrian. (13) Wellington. (14) USSR. (15) Malaya. (16) Rice.
(17) NAT0. (18) Once every two years. (19) Over one year. (20) Chinese.

■ Further reading

Augoustinos, M. and Walker, I. (1995) *Social Cognition: An Integrated Introduction*, London, Sage.

This book is a thorough introduction to the main topics in social cognition, with detailed discussions of research evidence. It also covers social representations theory and includes a chapter on criticisms of the cognitive perspective.

Joffe, H. (1999) *Risk and 'the Other'*, Cambridge, Cambridge University Press.

Joffe's monograph looks at ideas that exist across the social sciences regarding the human response to potential dangers. The concern of the book is how individuals, who are embedded within a set of cultural and societal representations, think about the dangers that are brought to their attention, often by way of the mass media. In particular, the focus is on the 'not me' response: the human sense of invulnerability to danger. The book is written for academics but is sufficiently clear in style to enable undergraduates access to its ideas.

Anand, P. (1993) *Foundations of Rational Choice Under Risk*, Oxford, Oxford University Press (especially Chapter 2 which surveys empirical evidence).

This monograph provides an overview of work on the nature of rational choice under risk. It deals mainly with logical and philosophical problems associated with expected utility and draws heavily on insights and experiments from the experimental literature on judgment and decision-making. It argues that some of the violations of expected utility found by experimentalists may call for new definitions of what it is for people to be rational.

Hastie, R. and Dawes, R.M. (2001) *Rational Choice in an Uncertain World*, London, Sage.

This book is as non technical as the subject permits and has been written as an introductory textbook with many everyday examples taken from decision making in such areas as medicine, finance and law.

Slovic, P. (ed.) (2000) *Risk Perception*, London, Earthscan.

This is a collection of the work by Slovic and colleagues over the past few decades. It contains the classic works in the risk and judgement field. This group's work is sometimes referred to as the psychometric approach to risk research. While the papers that it reprints are generally from journals targeted at academics, the clarity of its style allows undergraduates to gain an excellent sense of the issues in that field.

References

Bartlett, F. (1932) *Remembering: A Study in Experimental Social Psychology*, Cambridge, Cambridge University Press.

Bell, S.T., Kuriloff, P.J. and Lottes, I. (1994) 'Understanding attributions of blame in stranger rape and date rape situations: an examination of gender, race, identification and students' social perceptions of rape victims', *Journal of Applied Social Psychology*, vol.24, pp.1719–34.

Billig, M. (1987) *Arguing and Thinking: A Rhetorical Approach to Social Psychology*, Cambridge, Cambridge University Press.

Brown, R. (1986) *Social Psychology* (2nd edn) New York, Macmillan.

Darley, J.M. and Gross, P.H. (1983) 'A hypothesis-confirming bias in labelling effects', *Journal of Personality and Social Psychology*, vol.44, pp.20–33.

Douglas, M. (1994) *Risk and Blame: Essays in Cultural Theory*, London, Routledge.

Fischhoff, B. and Lichtenstein, S. (1977) 'Do those who know more also know more about how much they know?', *Organisational Behaviour and Human Performance*, vol.20, pp.159–83.

Fiske and Taylor (1991) *Social Cognition* (2nd edn) New York, McGraw Hill.

Gigerenzer, G. and Hoffrage, U. (1995) 'How to improve Bayesian reasoning without instruction: frequency formats', *Psychological Review*, vol.104, no.4, pp.608–704.

Graham, H. (1987) 'Women's smoking and family health', *Social Science and Medicine*, vol.25, no.1, pp.47–56.

Harris, P. and Middleton, W. (1994) 'The illusion of control and optimism about health: on being less at risk but no more in control than others', *British Journal of Social Psychology*, vol.33, no.4, pp.369–86.

Heider, F. (1958) *The Psychology of Interpersonal Relations,* New York, Wiley.

Heider, F. and Simmel, M. (1944) 'An experimental study of apparent behaviour', *American Journal of Psychology*, vol.57, pp.243–9.

Heine, S.J. and Lehman, D.R. (1995) 'The cultural construction of self-enhancement: an examination of group-serving biases', *Journal of Personality and Social Psychology*, vol.72, no.6, pp.1268–83.

Joffe, H. (1999) *Risk and the 'Other'*, Cambridge, Cambridge University Press.

Jones, E.E. and Davis, K.E. (1965) 'From acts to dispositions: the attribution process in person perception', in Berkowitz L. (ed.) *Advances in Experimental Social Psychology*, vol.2, New York, Academic Press.

Kahneman, D. and Tversky, A. (1973) 'On the psychology of prediction', *Psychological Review*, vol.80, pp.237–51.

Kelley, H.H. (1967) 'Attribution theory in social psychology', in Levine D. (ed.) *Nebraska Symposium on Motivation*, vol.15, Lincoln, NE, University of Nebraska Press.

Klein, W. and Radcliffe, N. (1999) 'Generalised and risk-specific unrealistic optimism and their relation to the processing of health information', *13th Conference of the European Health Psychology Society*, 1–3 October.

Kleinhesselink, R.R. and Rosa, E.A. (1991) 'Cognitive representations of risk perceptions: a comparison of Japan and the United States', *Journal of Cross Cultural Psychology*, vol.22, pp.11–28.

Lau, R.R. and Russell, D. (1980) 'Attributions in the sports pages', *Journal of Personality and Social Psychology*, vol.39, pp.29–38.

Moscovici, S. (1981) 'On social representations', in Forgas, J.P. (ed.) *Social Cognition: Perspectives on Everyday Understanding*, London, Academic Press.

McArthur, L.A. (1972) 'The how and what of why: some determinants and consequences of causal attribution', *Journal of Personality and Social Psychology*, vol.2, pp.171–93.

Miller, J.G. (1984) 'Culture and the development of everyday social explanation', *Journal of Personality and Social Psychology*, vol.46, pp.961–78.

Myers, L. and Brewin, C. (1996) 'Illusions of well-being and the repressive coping style', *British Journal of Social Psychology*, vol.35, pp.443–57.

Myers, L. and Renolds, D. (2000) 'How optimistic are repressors? The relationship between repressive coping style, controllability, self-esteem and comparative optimism for health-related events', *Psychology and Health*, vol.15, no.5, pp.677–87.

Neisser, U. (1976) *Cognition and Reality*, San Francisco, CA, Freeman.

Offir, J.T., Fisher, J.D., Williams, S.S. and Fisher, W.A. (1993) 'Reasons for inconsistent AIDS-preventive behaviours among gay men', *Journal of Sex Research*, vol.30, no.1, pp.62–9.

Peeters, G., Cammaert, M F. and Czapinski, J. (1997) 'Unrealistic optimism and positive-negative asymmetry: a conceptual and cross-cultural study of interrelationships between optimism, pessimism and realism', *International Journal of Psychology*, vol.32, no.1, pp.23–34.

Ruscher, J.B., Fiske, S.T. and Schnake, S.B. (2000) 'The motivated tactician's juggling act: compatible vs. incompatible impression goals', *British Journal of Social Psychology*, vol.39, pp.241–56.

Shrauger, J.S. (1975) 'Responses to evaluation as a function of initial self-perception', *Psychological Bulletin*, vol.82, pp.581–96.

Slovic, P., Fischhoff, B. and Lichtenstein, S. (1980) 'Knowing what you want: measuring labile values', in Wallsten, T.S. (ed.) *Cognitive Processes in Choice and Decision Behavior*, no.7, pp.117–41, Hillsdale, NJ, Erlbaum.

Storms, M.D. (1973) 'Videotape and the attribution process: reversing actors' and observers' points of view', *Journal of Personality and Social Psychology*, vol.27, p.167–75.

Taylor, S.E. (1989) *Positive Illusions*, New York, Basic Books.

Taylor, S.E. and Armor, D.A. (1996) 'Positive illusions and coping with adversity', *Journal of Personality*, vol.64, no.4, pp.873–98.

Taylor, S. and Brown, J. (1994) '"Illusion" of mental health does not explain positive illusions', *American Psychologist*, vol.49, no.11, pp.972–3.

Taylor, S.E., Kemeny, M.E., Aspinwall, L.G., Schneider, S.C., Rodriguez, R. and Herbert, M. (1992) 'Optimism, coping, psychological distress, and high-risk sexual behaviour among men at risk of AIDS', *Journal of Personality and Social Psychology*, vol.63, pp.460–73.

Thomas, K. (1981) 'Comparative risk perception: how the public perceives the risks and benefits of energy systems', *Proceedings Royal Society of London A*, vol.376, pp.35–50.

Thomas, K., Swaton, E., Fishbein, M. and Otway, H.J. (1980) 'Nuclear energy: the accuracy of policy makers' perceptions of public beliefs', *Behavioural Science*, vol.25, pp.332–44.

Weinstein, N.D. (1982) 'Unrealistic optimism about susceptibility to health problems', *Journal of Behavioural Medicine*, vol.5, pp.441–60.

Weinstein, N.D. (1987) 'Unrealistic optimism about susceptibility to health problems: conclusions from a community wide sample', *Journal of Behavioural Medicine*, vol.10, pp.481–95.

Wright, G. (1984) *Behavioural Decision Theory: an Introduction*, Penguin, Harmondsworth.

Commentary 7: Perceiving and understanding the social world

Chapter 7 is the second of three chapters, Chapters 6, 7 and 8 (and Section 3 of Chapter 3), that address cognitive processes – that is, 'what goes on in the mind'. In Chapter 7 the emphasis is not on the particular processes that constitute social perception and understanding, but rather on the way that perceiving, attending, thinking and judging are affected by social, cultural and motivational factors. Nevertheless, the same basic method is used – that of experimentation. The application of this method to social perception and social cognition is an important instance of a psychological perspective called experimental social psychology.

Theory

1   Assumptions about 'what people are like' underpin all psychological perspectives. Psychological investigation of social perception and social cognition has used theories that assume people pursue the truth rationally. This assumption is associated with a prescription that people *should* process information with machine-like logic. When this does not happen, people are seen as irrational and their information processing as flawed. However, humans often have cognitions or make judgements that are *reasonable* – given their motivations and information-processing capacities.

Methods

2   Experimental social psychology tries to bring the complexity of social perception, cognition and attribution into the laboratory. One way in which this has been done is through asking research participants to respond to vignettes constructed by the researcher.
3   It is difficult to reproduce in the laboratory the ways in which information is encountered and gathered in the everyday world, and the urgency and emotive content of social cognition in ordinary life. Both of these difficulties raise issues about ecological validity.
4   The experimental study of social perception and cognition seeks to make generalizations about how people process information in, and about, the social world. Such findings can also contribute to a holistic understanding of people by providing information about personal motives.

Themes

5   The schemas we hold can constrain, or even determine, how new and/or ambiguous information is processed – without our being *aware* of how and when this happens. This can promote fixity and make change difficult.
6   The interplay between nature and nurture can be seen in the suggestion that survival requires quick and effective decision making under conditions of uncertainty – with the result that these processing capabilities have been selected for in evolution.

■ Thinking about theory

Converging traditions

Perceiving and understanding in the social world, as it is studied within the perspective of experimental social psychology, has roots in two psychological traditions. The first, cognitive psychology, has grown as a force in psychology primarily through using laboratory experimentation. The second tradition, social psychology, has had as its goal the understanding of social behaviour. Here, the focus has been, not on cognitive processes in their own right, but on ways in which cognitive processes, such as having systems of beliefs and attitudes and making attributions, can mediate between the social world and what people do. And, again, the primary method has been experimentation, with an additional focus on measurement using questionnaires. The perspective in Chapter 7 could be seen as a convergence of these two traditions. What is important to note is that this convergence was possible only because the underlying assumptions about *what people are like* are very similar in the two traditions. Cognitive psychologists adopt an information processing approach – people's cognitive processing is likened to the workings of a computer. Social psychologists interested in social perception and cognition have an 'intuitive scientist' model of how people understand their worlds – *people seek 'truths' in a logical and rational way*. So both are able to embrace a scientific, experimental approach as a way of understanding their subject matter – how 'rational people' process information about their worlds.

Theoretical assumptions can become prescriptions

All psychological perspectives are built on assumptions about people – the subject matter. Such assumptions are a big part of what a perspective is and they play a central role in what is accepted as the appropriate methods to use and data to collect. But psychologists' perspective-bound assumptions about people can lead them to *expect* certain results from their studies – in this case, computer-like information processing and rational truth-seeking. The chapter you have just read shows how experimental social psychology tends to add to the expectation of rationality because the very nature of the stimulus material used means that there is, very often, an objectively *correct* answer and, therefore, also an incorrect one. This is demonstrated by the availability heuristic: participants' failure to use all the relevant information that the experimenter knows has been provided is defined as 'not correct'. In attribution experiments, on the other hand, there may *seem* to be a correct answer, such as 'information should be processed without extra weighting on the internal factors'. But who is to say that this is correct with respect to maximizing social efficiency?

The chapter has vividly demonstrated that people do not always operate as scientists, they are not rational in the way that was expected. This doesn't mean that people always make mistakes – just that we can find and replicate situations where they do not behave as some accounts of rationality suggest they would behave. For example, they do not use all the information that is available to them; they seem to weight information from different sources (knowledge of the environment and knowledge of people) in ways that serve motivational purposes. But you also saw that researchers' *expectations* of rationality have tended to slip into *prescriptions* about rationality. So, when the empirical findings were not as expected, this was seen as evidence of failures of cognitive processing and/or failures of people – 'people don't operate in the ways they should, and therefore people are irrational.' The general point is that, whilst perspectives, and the theories they produce, need assumptions as starting points, these assumptions and their implications have to be kept visible and continually questioned.

■ Thinking about methods

Experimentation and social psychology

We have seen that psychologists who study social perception and cognition rely largely on experiments. They simplify the variables, define them carefully and control all but two, the independent variable and the dependent variable. Since the intent is to understand social behaviour in the flow of everyday life in ordinary environments, ways have to be found to bring aspects of this complexity into the laboratory. You saw that a common method is to use vignettes. These can contain quite complex, fictitious information about people and situations presented as short summaries of what might be encountered in everyday life. But, at the same time, they are in a form that permits just one variable (such as a person's socio-economic status) to be manipulated in the experimental condition. Sometimes the designs are closer to 'natural' experiments. For example, in Lau and Russell's study of attributions of success and failure in baseball and football games, the sports stories were not created especially for the study; they were already-existing texts, selected from newspapers so as to represent the two experimental conditions.

You may remember that the problem of ecological validity was raised towards the end of Chapter 6 ('Perception and attention'). It was suggested there that findings from laboratory studies can sometimes be different from those in the outside world because the experience of the task in the laboratory is, by definition, different from what it would be in ordinary life. Driving on a simulator will never carry the risk of driving on the roads. A similar problem exists in the experimental study of social perception and cognition. Doing information-processing tasks and making attributions in the laboratory may be different from doing them outside the laboratory because the information is presented in a fashion that is so unlike the ways we usually gather information. It is also difficult to impart the urgency and the emotive content of much of what we process ordinarily. For example, the experiment carried out by Ruscher *et al.* (Box 7.3) testing the 'motivated tactician' model doesn't really reproduce the motivational impact that other people can have on us and that often drives our everyday 'impression formation' – our impressions of what people are like.

You saw, in the discussion of risk at the end of Section 4 and in the case study in Section 5, that understanding how people think about risk can benefit from using other methods, in addition to experiments, to tap how people think about risk naturalistically. In other words, a different picture can emerge about how people think about risk in their own environments and with their own knowledge and language, compared with how they express their beliefs and knowledge via responses to questionnaires that inevitably have demand characteristics.

The study of general processes also contributes to holistic understandings

The experimental study of social perception and cognition sets out to make generalizations about how people process information in and about the social world. As this perspective has accumulated knowledge, the important role of motivational factors has been highlighted. Whilst some generalizations can be made about processing, *and* about the role of motives, such findings can also contribute to a more holistic understanding of people. These generalizations draw attention to the important influence of personal motives, meanings and social representations on how each of us processes information and operates in the world.

■ Thinking about themes

Fixity and change

In Chapter 7 we have seen yet another way in which the possibility of fixity arises. We saw in Section 2 that direct experiences in the social world, and indirect experiences through the media, provide knowledge that we organize into relatively fixed structures called schemas. The evidence presented in the chapter suggested that schemas can constrain how we deal with new information and with ambiguous information. Furthermore, and very importantly, we are not *aware* of how and when this happens. It was suggested therefore that we might be 'stuck in our schemas' – a rather dramatic expression of fixity. Cognitive processing might also affect what we 'see' in the world through the related process of categorization which leads inevitably to overgeneralization of differences between categories and of similarities within categories. On the other hand, some psychologists have suggested that we are not so unthinking or so fixed and can debate positions with ourselves; perhaps the question is not whether we *can* but whether we *do*.

One of the clearest and perhaps most unexpected findings of the work on social perception and cognition is that a great deal of our processing and efforts to understand proceed below the level of conscious awareness; that is, unconsciously. Even with effort we cannot track the processing we are doing. There are two very important implications of this for questions about fixity and change. The first, as we saw above, is that, to the extent that we are limited by our schemas and categorical processing, we are not able to be flexible about the way we see the world. The second is that this finding emphasizes the importance of our embeddedness in particular social contexts that define the information we encounter. What we are exposed to early in life defines the structure of cognitive systems that thereafter constrain, and perhaps determine to some degree, what we 'see' and 'do'.

Nature and nurture

In Commentary 6, *nature and nurture* as an explanatory scheme was expanded to include nature in the sense of the biological structures and processes that develop during life, and nurture as our experience of environments of all kinds. We have seen in Chapter 7 that our schemas and categories are formed under the influence of our environments. Once formed, these mental structures (and presumably in some sense biological structures) have a powerful influence on how we 'see' and interpret the world around us – they *become* a kind of 'wiring'. You may remember the suggestion in the cognitive psychology section of Chapter 3 that some of this categorical structuring is already present at birth.

The material in Chapter 7 has also contributed to thinking about the evolutionary aspects of nature and nurture with respect to how people process information and think. In Chapter 2 ('Evolutionary psychology'), an argument was made for the idea that our cognitive abilities, for example, in relation to theory of mind, evolved in an essentially social environment. In Chapter 7 we have seen that perceiving and understanding the social world is not primarily about logical and rational information processing, but about processing that enables quick and effective decisions to be made under conditions of uncertainty – in the service of survival. There is also an argument from evolutionary psychology that we process information best when it is presented in the same ways that it is encountered in naturalistic environments.

In Chapter 8 ('Memory: structures, processes and skills') the discussion of the broad topic of cognitive psychology is continued.

CHAPTER **8**

Memory: structures, processes and skills

Nicky Brace and Ilona Roth

Contents

Aims

This chapter aims to.

- provide an understanding of the fundamental role of memory in cognition and behaviour
- introduce the brain structures and mechanisms that play a role in memory
- consider the key factors that have been found to enhance memory processes
- explore the diversity in memory functioning and memory skills
- illustrate the pervasive role of memory with examples of the operation of memory in everyday life
- explore the range of research methods employed in studies of memory
- help you gain insights into the working of your own memory.

1   Introduction

Memory is vital to us in everyday life. It involves storing and retrieving information and experiences that not only enable us to keep track of our activities but also help us to understand who we are and how we should interact with others. We use our memory in almost all daily activities. Memory lapses can be annoying, embarrassing or have important consequences. Indeed, we are usually more aware of our memory failures than our successes; we may not realize just how much we use our memory and how well it functions most of the time.

Memory is not easy to investigate because, like many psychological phenomena, it cannot be observed directly. We infer its existence because we know that we are not constantly relearning the same things. We also refer to memory in different ways, sometimes describing it as a structure or system that can fail: "my memory has failed me" (and, with advances in methods for investigating the brain, we now know a bit about the brain structures and neurotransmitters that are involved). At other times we talk about memory as if it were a skill that can be improved or that differentiates people: "my memory is not as good as yours", or "my memory for faces is better than my memory for names". In this first section of the chapter, we shall explore how psychologists have conceptualized memory.

1.1 Key processes in memory

Psychologists have found it useful to break memory down into a set of component processes and to consider the factors that affect their operation. Research has considered three kinds of processes (see Figure 8.1):

Figure 8.1   Key processes in memory

Encoding processes are involved in putting information into the memory store. Information from the external world is acquired and is transformed into a code. There are a number of ways in which information can be encoded: a visual code captures the word 'dog' in a form based on its visual appearance; an acoustic code captures the sound of the word 'dog'; and a semantic code encapsulates the meaning of the word 'dog'. Alternatively, if the information to be stored is in the form of an action or skill, it might be represented as a motor code (e.g. containing information on how to balance on skis). Little is known yet of how other sorts of information such as pain, emotion, smell and taste might be represented.

Storage processes are involved in maintaining or holding this encoded information in the form of internal representations. The precise form that these representations take is a matter of debate. At the physical level, it is thought that learning or memory formation entails a change to the pattern of the synaptic connections between neurones in the brain. (See Chapter 4 for an explanation of these terms.)

Retrieval processes are involved in getting information out of the memory store and include recognition and recall. **Recognition** is a form of retrieval process that involves searching our memory for a match for something we are perceiving (an internal representation from a previous experience, e.g. words, faces, actions etc). **Recall** is a form of retrieval process that involves reclaiming something stored in our memory and bringing it into consciousness, as when you remember where you safely stored your passport or spare front door keys.

Encoding, storage and retrieval processes do not operate in isolation from one another: how well information is encoded will influence how it is stored, and how easily it is retrieved. As we will see later on in this chapter, there are some things that we are unlikely to forget, for instance a favourite joke. Because we enjoyed the punch line, we paid close attention to it and then went on to retell it several times. Sometimes, however,

Encoding processes
Used to code the information acquired through the senses and to enter it into the memory system.

Storage processes
Used to retain coded information in the memory system as internal representations.

Retrieval processes
Used to recover or get access to the information stored in the memory system.

Recognition
The type of retrieval process that involves finding a match in memory for something that is in the external world.

Recall
The type of retrieval process that involves searching for something stored in memory and bringing it into consciousness.

poorly encoded material can be remembered because there is a lot of information available at the retrieval stage to help us. We may remember something said to us because we are prompted with cues about when it was said, by whom, in what context etc. These are known as **retrieval cues.** Therefore, these three memory processes should be thought of as operating together.

Retrieval cues
Cues or prompts available at retrieval that may help us find the information we are searching for in memory.

1.2 Key subsystems in memory

Memory not only includes different processes but also comprises a number of different subsystems that work together. Different models have been proposed to describe these subsystems. One of the first psychologists to conceptualize memory as involving different systems was William James (1890), who proposed a primary memory permitting conscious mental activity, and a secondary memory responsible for storing knowledge. Many since have differentiated between three main subsystems as shown below.

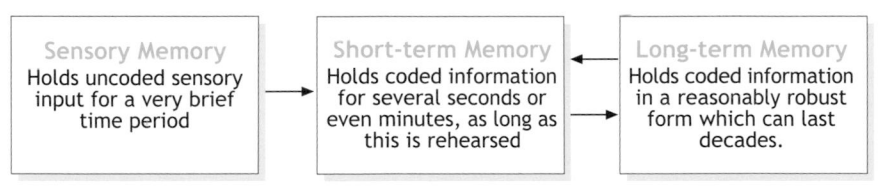

Figure 8.2   Key subsystems in memory

Models such as the one depicted in Figure 8.2 are examples of the information processing approach to memory, which has stimulated a great deal of research. This has been, and remains, an important strand of research within cognitive psychology and you have already met other examples of this information processing approach in Chapter 6 and Chapter 7. In memory research, the information processing approach sees memory as a flow of information through a series of sub-systems. Information is recoded as it moves from one sub-system to the next in a fixed sequence, and the capacity of each of these sub-systems is limited.

Information about the environment is picked up through our senses and is held in its raw, uncoded form in sensory memory. This perceptual record, containing the sensory characteristics of the information, lasts for an extremely short period of time, certainly no more than a few seconds. The capacity of sensory memory has been difficult to establish because of its short duration, but different stores or buffers for the different sensory modalities are thought to be involved. It is perhaps appropriate to consider this first stage as part of the perceptual process and it is through the processes of selective attention and recognition (see Chapter 6), that some of the information is coded and stored in short-term memory (STM).

Research suggests that only a limited amount of information can be stored in STM for a limited amount of time. A classic example of STM in operation is dialling a new telephone number. Having looked up the number, you might remember it long enough to dial (about 6–12 seconds), but not much longer than that. If, however, you studied the number long enough or dialled it on a regular basis, then it is likely that the number would enter into LTM and be remembered for longer. LTM is considered to be unlimited in its capacity and indeed many people find that they can continue to learn new things and remember new experiences throughout their lives. However, sometimes, there may be difficulty in retrieving these from memory – either we cannot remember them at all or we can only partially remember them.

Now try the following activity to test the limits of your STM.

Activity 8.1   Primacy and recency effects

Read the following set of digits once and then close the book and write down as many as you can remember in the correct order.

8   5   9   2   4   1   6   3   7

Experiments have found that most people remember about seven digits, although scores vary from five to nine digits. The amount remembered is referred to as your **memory span** and this span was thought to reflect the capacity of STM.

What happens if the amount of information to be remembered exceeds the capacity of the STM, i.e. the memory span? Try learning the following in 20 seconds and then close the book and write down as many as you can remember in the correct order. Then read the comment below.

A I J Z D S U B L P X C M T N E O Y

Comment

It is likely that you forgot some of the items. Usually, when the list exceeds nine items, the middle items are the ones not retrieved at test. Experiments have shown that participants are more likely to recall the first few items, the **primacy effect**, along with the last few items, the **recency effect**. The proposed explanation was that the first few items are recalled from LTM; as they are early on in the list they will have been rehearsed (repeated to oneself) and entered into LTM. The last few items are recalled because they are still available in STM (i.e. the recency effect). The recency

---

Memory span
The number of items that can be repeated back in the correct order just after a list of items has been presented in a memory experiment.

Primacy effect
The finding, in memory experiments, that participants are more likely to remember the first few items from a list of items.

Recency effect
The finding, in memory experiments, that participants are more likely to remember the last few items from a list of items.

effect was found to disappear if participants were asked to perform another task immediately after learning, such as counting backwards in 3s from 501, before attempting recall.

Short-term memory as 'working memory'?

We may have given you the impression that STM is simply a temporary store for holding information for a brief period. However, in contemporary approaches it is seen as much more than this. Baddeley and Hitch (1974) argued that to understand what STM is, we should think about what it is used for. They have characterized STM as having several functions. For instance, one key function is to concentrate on processing new inputs, and rehearse and code them for transfer to long-term memory. Another function is to retrieve relevant stored knowledge to assist in making sense of these inputs. Yet another is to hold information temporarily while performing some kind of calculation, either a mathematical or a reasoning task. For example, imagine someone giving you the clue to a question in a crossword puzzle along with the number of spaces the word fits into. You need to match words retrieved from LTM against the new input, the clue and the number of letters the word has to have. In their model, Baddeley and Hitch use the term **working memory** to describe STM. They emphasize that STM is an *active* store holding the information that we are consciously thinking about – it is an attention-limited 'workbench' system of memory. In other words, it is like a mental workspace in which we pull together new inputs and old memories and carry out a variety of processing operations. It is limited in terms of the amount of attentional resources that are available, as you saw in Chapter 6.

Working memory
An alternative conception of short-term memory which reflects its active role in cognitive processing.

1.3 Ways of studying memory

Psychologists have used a variety of techniques to study memory, including controlled laboratory experiments, quasi-experiments and field experiments as well as diary studies and cross-sectional studies. Valuable data have also been derived from the development of computational models (such as computer-based face recognition systems that mimic human cognition) and from neuropsychology. Neuropsychological case studies have provided insights into the patterns of cognitive deficits arising from brain damage and valuable information for the construction of models of memory. Brain-imaging techniques allow brain functioning to be explored in individuals with and without brain damage. Case studies and imaging research have shown that many different areas and structures of the brain are implicated in memory. You will come across most of these methods in this chapter. Computational modelling however will be explored in the third level course on cognitive psychology.

| Summary | Section 1

- Memory is involved in almost all daily activities.
- Three key memory processes are encoding, storage and retrieval.
  It is important to remember that these operate together.
- Models have distinguished different subsystems relating to sensory
  memory, short-term memory and long-term memory.
- A variety of methods is used to explore different aspects of memory,
  ranging from controlled experiments to case studies of memory
  deficits.

2   Memory processes

In this section, we shall consider factors that have been shown to enhance
memory. As an Open University student you may find the following
discussion of practical help in your own study of this course.

Activity 8.2

Think of the new knowledge you have gained so far in this course, including the ICT
and research skills you have acquired and the material you have read in the earlier
chapters of this book. What knowledge do you think you will remember in a year's
time? Will it be statistical information, theoretical perspectives or names of
psychologists?

Martin Conway and colleagues investigated how well students would retain
information over a 12–year period following completion of a course in
cognitive psychology (Conway *et al.*, 1991). They tested for names and
concepts, general principles and specific facts, as well as knowledge about
experimental design and statistics. They found that some forgetting took
place over the first three to four years, followed by a period of stability for
the remaining eight years. The same pattern was obtained for different
kinds of information, although memory for names initially declined more
than the other types of knowledge. You may find it interesting to know
that very little was forgotten about the principles of experimental design
and statistical analysis.

Why were the participants in the above study able to remember the
information from their course over such a long period of time? What are
the factors that enhance memory? These factors come into play either at

encoding or at retrieval, or both. It seems plausible that certain factors operating at encoding also lead to better storage but, alternatively, they may facilitate retrieval. As pointed out previously, these three processes should be considered as operating together. Our discussion will serve the dual purpose of providing practical advice and highlighting research findings.

2.1 Factors operating at encoding

Study skills books provide advice on how best to study and prepare for examinations. For example:

- make summary notes when reading and test yourself;
- space out your revision sessions;
- restructure your notes when revising; and
- avoid working for long stretches.

In this section, we shall examine the psychological principles underlying these tips, drawing on relevant theoretical frameworks and experimental laboratory research.

Why make notes when reading and why test yourself?

The retention of material in LTM depends largely on how the information is encoded once it has been registered. Craik and Lockhart (1972) proposed the **levels of processing theory,** which sees the depth to which information is processed as determining later retention. At the 'shallow' level, individuals simply code the information in terms of its physical characteristics, for example they attend to the visual characteristics like the typeface or the acoustic features like the sound of the words. If you just copy down the material you are reading without extracting meaning, you would only encode at this level. At the 'deep' level, individuals code the information in terms of its meaning (this is referred to as semantic processing). By forcing yourself to make summary notes of the key points while reading, you ensure that you carry out this type of deep processing. Deep level semantic processing is likely to assist retention in LTM because it tends to involve **elaborative rehearsal**; this means that you are processing the material more extensively because you are activating different aspects of its meaning and linking it to other associated items. In contrast, so called **maintenance rehearsal** is simply the repetition of information in your head or out loud without any further processing (like saying a phone number out loud until you dial it). By testing yourself rather than simply reading your notes, you will be carrying out elaborative rehearsal and will be more likely to remember your revision notes later on.

Levels of processing theory
The theory that the retention of material in memory is dependent on how deeply it is processed at encoding.

Elaborative rehearsal
The process of thinking about information to be remembered in terms of its meaning and associations to other stored material.

Maintenance rehearsal
The process of memorising by simply repeating information without any further processing.

Orienting tasks
Task instructions designed to influence the processing performed on material to be remembered, such as words.

Incidental learning
Learning that occurs in the absence of explicit instructions to learn when an experimenter presents a set of items for later memory testing.

Intentional learning
Learning that occurs when an experimenter has specifically told participants that their memory for presented items will be tested.

Researchers have investigated the levels of processing theory by using **orienting tasks**. An orienting task is a set of instructions giving participants a specific task to perform on the stimulus material. Orienting tasks are designed to test **incidental learning**, as participants are not told that they should try to remember presented stimulus words. If participants are told explicitly that their memory for the items will be tested, then **intentional learning** is being investigated.

In one experiment reported by Craik and Tulving (1975), participants were shown 60 words one at a time to make 'yes' or 'no' decisions about, as each word was accompanied by one of the following orienting tasks:

- Structural orienting task – is the word in block capitals?
- Acoustic orienting task   does the word rhyme with ... (e.g. 'bat')?
- Semantic orienting task – does the word fit the sentence ... (e.g. 'The cat sat on the ...')?

For half of the 20 words linked to each orienting task, the correct response was 'no' and for the other half it was 'yes'. Later, unexpectedly, participants were given a recognition task and asked to identify in a list of words those that they had seen previously when completing the orienting task. This list comprised the 60 original words plus 120 new words (known as distractors).

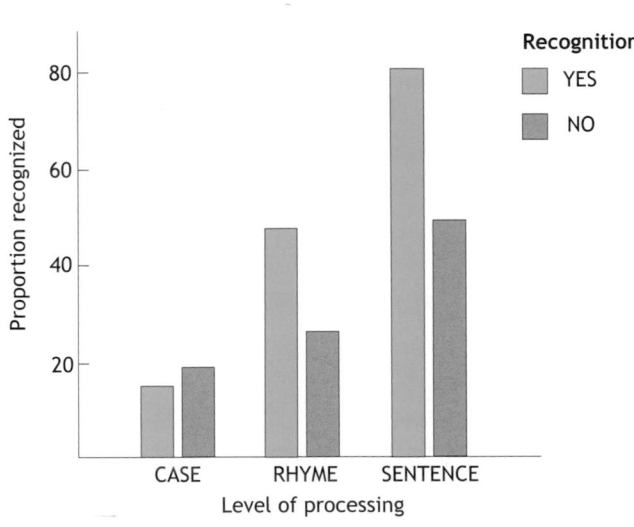

Figure 8.3   The effect of orienting task on recognition performance (Source: adapted from Craik and Tulving, Figure 1, 1975)

The results presented in Figure 8.3 indicate that the semantic orienting task ('sentence') generated the highest amount of incidental learning, the structural orienting task ('case') the lowest amount and the acoustic task ('rhyme') an intermediate amount. This pattern was evident for both recognition of 'yes' words and recognition of 'no' words.

Numerous other studies have demonstrated the effect of processing depth and there is evidence that it extends beyond verbal items. However, of interest here is the finding known as the **generation effect**. Imagine that you have been given a list of words and are asked to generate words that rhyme with each, thus creating word-pairs. You are more likely to remember the words you generated than words that were provided as rhymes and that you had simply read. In terms of depth of processing, the interpretation of this effect is that the self-generated words, the words you thought of as rhymes, have received deeper processing. In a similar way, if you use your own words to paraphrase the material you want to learn for an exam (i.e. by self-generating), your memory should improve as a result of deeper or more elaborate processing.

generation effect
An effect in which participants are more likely to remember the items that they generated in a word association test, rather than items they simply read.

Why space out your revision sessions?

Students who distribute their sessions of studying a particular topic over the week, for example one hour per day, should retain more information than students who revise the same topic for seven hours in the same day. Each time they return to the same topic, they are creating, extending or strengthening memory representations of that topic. Additional study opportunities allow the learner to use knowledge gained in previous study sessions to encode the new material more elaborately. For example, Mayer (1983) found that those who were repeatedly exposed to a science passage showed an increase in recall of the conceptual principles outlined in the passage. He suggests that the content and the structure of learning changes qualitatively with repetition; the earlier study opportunity provides learners with a conceptual framework which can be used during subsequent study sessions to focus attention and reorganize the conceptual ideas contained in the passage.

The benefit of spreading out learning rather than confining it to one session was observed by Hermann Ebbinghaus (1885) while he was studying the learning of meaningless material. Subsequent research has confirmed this **spacing effect** using many different types of learning tasks and stimulus material, including words, pictures, sentences and texts.

Spacing effect
An effect in which memory is enhanced because learning is spread out across several sessions, rather than confined to a single session.

BIOGRAPHY   *Hermann Ebbinghaus 1850–1909*

Ebbinghaus was not the first to think about memory but he is considered to be one of the first to study it scientifically. He wanted to explore how long it would take to learn something, what factors would affect learning speed, how quickly this learning would be forgotten, and how quickly it could be relearned. He was the sole participant in his experiments and so to study memory objectively and avoid confounding variables, he devised stimulus material that he had not encountered before in his daily life and that had no meaning. He created thousands of **nonsense syllables**, i.e. consonant – vowel – consonant trigrams that were pronounceable but had no meaning, such as TUV and BUX. One of his findings (a result that has been replicated by other researchers) is that the forgetting rate is initially quite rapid, but then slows down. A lot of what he learned was forgotten within the first 24 hours but after 30 days he was still able to remember much of what he could remember after 5 days.

Hermann Ebbinghaus, 1850–1909

Why restructure your notes when revising?

Restructuring and organizing your notes helps because this constitutes an additional study opportunity and requires you to engage in deep processing. By organizing items into larger, more meaningful units, you are also reducing the number of chunks of material to be learned.

For example, look at the following list: **Skinner; Identity; Psychometrics; Learning; Erikson; Cattell; Adolescence; Conditioning; Personality.**

As you may remember from earlier chapters, you can organize the list into three blocks:

Erikson	Cattell	Skinner
Adolescence	Psychometrics	Conditioning
Identity	Personality	Learning

Studies have found that memory improves if items to be remembered are presented in blocked form, i.e. with all the items in one category together, than if they are randomly presented. Bousfield (1953) found that even if items were not presented in blocked form, participants spontaneously grouped items. Although they were invited to recall the items in any order, known as **free recall**, they chose to recall them from the same category together, known as **clustering**.

On this course, you will find that you can organize your notes in clusters, and that these clusters themselves can be linked together, in a logical way (maybe even hierarchically organized). For example, the information on memory processes so far may be organized like this:

Free recall
A memory recall task in which participants can recall the items in any order they wish.

Clustering
Seen in memory recall when participants recall the items in clusters according to category or some other dimension.

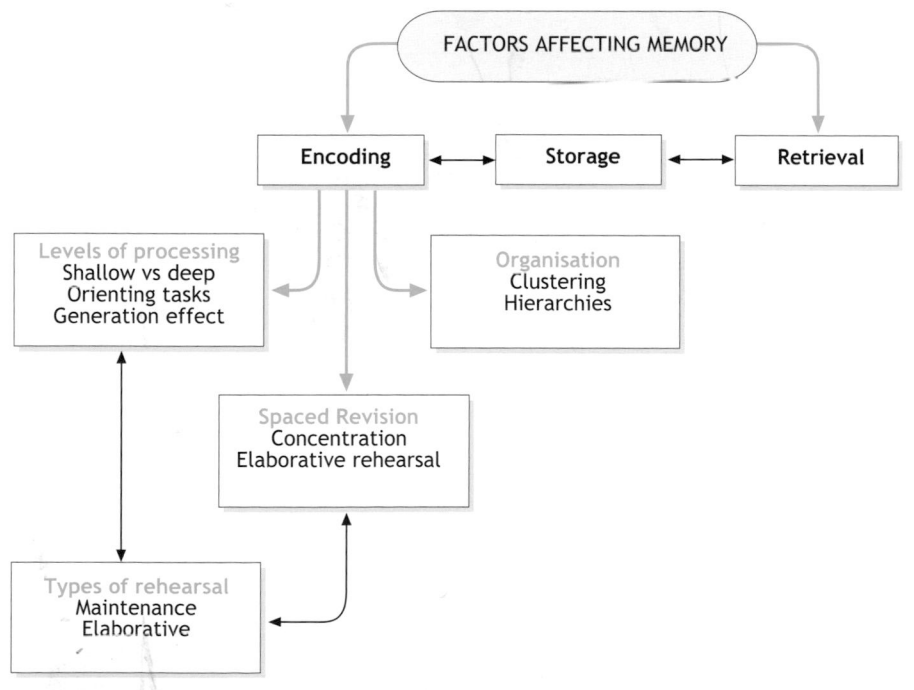

Figure 8.4 Factors affecting memory

Bower, Clark, Lesgold and Winzenz (1969) presented the names of different minerals laid out in a hierarchical manner, i.e. subdivided into metals and stones with each of these categories subdivided further. After one trial, participants remembered 65 per cent of the words and after three trials recall was 100 per cent. A control group of participants were shown the same number and hierarchical pattern of words but the actual words were unrelated to each other. After one trial, they remembered 18 per cent of the words and after three trials 47 per cent. These findings demonstrate that a hierarchical organization can assist memory.

In everyday life, people organize information in all sorts of ways to assist their memory. Stevens (1988) found that waitresses reorganized and clustered customers' orders so that they mapped onto the layout of the restaurant. Visual imagery has proved to be a powerful organizing method. Figure 8.4 shows you how you can draw up an overview of an area that can be visualized and used when you come to sit your examination. Imagery is also the basis for many **mnemonic** techniques (memory enhancing techniques). For example, if learning the vocabulary of a foreign language, you can associate the foreign word with its English counterpart via a keyword by creating a visual image. This image will allow you to access the foreign word when you need it. For example, the Spanish word for postal letter is 'carta' so the keyword could be cart and you might form a mental image of pushing a grocery cart full of letters.

Mnemonic
A technique or strategy that will increase the memorability of material to be remembered, such as adding meaningful associations or bizarre images.

Why avoid working for long stretches?

There are a number of mostly common-sense reasons why you should follow this advice. First, the amount of time during which one can concentrate is limited. Elaborative rehearsal, which you should be undertaking in your study sessions, is demanding and requires a considerable amount of attentional resources and these are limited (see Chapter 6). Remember also that you need to remain motivated, and to help you it is best to break down the revision task into smaller units, set yourself achievable goals and reward yourself when you reach them. Finally, studies have shown that a person's physical condition and diet can affect their performance, so find the time to eat, sleep and exercise properly during your revision period.

2.2 Factors operating at retrieval

Once material has been encoded into memory, is there anything that will help to recover it? Here, we turn our attention to the retrieval stage and the factors that may affect our ability to access the information stored.

Activity 8.3

Take a moment to remember an event you witnessed or experienced that was a little upsetting, for example a minor car accident or losing important documents. Write down what you remember. How complete is your memory for this event? Do you think your memory for this event is as good as your memory for a pleasant event, such as a wedding? Would it help your memory to picture in your mind where the event took place?

Comment

Police officers are trained to assist witnesses in police interviews to recall as much as they can. Stress can limit how easily we can retrieve information and witnessing a crime can be quite traumatic. The training that police officers receive has been informed by research undertaken by cognitive psychologists. Four retrieval techniques, described below, have been highlighted.

Retrieval-enhancing techniques

- *Context reinstatement*: in this technique, the police ask a person to remember a witnessed event *just as they experienced it.* The witness is encouraged to think about the physical surroundings including temperature and lighting, as well as how they were feeling at the time. There is convincing evidence that this context reinstatement can assist retrieval. You may have experienced this yourself. When looking for your keys or glasses you may have thought back to when you last had them, including where you were and what you were doing. Alternatively you may have found that a certain smell, taste or a particular piece of music will bring back particular memories. The police may also organize a crime reconstruction in an attempt to jog the memories of witnesses who have not yet come forth. Every attempt is made to re-enact the crime exactly as it is thought to have occurred.
- *Recalling everything*: witnesses are encouraged to recall everything that they can remember, regardless of whether they think it is important. Providing one piece of information can lead to the retrieval of others, so that remembering an apparently minor detail can provoke retrieval of potentially important information. Furthermore, at the beginning of a police investigation, the potential importance of any given piece of information is not known. It is therefore desirable to start the interview by obtaining as full an account as possible of the event, and then return to specific episodes by using open-ended questions.
- *Recalling in different temporal orders*: witnesses may be encouraged to recall the information not just forwards from the first thing they

remember about the event, but also backwards starting with the very last thing they can remember. Sometimes, a witness may wish to start with what he/she felt to be the most salient aspect of the event and work forwards and backwards from that point.

- *Changing perspective*: witnesses may be asked to recall the event from different perspectives, for example from both their own perspective and that of the victim, or from the viewpoint of another witness to the crime. By activating this alternative perceptual perspective, more information may be retrieved.

The techniques outlined above formed the basis of the original version of the 'cognitive interview', developed by Geiselman and Fisher (e.g. Geiselman *et al.*, 1984). The cognitive interview has been found to be effective in aiding recall in a police interview. Next, we shall consider why these retrieval techniques may assist memory.

Theoretical rationale for retrieval-enhancing techniques

Encoding specificity principle
The notion that retrieval of information from memory depends on an overlap or matching of the cues that are available at retrieval with those registered at encoding.

The techniques are based on several different theoretical frameworks, including the **encoding specificity principle**, presented by Endel Tulving (1975, 1983), which has been an influential theoretical framework in the field of memory for decades. This centres on the relationship between encoding and retrieval, and suggests that we remember more if the cues that are available during retrieval overlap or match with cues that were registered at encoding. Indeed, the effectiveness of a retrieval cue is dependent on how many properties or features it shares with the item that is being retrieved. More elaborate processing at encoding creates a richer network of associations, increasing the number of features or cues available for overlap. Recognition tests provide more retrieval cues than recall tests, increasing the likelihood of overlap between the features.

Tulving suggests that there may be several retrieval paths to the information that was encoded, so that information not accessed via one retrieval cue could be accessed via an alternative retrieval cue. For example, 'Thomas' might be accessed via the cue 'Welsh poet' or the cue 'Dylan'.

Retrieval techniques can work in the following ways:

- Reinstating the context increases the likelihood that cues available at encoding will also be available at retrieval.
- Encouraging witnesses to report incomplete information may overcome their reluctance to report something they remember only sketchily and also to report information they feel uncertain about. Furthermore, recalling one bit of the information may provide the necessary retrieval cues to access the missing information.

- Recalling in different orders will increase the number of retrieval routes and potential retrieval cues available.
- Recalling from the perspective of another person at the scene of the crime may generate additional retrieval cues and assist memory.

8.2 Context reinstatement

The beneficial effect on memory of reinstating context has been researched empirically. Godden and Baddeley (1975) demonstrated the effects of physical context in a study involving divers. Half of the participants learned a list of 40 words while 15 feet underwater and half learned the list on the beach. The recall test then took place in the same or an alternative environment.

As Figure 8.5 below shows, recall was roughly 40 per cent higher when the test environment was the same as the learning environment. Those learning and recalling underwater remembered more than those who learned underwater but were asked to recall on land; similarly those learning and recalling on land remembered more than those who switched context and were asked to recall underwater. This finding has important implications for divers as they usually train and receive instruction for their day's work on land.

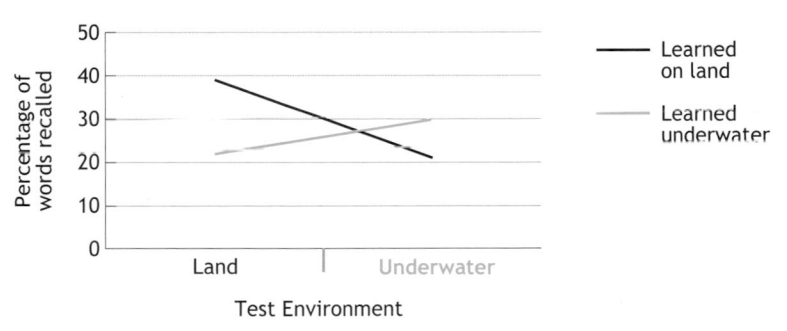

Figure 8.5 The effect of environmental context on word recall (Source: adapted from Godden and Baddeley, Table 1, p.328, 1975)

Godden and Baddeley did not find such a result in a subsequent experiment testing recognition rather than recall (Godden and Baddeley, 1980). One key difference between recall and recognition is that in the latter the original information is re-presented and hence many of the cues that were available at encoding are also available at retrieval. In free recall tests, cues are normally scarce as these tests require you to generate the information from your own memory. The beneficial effect on recall of reinstating the context could therefore be explained in terms of the extra cues that become available.

2.3 Retrieval difficulties

As we have seen above, retrieval failure is sometimes temporary. We think we have stored something yet cannot access it. This suggests the need to distinguish between availability and accessibility, well illustrated by the **tip-of-the-tongue phenomenon**, which occurs when you cannot remember a word or a name that you know you have stored. There is a feeling that what you are trying to remember is 'on the tip of your tongue'.

Brown and McNeill (1966) induced this state in experimental participants, by reading definitions of rare words. The task was to identify the word that was being defined, the target word. They found that participants often recalled some information about the target word such as the first letter, or recalled related words that resembled the target word in sound or meaning. This conscious searching is an example of active, effortful retrieval and is known as **indirect access**. We may use sound, meaning or, as we saw above, reinstatement of context to locate the information we want to remember. This sort of retrieval contrasts with automatic effortless retrieval, known as **direct access**, which occurs, for instance, when remembering your own name.

Another feeling that we have all encountered is that a piece of information is familiar even though we may not recollect when we encoded or learned it. An example of this is when we meet someone outside his or her usual context. The person's face will be familiar but we may not remember from where. Often, with a bit of effort, this can be recalled, and we find that we can remember the person's name and other useful information. Endel Tulving (1985) distinguished 'remembering' and 'knowing' as two different cognitive states reflecting the subjective experience of memory. 'Remembering' is a state in which you can consciously remember specific details, such as your thoughts or feelings at the time when you saw the person or item. 'Knowing' is when the item feels familiar and you are convinced you have seen it but cannot recall this occurrence.

How might this distinction between 'remembering' and 'knowing' relate to a student's retention of information acquired on his or her course? Martin Conway and colleagues investigated change of memory awareness during students' studies (Conway *et al.*, 1997). Psychology students in their first year of study were asked to complete multiple-choice tests as part of both lecture-based and research methods courses. Students were re-tested at the end of the academic year in just one of these courses, namely the lecture-based course 'Introduction to Psychology'. After selecting an answer for each test item, they were asked to indicate

Tip of the tongue phenomenon
The feeling that although you cannot remember something it is there stored in memory just out of reach.

Indirect access
A type of retrieval that involves deliberate and conscious searching in memory.

Direct access
A type of retrieval that is effortless and occurs automatically without searching in memory.

which of the following states of memory awareness accompanied their response:

- remember (memory of a specific episode from a lecture)
- know (a feeling of 'just knowing' the answer)
- familiar (the selected item felt more familiar than the others)
- guess

Conway *et al.* observed that when knowledge acquisition was assessed immediately after the lecture course had been completed, students achieving higher marks did so because they 'remembered' more. The authors suggest that these students may have attended to the lectures more fully and carried out more elaborative processing, allowing them to relate concepts and organize the material more efficiently. Of interest is that in the re-test for the course 'Introduction to Psychology' the higher performing students differed because they now 'knew' rather than 'remembered' more. For all students there was a shift from the state of 'remembering' to that of 'knowing', however, this shift was stronger for students obtaining higher marks. The authors suggest that as a result of encountering the same concepts in different classes, the contextual information associated with their first encounter of those concepts became lost and the knowledge representations in long-term memory became stronger. The elaborative processing that the higher-achieving students engaged in would facilitate this strengthening of knowledge representation. Finally, the shift occurred faster in the research methods courses as the tests in these courses revealed that all the higher-achieving students performed better because they 'knew' more. The authors explain that in these courses, students are asked actively to engage with the material taught, fewer topics are covered and these tend to be repeated in different contexts in relation to different research problems.

If you think about the way in which you are acquiring your knowledge about research methods, you will discover that you are encountering this material in many different contexts. There are dedicated research methods booklets, Featured Methods Boxes in book chapters, material in your statistics book and related exercises in TMAs involving SPSS. As a result, hopefully your knowledge representations for this material will endure and you will forget very little of this material (like the students who took part in the study at the beginning of this section.)

Summary Section 2

- Levels of processing theory suggests that retention of material is dependent upon depth of processing.
- To ensure retention you should use elaborative rehearsal that explores the meaning of the material and link it to other associated material.
- By organizing your notes you reduce the number of chunks of material to be encoded.
- Retrieval-enhancing techniques include reinstatement of context, which maximizes the number of retrieval cues available for overlap with encoding cues.
- 'Remembering' and 'knowing' are different cognitive states reflecting our subjective experience of memory. Information that we 'remember' may over time become information that we 'know' and the contextual information associated with the original learning may be lost.

3   Constructing and reconstructing memories

In the previous section, we looked at how memory could be enhanced at encoding and retrieval stages. An important factor that we shall consider in more detail here is the close interplay between knowledge already stored and the processing of new information. Existing knowledge will direct our attention to what is important, as we saw in Chapter 6. Like perception, memory involves an active, selective and constructive process rather than a passive mechanism for recording external information for later reproduction. It is not surprising, then, if many of our stored memories are neither accurate nor complete.

3.1 'Effort after meaning'

The notion of memory as a constructive and dynamic system was highlighted by the work of Bartlett, in the 1920s. Below is the most famous of the stories that Bartlett used (Bartlett 1932, p.65). Read the story and then have a go at the subsequent activity. The story may sound strange if you are from a Western cultural background.

Sir Frederic C. Bartlett *1886–1969*

Bartlett, like Ebbinghaus, investigated memory experimentally rather than employing introspection as a method. However, unlike Ebbinghaus, he chose not to use meaningless material to study memory. Bartlett sought to study the effects of past experiences on the acquisition of new material, and he deliberately chose meaningful stimulus material such as pictures, figures and stories, so that his studies reflected everyday and meaningful phenomena. His best-known book is *Remembering: A Study in Experimental and Social Psychology,* published in 1932. Bartlett's work was important in highlighting the influence of social factors on memory and the need to conduct research that reflects everyday and meaningful phenomena.

Frederic C. Bartlett, 1886–1969

THE WAR OF THE GHOSTS

One night two young men from Egulac went down to the river to hunt seals, and while they were there it became foggy and calm. Then they heard war-cries, and they thought, 'Maybe this is a war party.' They escaped to the shore, and hid behind a log. Now canoes came up, and they heard the noise of paddles, and saw one canoe coming up to them. There were five men in the canoe, and they said, 'What do you think? We are going up the river to make war on the people.' One of the young men said, 'I have no arrows.' 'Arrows are in the canoe,' they said. 'I will not go along. I might be killed. My relatives do not know where I have gone. But you,' he said, turning to the other, 'may go with them.' So one of the young men went, but the other returned home. And the warriors went up the river to a town on the other side of Kalama. The people came down to the river, and they began to fight, and many were killed. But presently the young man heard one of the warriors say: 'Quick, let us go home: that Indian has been hit.' Now he thought: 'Oh, they are ghosts.' He did not feel sick, but they said he had been shot. So the canoes went back to Egulac and the young man went ashore to this house, and made a fire. And he told everybody and said: 'Behold I accompanied the ghosts, and we went to fight. Many of our fellows were killed, and many of those who attacked us were killed. They said I was hit, and I did not feel sick.' He told it all, and then he became quiet. When the sun rose he fell down. Something black came out of his mouth. His face became contorted. The people jumped up and cried. He was dead.

Activity 8.4

Put this chapter aside for a moment and try to write down as much as possible of the story that you've just read. Then, come back to the chapter and see how many of the key ideas you were able to recall, and which kinds of material you did remember and which you failed to remember. In the next paragraph you will read about other people's memory of this passage. Compare your own recall to theirs.

Bartlett found that, when people tried to recall the story, the one they told was different from the original. There was omission of material that could be deemed irrelevant (for example, that when the main character came back home, he made a fire) and of material that was unfamiliar or inconsistent with the reader's own experience (for example, the supernatural elements of the story). There were transformations, such that unfamiliar elements were changed into familiar ones (for example, 'foamed at the mouth' was remembered rather than 'something black came out of his mouth'). Other changes resulted from what Bartlett termed rationalization (for example, 'that Indian has been hit' was remembered as 'An Indian is killed' or 'he had been wounded by an arrow'). These errors were a result of going beyond what was explicitly stated in the story. Brewer (2000) points out that when Bartlett discussed these omissions and transformations, he used the term 'unwitting', suggesting that these were memory processes operating outside conscious awareness.

In his later work, Bartlett suggested that when we are presented with new material, we use our knowledge and past experiences to make sense of the material – Bartlett referred to this as *'effort after meaning'*. Bartlett uses the term 'schema' to refer to mental representations that are constructed as a result of past experience; any new perceptual input is interpreted in terms of these schemata (plural of schema). Using more recent terminology, Bartlett was suggesting that the knowledge contained within schemata operates in a *top-down* fashion to influence the processes of perception and memory (see

Section 1 of Chapter 6 and Section 2 of Chapter 7 for a discussion of top-down influences).

Bartlett's work on memory was ignored in the early days of cognitive psychology because it was at odds with the more rigorous, experimental approach of Ebbinghaus. Bartlett's work coincided, approximately, with the beginnings of the behaviourist tradition with its focus on overt behaviour. Interest in 'what goes on in the mind' and internal representations of knowledge was unfashionable for several decades, only regaining influence in the 1970s and 1980s, when researchers turned to look at more practical issues, and when interest in schema theories re-emerged. You have already met the more current notions of schemas and scripts, which are schema-like structures for events, in Chapter 7.

3.2 The pliability of memory

Bartlett demonstrated how the accuracy and completeness of our memory can be influenced by our own knowledge and expectations. One research area related to this concerns the effect of *leading questions*: how the wording of a question can influence what we remember of an event. This research has obvious implications for the testimony of witnesses. Here, the work of Elizabeth Loftus has been influential.

8.3 Misinformation effect

Loftus and Palmer (1974) showed video clips of car accidents to 45 participants who were then asked to describe what had happened and were posed a number of specific questions. Critically, some were asked "About how fast were the cars going when they hit each other?", whereas others were asked the same question but with the verb 'hit' replaced by one of the following: 'smashed', 'collided', 'bumped' or 'contacted'. Participants' responses showed that estimates of speed increased with the increased violence implied by the verb:

verb	average speed estimated (mph)
Smashed	40.8
Collided	39.3
Bumped	38.1
Hit	34.0
Contacted	31.8

In a second experiment, 150 participants were asked to view a film showing a multiple car accident. One third were asked "About how fast were the cars going when they smashed into each other?", one third "About how fast were the cars going when they hit each other?" and one third acted as a control group who were not posed a question about speed. One week later, all were asked questions about the film, including "Did you see any broken glass?". None had actually appeared in the video clip, but the number of sightings increased with the vigour of the verbs used one week earlier. Of those asked about estimated speed using the word "smashed", 32 per cent said they had seen broken glass. This compares with 14 per cent asked using the word "hit" and 12 per cent for those in the control group. Thus the information implicit in the question asked after participants saw the video affected their subsequent judgements and recall of the accident. This 'contamination' of memory by post-event information (here contained in the question) is known as the **misinformation effect.**

Misinformation effect
An effect in which later information influences the accuracy of memory for earlier information

Why do leading questions influence the accuracy of memory? The exact psychological mechanisms responsible for the misinformation effect have attracted much debate and there are several different explanations under consideration. Imagine you see a pair of scissors on the table as you walk through a kitchen and are later asked if you know the whereabouts of the knife that was on the table. The information in the question may become merged with, and hence alter your memory, for the original event (e.g. you now remember having seen a knife). Alternatively, misinformation may be accepted because your memory for the original event was not encoded properly or was already forgotten (e.g. you cannot quite remember what you saw on the table and are prepared to accept that it was a knife). Finally, the information given in the question may exist in your memory separately from your memory for the original event. It influences your reconstruction either because it is the more recent information (e.g. we still have a memory of seeing scissors but are thinking about a knife because we just heard it was a knife) or because we misremember the origin of an experience (known as 'misattributing the source'). This last suggestion implies that we will believe something that was suggested to have really happened. You may have experienced this yourself when confusing actually doing something with only thinking about doing it, or confusing something that happened in a dream with reality.

Although the misinformation effect may be brought about by intentional implanting of false information, we normally have access to many different sources of post-event information, including what we hear from others, what we read in the media and our own general knowledge about the world. Further, common sense tells us what is probably true most of the time in relatively familiar situations. All of these will influence the construction or reconstruction of our memory for a particular event.

Crombag *et al.* (1996) showed how both our prior knowledge of situations and our own mental image may influence what we remember about an event that we witness. Their findings also suggest that we may be unable to distinguish between memories produced by 'perception of external stimuli' and those produced by 'thought', especially when the event is of a highly dramatic nature (which almost inevitably evokes strong and detailed imagery). Their Netherlands-based studies looked at memories of the collision of a Boeing 747 into 11-storey apartment buildings in Bijlmermeer, a suburb of Amsterdam. At the time, the disaster was extensively broadcast, but, of the considerable amount of footage shown, none depicted the actual moment of collision. In their investigations, 10 months after the crash happened, they found that over half of the participants responded 'yes' to the question: "Did you see the television film of the moment the plane hit the apartment building?" Furthermore, many claimed that the plane hit the building horizontally and quite a few that the body of the plane disintegrated after impact. According to the experimenters, news coverage revealed that the fire started immediately, the plane crashed nose down and almost vertically, and the body of the plane fell to the ground. Yet participants had apparently formed their own images about the moment the plane crashed into the building, and subsequently thought that this memory derived from what they had seen on television.

Bijlmermeer plane crash, Netherlands

3.3 Enduring memories

In contrast, our memory for certain types of information can be very accurate and durable. For example, lyrics from songs, poems, jokes and the faces of familiar people are often well remembered. Bahrick *et al.* (1975) asked 392 participants, ranging in age from 17 years to 74 years, about the members of their own high school graduating classes. Using each person's own yearbook (a record including the photographs and the names of everybody in the class), the experimenters designed different kinds of memory tasks. They asked the participants to choose the name (or face) of their classmate from among five names (or faces) of non-classmates. A matching task required that the correct name and face be paired. In a picture cueing task, a face was shown and participants were

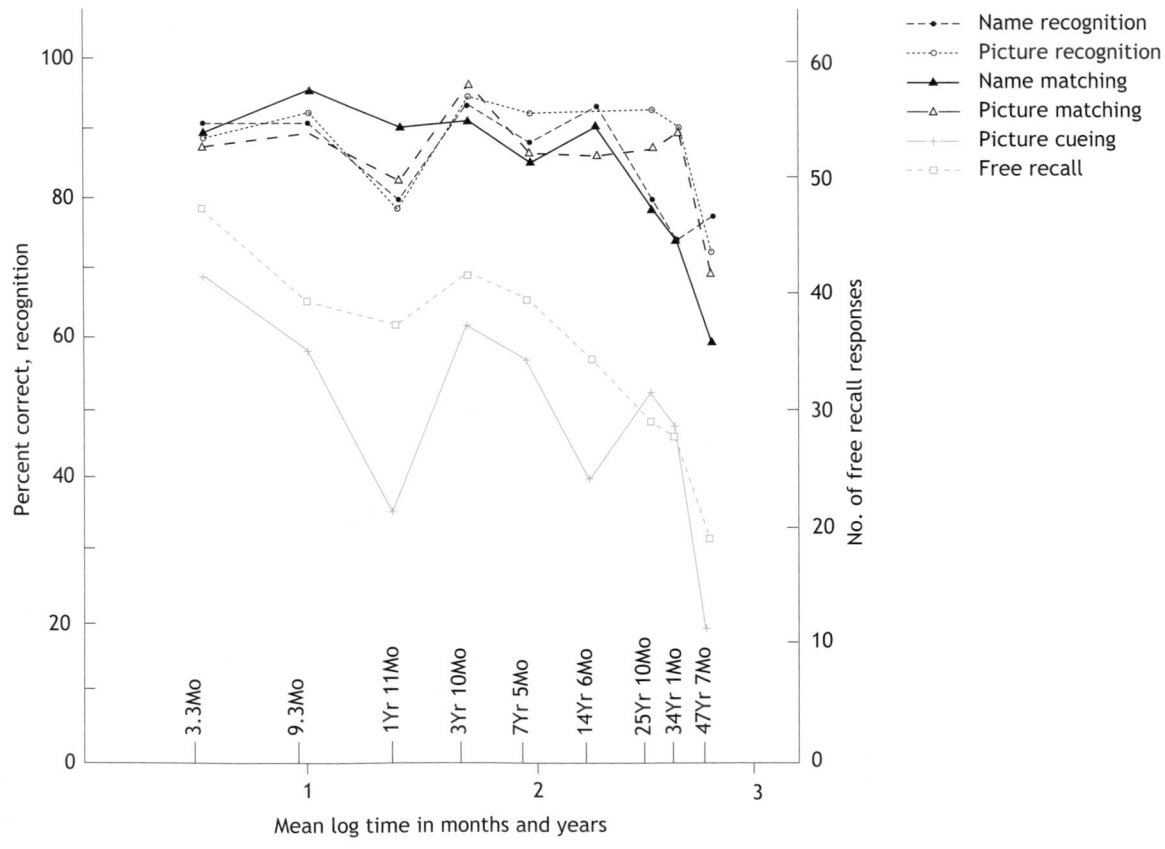

Figure 8.6   Memory for faces and names over time (Bahrick et al., Figure 1, p.66, 1975)

Note: recognition tasks are represented by black lines and are plotted against the left axis; recall tasks are represented by coloured lines and are plotted against the right axis

asked to recall the name. In a free recall task, participants were asked to retrieve as many names of classmates as possible with no cues provided. For the youngest participants these memory tasks involved a fairly small retention interval of just two weeks as they had only just graduated, and for the eldest participants, the retention interval was much larger, nearly 57 years.

The recognition and matching tests revealed that hardly any forgetting took place during the first 35 years after graduation. The authors of this study suggest that this is because the material being retrieved involved repeated learning: it was acquired over a long period of time and with distributed practice, as the names and faces were constantly being recognized and recalled. (These two factors were mentioned previously in Section 2 of this chapter, and have been found to aid long-term retention.)

The authors also found that recognition was better than recall. Performance on the free recall task indicated that even after 3 months, only around 50 names were accurately recalled from an average size of graduating class of 294.

The study revealed a decline in recall and recognition in the very oldest group of participants (the authors noted that this might be due to factors related to physical ageing).

8.4 FEATURED METHOD

Experiments IV: A quasi-experiment

The essence of doing experiments is to hold all the variables constant, except two. One of these is the independent variable, the one that is deliberately manipulated by the experimenter as the 'cause'. The other is the dependent variable, the 'effect 'which is measured. You saw examples of this in the first Featured Method Box in Chapter 3 and in Chapters 6 and 7 where the focus was on other aspects of experimentation – such as how vignettes are used in experimental social psychology and how experiments are designed to allow inferences about cognitive processes. The experiment on enduring memories by Bahrick et al., described above, is not a typical experiment because in this study the experimenters did not actually *manipulate* the independent variable. Hence the study was a quasi-experiment. The experimenters selected participants who varied in age so that the time interval between initial learning phase and test phase varied (this was the independent variable). The participants were divided into nine groups according to the elapsed time since graduation (for group one the mean was 3.26 months and for group nine it was 570.73 months).

Laboratory investigations of memory are usually longitudinal in approach in that they involve both the learning and the testing of the material, and conditions are carefully controlled. The approach taken here is cross-sectional, with participants chosen so as to represent the different levels of the variable under investigation. Here, the use of a very large number of participants was necessary as participants could only be allocated to one of the nine groups as if in a 'between participants' design.

The study was high in ecological validity, that is, the experimenters were testing 'real world' learning. Their participants were motivated to learn material of relevance to them in a real context over a period of time and the retention interval that was tested exceeded what would be possible in a laboratory. However, as with all quasi-experiments, participants were not *randomly allocated* to the nine groups, so the authors had to consider whether their 'pseudo-manipulation' of the independent variable was responsible for any change observed in the dependent variable. Did the observed drop in recall occur because of increased time lapse or because of uncontrolled confounding variables?

There were many uncontrolled variables, such as whether individual participants stayed in contact with friends from school, whether they frequently went through their own yearbooks to remember their early school days and how well and how many friends the participants had made at school. Because they were aware of this lack of experimental control, the experimenters employed statistical control. They asked questions about participants' contacts and relationships with classmates, about attendance at reunions, and about time spent examining yearbooks and checked that these were not confounding variables. As you might expect, they observed that the nature of the interpersonal relationship was an important variable, but this was the case for all groups. The names of close friends and romantic interests were almost always recalled.

3.4 Autobiographical memories

Autobiographical memories are episodes remembered from our individual life, including biographical information and past experiences. Martin Conway (1996) writes that these memories include the location and time period in which the episode took place; this is known as *spatiotemporal* knowledge. However, we also place the episode in our own personal history as in 'this was my first trip abroad' or 'this was my first day at secondary school', so that these memories will also include *factual* knowledge. Conway stresses that these memories are our personal interpretations of events and not veridical or accurate representations of past experiences.

Diary Studies

In a pioneering study of autobiographical memory, Marigold Linton used a memory diary as a way of investigating her own autobiographical memory. In a six-year long study, she recorded daily at least two events from her own life. Every month, she randomly selected records in pairs from the accumulating pool of records, and tried to estimate the chronological order in which they had occurred and the date of each recorded event. She also rated these events for salience/importance and for emotionality, both at the time of writing the description and again at the time of recall. After six years she had amassed 5,500 items and tested/re-tested herself for 11,000 items (about 150 items each month).

By the sixth year of the study, 30 per cent of the events recorded had been totally forgotten (Linton, 1982, pp.77–81). She found that her memory for real-life events faded at about the rate of 5 per cent a year. Some loss was associated with repetitions of the same or similar occurrences – the distinctiveness of these repeated events decreased over time. For example, she regularly attended committee meetings but found that the first meeting and the most recent meetings were the ones that remained distinctive; the rest could not be differentiated from each other in memory. In another form of forgetting, she simply could not remember the event happening. She found that the number of events forgotten in this way increased steadily with each year that elapsed since their occurrence. Interestingly, she did not find any strong relationship between rated importance and emotionality, and subsequent recall. One might predict that something that strikes us as important or rouses passions might be recalled better, but Linton found that the emotionality and importance ratings she gave to an event initially did not correspond closely with those given later. Thus she found it difficult to make accurate and stable judgments about the long-term significance of events.

Linton (1986, pp.50–67) reported that many events were organized chronologically and could be recalled by a temporally ordered search. Other events were organized according to categories or themes (e.g. interactions with loved ones) and hence were retrieved by working through named categories. Indeed, for events older than two years, there was a shift from a chronological search towards a greater use of a thematic search. She also noted that events seemed to be organized in terms of lifetime periods such as a job, a marriage or living in a particular place. Linton's conclusions are consistent with those of other researchers who see autobiographical memories as organized hierarchically, with interlocking structures of time periods and themes (e.g. Conway, 1996).

Criticism of diary studies

Many other researchers have since undertaken diary studies. The methods used in these studies may be criticized for several reasons, including the problem of selectivity (which events get recorded or remembered and what is recorded about the event) and the effect of recording the event (whether the act of recording an event makes it more memorable). Some consistency in results has emerged, particularly with regard to the organization of autobiographical memories. The effects of the intensity of the event and the pleasantness of the event are less clear. There is a trend favouring better recall for pleasant rather than unpleasant events, but there are inconsistencies in the findings reported.

Activity 8.5

Try to answer the following questions:

Can you remember when you first heard that planes had crashed into the World Trade Center's twin towers in New York? Do you remember what day of the week it was? What were you doing? How did you find out? Who was with you? Do you think this is something you will always remember? Can you think of reasons why someone may not accurately remember these events?

'Flashbulb' memories

Brown and Kulik (1977) coined the term 'flashbulb memory' to refer to an autobiographical memory for the personal circumstances during which we first learn of a very surprising and emotionally arousing event. They looked at 10 events, including the assassinations of J.F. Kennedy, Martin Luther King and Malcolm "X" and found that if certain conditions were met, then a detailed and stable memory was formed (with "almost perceptual clarity", p.73) of the circumstances in which people learned of the event. People remembered particular details which are referred to as the *reception* event: where they were, who they were with, what they were doing, who told them, how they felt about it, and what happened afterwards, as well as other trivial items. Brown and Kulik found that the two main determinants of flashbulb memory were considered to be high levels of surprise and personal consequentiality. For example, the assassination of Martin Luther King generated a high incidence of flashbulb memories among black North Americans compared with a lower incidence among white North Americans.

In support, Martin Conway *et al.* (1994) found that more than 86 per cent of 215 UK participants were able to recall an accurate and full account of *reception* event details nearly one year after the resignation of the British Prime Minister, Margaret Thatcher. This compared with only 29 per cent of 154 non-UK participants showing such good recall - the remainder forgot or erroneously reconstructed the event. They found that the level of importance attached to the event was critical, but those with flashbulb memories also showed more detailed prior knowledge and higher levels of affect (emotional response). In this particular research area, there has been debate over whether these memories are unusually accurate, whether a special memory mechanism is involved, and what actually determines their formation and maintenance. Despite this debate though, the evidence does concur that 'flashbulb' memories are more detailed, vivid and durable than other autobiographical memories and reminds us that some memories can be highly accurate.

The retention of autobiographical memories over time

Other studies have looked at the retention of autobiographical memories over time and at how they are distributed across the life span. One way of doing this is to appraise individual memory in an unrestricted way, by providing words as cues and requesting memories as responses. So, for

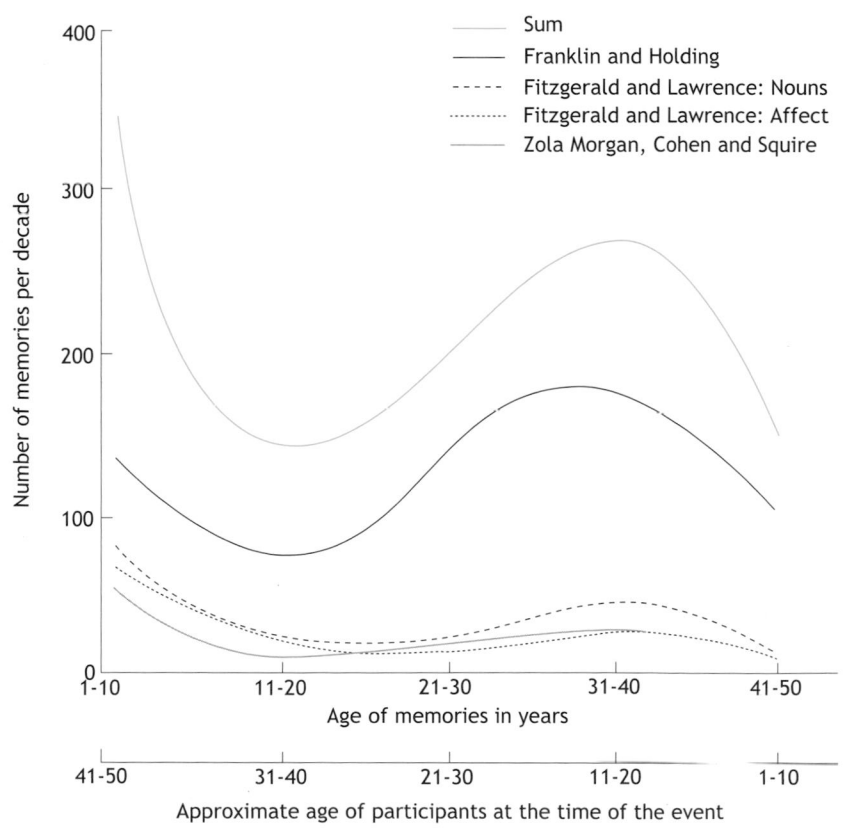

Figure 8.7   Distribution of personal memories across the life span (Source: Rubin *et al.*, Figure 12.1, p.211, 1986)

example, you would be asked: 'What incident in your life are you reminded of by "car", or "hand", or "dog"? When did each of these incidents occur?' The distribution of memories in relation to date or elapsed time provides an indication of how accessible they are across the life span. Rubin *et al.* (1986, pp.202–21) have collated the results of three such studies.

Figure 8.7 above shows the distributions of memories obtained from 50 year-old respondents (this same pattern is also seen in the distributions of memories obtained from 70 year-old respondents). The top curve combines the findings from the three studies and displays the pattern most clearly. The figure shows that the mean number of memories elicited declined as a function of the age of the memories (this is the higher of the two x axes), there were many more recent memories and fewer remote ones. Interestingly, a disproportionate number of memories are recalled from between birth and 30 years old. This is known as the **reminiscence bump** (participant's age is shown in the lower of the two x axes and reads right-to-left). Conway (1996) notes that this phenomenon is reliable. That is, it has been observed by many using different experimental procedures, and cannot be explained in terms of either the number of significant events during this period or in terms of differential rehearsal (i.e. it is not the case that the events that occur during this age are recounted more frequently than other events). It also seems unlikely that these events were encoded in a different way. Instead, it has been proposed that this bump occurs during the formation of the *self*. The memories from that part of our lives are more elaborate because they place the developing self in a social and cultural context.

Reminiscence bump
The disproportionately higher number of memories recalled from the adolescent and early adult period compared to other life periods

---

You may remember from Chapter 1 that Erikson considered adolescence to be particularly important in identity development. The reminiscence bump suggests that there is a strong relation between memories and the development of the self during adolescence and early adulthood. In the next section we will see that memories play a very important role in helping us to construct our personal identity and our self-history.

3.5 Collective memories

By pooling our experiences of important past events we can create shared or collective memories. We may even recollect events that took place early on in our lives simply because others have shared these with us. In his autobiography, the Chilean playwright Ariel Dorfmann writes of how, as a Spanish-speaking boy brought to the USA, he caught tuberculosis and was hospitalised knowing no English. He has clear recollections of the decision he took not to speak Spanish again at three years of age. However, he now believes that he cannot really remember this. Instead, his parents' memories and retellings provided the framework for his reconstruction of the event. The eminent Swiss psychologist Jean Piaget had a somewhat comparable experience. He retained a vivid memory of an attempt to kidnap him as a child while he was being looked after by his nurse, despite the fact that when he was fifteen the then ex-nurse involved wrote to his parents claiming that she had made up the whole story. Writing fifty years after the event, he recalled that: *'I was sitting in my pram which my nurse was pushing when a man tried to kidnap me. My brave nurse tried to stand between me and the thief. She received several scratches and I can still see vaguely those on her face... I can still see the whole scene and can even place it near the tube station.'* (Piaget, 1960, p.188). Family stories become collective memories because they are repeatedly discussed and details are negotiated. Miller (2000) suggests that collective family memories serve to express a common family identity and to transmit it from one generation to another so that traditions and family characteristics are maintained.

According to Gergen (1999), collective remembering can help to construct and reconstruct national history. Nowhere was this process more evident than in South Africa in the late twentieth century when the Truth and Reconciliation Committee was set up. This aimed to make public the atrocities that had occurred under apartheid, in order that black and white members of the society could become reconciled to each other. This 'negotiating of the past' was an attempt to (re)shape collective memory through the production of public accounts of individual testimony (Nuttall and Coetzee, 1998).

It is not as unusual as one might expect for nations to attempt to produce new memories. Leonard (1997) points out that there have been various periods in British history when traditions were invented and then collectively treated as if they were longstanding. *'Highland dress, for example, was invented by an Englishman after the Union of 1707, the differentiated 'class tartans' are an even later invention and the word 'kilt' didn't exist until twenty years after the Union.'* (Leonard, 1997, p.26). The process of 'inventing tradition' is one that fits well with the ideas of social constructionism, a perspective that you met in Section 5 of Chapter 1.

Summary   Section 3

- Memory is active, selective and constructive.
- The early work of Bartlett demonstrated how we use our knowledge and past experiences to make sense of new material.
- Memory can be pliable and our recollections can be influenced by post-event information and our own mental images or thought processes.
- Other memories are more accurate and enduring, and a special form of vivid memories may exist for public events that are shocking and have personal consequences.
- Autobiographical memories comprise memories for knowledge about our self, our personal life history and life events.
- Memory for our past can be collectively constructed.

4   Atypical memory functioning

We have seen how memory for factual information, events and personal experiences can be enhanced by the use of efficient encoding and retrieval strategies, and can also be shaped and distorted by influences such as time, context and suggestion. Though the specific memory outcomes of these constructive processes vary from person to person, we have implied that memory operates in broadly the same way for most people, and is subject to the same constraints.

Yet you may think that some people's memory functions better than your own, or that your memory works better for some tasks than for others. For instance, you may regularly forget people's names and yet remember in great detail experiences such as the birth of children, places and people visited. You may also know someone – perhaps an older person with Alzheimer's disease – who has a severe memory loss.

Activity 8.6

Take a few moments to consider what strengths and weaknesses you are aware of in your own memory and that of family and friends. For instance, is there someone who never remembers where they put their glasses or their keys? Why do you think that is?

In this section we highlight diversity in memory functioning by considering studies of individuals with substantial memory deficits and people with exceptional memory skills. Such in-depth **case studies** of individuals with atypical cognitive functioning have elucidated just how widely memory can vary from person to person, as well as some of the specific processes, mechanisms and structures that make up the memory system.

Case study
An in-depth study of a single participant often focusing on atypical psychological functioning

4.1 Neuropsychological impairments and the memory system

The phenomenon of serious memory deficits, usually resulting from accidental damage to one or more brain areas, provides very powerful support for the claim that memory consists of separate subsystems or components and suggests that different parts of the brain play a key role in these. This general idea – known as **localization of function** – has a long history, but started to gain ground in the nineteenth century, when neurologists such as Broca and Wernicke deduced from studies of brain lesions that specific brain areas were involved in the production and understanding of language. The key features of the contemporary approach that uses case studies to 'map' the role of different brain structures in memory are outlined in Box 8.6 below.

Localization of function
The theoretical approach that assumes that particular areas of the brain play a key role in functions such as motor control, perception, memory, emotion, etc.

8.6 FEATURED METHOD

Studying memory using case studies of neuropsychological impairment.

Injury to the brain can result from diseases such as encephalitis, from 'trauma', for example after a car crash, or as an unavoidable side effect of brain surgery for conditions such as epilepsy. The initial diagnosis and treatment of the injury, and assessment of its effects, is the role of medical specialists. Neuropsychologists are often involved in the longer term evaluation of consequences, and in helping the patient with rehabilitation. In this context the brain injury is carefully mapped, and the patient will undergo a wide range of tests of cognitive and motor functioning. Brain scanning technologies, such as positron emission tomography (PET) and functional magnetic resonance imaging (fMRI) (see Chapter 4 for PET) are used to study the patient's brain activity during task performance, and to compare it with intact brain activity. In this way the neuropsychologist is well placed both to design a rehabilitation programme targeted to the deficits and needs of the individual patient, and simultaneously to construct theories about brain function.

Neuropsychological case studies are most informative when two or more patients display a *converse* pattern of impairment in two distinct cognitive

Double dissociation
Different patients display converse patterns of deficit within memory function or other cognitive domains. This can yield important insights when linked to damage in different areas of the brain.

functions – this is known as **double dissociation**: one patient displays deficits in memory function A, but not in memory function B, while another patient displays the opposite pattern. For instance, studies of patients with amnesia (loss of memory) have revealed that in some patients STM can be severely impaired whilst LTM remains relatively intact. In others the opposite can be found: impairment of LTM whilst STM is relatively intact. When this pattern of opposing deficits in memory function is accompanied by clear evidence that a *different* part of the brain has been damaged in the two patients, it is possible to draw conclusions about the role of the damaged areas in normally functioning memory.

However, this is a complex and controversial methodology, since accidental brain damage is rarely 'tidy' and rarely affects a single, well-defined area of tissue. Neuropsychologists often have to work with lesions centred on one brain structure but also invading adjacent structures (this is one reason why some researchers opt to do 'animal studies' involving carefully targeted experimental lesions). Another problem for research – though good news for the patient – is that during the post-injury phase some brain areas may 'take over' from, or compensate for, the injured structure, resulting in partial recovery of lost memory skills. This is particularly so when the patient is a child, since the brain has most **plasticity** during development. Finally, even if normal memory skills are to an extent 'localized' in the brain, this does not necessarily mean that the structures work in isolation. If different areas normally work together as a *system*, then damage to one bit of the system may have 'knock on' effects for other bits. For all these reasons, the enterprise of linking specific memory functions to specific brain areas is a tricky one.

Plasticity
The capacity for organised alteration or development in the structure and/or function of the nervous system, typically with beneficial outcomes.

In the introductory chapter, you were introduced to four kinds of data. Most of the studies in this chapter have been concerned with behavioural data obtained by measuring participants' performances on memory tasks. Case studies of participants with neuropsychological impairment provide an additional kind of data: 'material' data in the form of information about brain lesions. These are used in conjunction with behavioural data to draw inferences about which areas of the brain are involved in memory functioning. They provide valuable information for those seeking to construct models of memory.

Figure 8.8 shows some of the areas and structures thought to be involved in the human memory system. In the discussion that follows we will look at case studies involving lesions to some of the areas shown, and consider their implications for the memory system.

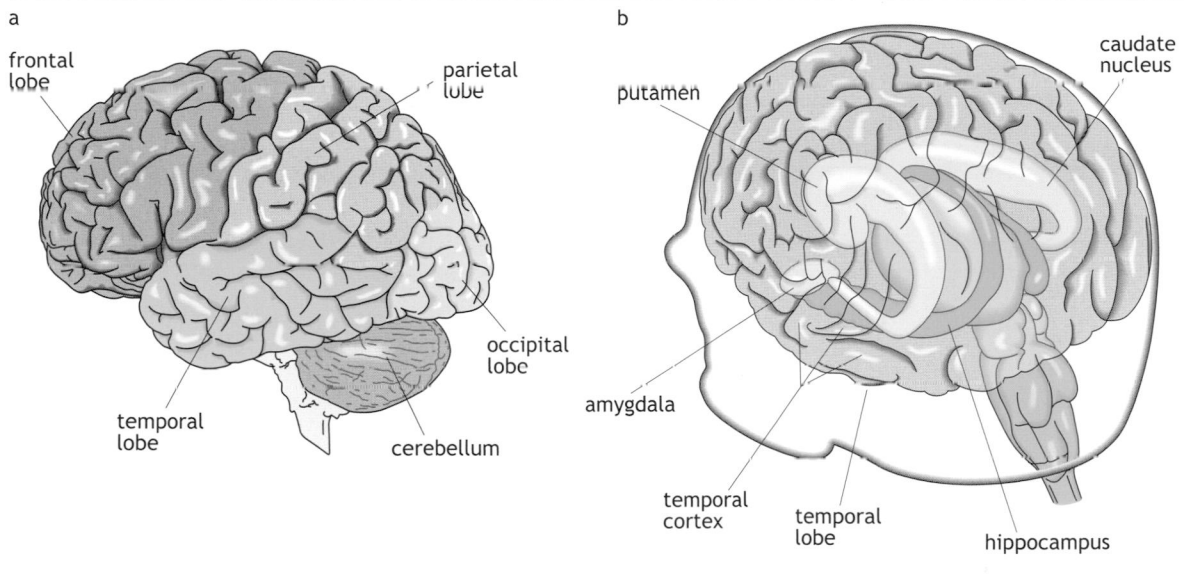

Figure 8.8   Some brain areas and structures thought to be implicated in human memory
(Source: adapted from Carter, p.264, 1998)

Note: Figure 8.8a is a side view of the outside of the brain, showing the position of the main lobes (frontal, parietal, occipital and temporal) and the cerebellum. Figure 8.8b is a three-quarters view of the brain showing the position of the hippocampus and other internal structures in relation to the temporal lobe.

Selective impairments within short- and long-term memory

A patient, referred to as 'KF' suffered injury to the left parieto-occipital lobe (an area comprising both the parietal and the occipital lobe) as a result of a motorcycle accident. Consequently, he was found to have a very reduced short-term memory span of only one or two items, but had no problem with long-term memory (Warrington and Shallice, 1969). Another patient, referred to as 'HM', was found to display a different type of amnesia. HM underwent an operation for epilepsy in which parts of the temporal lobe (including the hippocampus and the adjacent temporal cortex tissue) in each hemisphere were removed (Scoville and Milner, 1957). After surgery, it emerged that HM was unable to form any new long-term memories. Because of his intact STM *and* because he was able to remember experiences and events from his life before the operation, HM was found to be able to conduct conversations, watch television and complete crossword puzzles. But he could not remember more than the last few words in the conversation, would repeat things he said, watch the same television programmes and do the same crossword puzzles repeatedly. Observation showed that he was unable to retain any new information or experiences for more than a few seconds.

The pattern illustrated by these two cases meets the broad criteria for double dissociation, since the patients had approximately 'mirror image' memory deficits. As their lesions were in different areas, these findings support the notion that STM and LTM are structurally and functionally distinct. KF's lesion, which affected the parieto-occipital lobe, impaired STM and left LTM intact. HM's brain lesions, which affected temporal lobe structures, including both hippocampus and temporal cortex, resulted in a global inability to form long-term memories, suggesting that both the hippocampus and temporal cortex play a contributory role in this process.

Next, we will look at the selective memory impairments that occur when either *just* the hippocampus or *just* the temporal cortex is damaged, and consider what role each area plays in memory.

Episodic and semantic memory

Vargha-Khadem *et al.* (1997) reported three case studies of young people in whom the hippocampal area was damaged at birth or during childhood, while adjacent temporal cortex tissue was left intact. All three children experienced extreme difficulty remembering specific episodes and personal life experiences:

> ... *none (of the children) can provide a reliable account of the day's activities or reliably remember telephone conversations or messages, stories, television programs, visitors, holidays, and so on. According to all three sets of parents, these everyday memory losses are so disabling that none of the patients can be left alone, much less lead lives commensurate with their age, circumstances and aspirations ...*

> *(Vargha-Khadem et al., 1997, p.377)*

Despite these difficulties, all three children were in mainstream school and had acquired adequate knowledge of reading, writing and other academic subjects. In other words, they retained the ability to store general knowledge in LTM.

In a mirror image of this pattern, Warrington (1975) and more recent researchers including Bozeat *et al.* (2000), describe cases where damage to the temporal cortex, sparing the hippocampus, leads to the loss of factual information such as the names and properties of objects and the meanings of words. Episodic memory for personal experiences, however, is retained. Hodges and Graham (1998) comment: "Patients are well orientated in time and place, can produce, albeit **anomically,** autobiographical memories from the recent past and report few difficulties with remembering appointments, routes, etc." (pp.803–4)

Anomically
Describes the inability to generate names for people or objects, typically as a result of a brain injury

This double dissociation between memory for specific episodes and personal experiences, and memory for factual knowledge has been interpreted as supporting Tulving's (1972) suggestion that long-term memory should be subdivided into an **episodic** component concerned with temporally dated episodes or events, and a **semantic** memory component concerned with general knowledge about the world. The fact that the children in the Vargha-Khadem study had episodic memory difficulties associated with hippocampal damage, while Hodges and Graham's patients had problems with general knowledge associated with damage to the temporal cortex, suggests that the hippocampus is central for episodic memory, while the temporal cortex plays an important role in semantic memory.

Episodic memory
A subsystem of long-term memory concerned with personal episodes or events which include information about the place and the time in which they were acquired.

Semantic memory
A subsystem of long-term memory concerned with general facts or knowledge about the world, and lacking reference to the specific contextual episodes involved in their original acquisition.

Note that, in Section 3.4 of this chapter, we described memory for personal experiences as constituting autobiographical memory. There is considerable overlap between the concepts of episodic and autobiographical memory, and differing views on how they are distinguished. For instance, Conway (2001) sees episodic memory as a transient memory, while autobiographical memory comprises a person's enduring memories of personally significant experiences. But the research described here sees episodic memory as a more general and enduring type of personal memory of which autobiographical memory is a part.

Although these findings suggest that episodic and semantic components of LTM are functionally and physically separable, it seems probable that they interact. Conway *et al.* (1997) and others have argued that repeated episodic experiences are necessary for the formation of general knowledge representations, and that episodic memory thus provides the initial basis for semantic memory. According to this account, a young child stores personal experiences of, say, furry four-legged creatures with pointed ears as individual memory episodes (seeing one in the garden, being shown one in a picture book) as a stage in acquiring the general semantic category 'cat'. In Chapter 3 the authors considered how we organize our experiences into categories, and how categories are acquired. A neuropsychological model of how new semantic information such as conceptual categories for animals or plants is acquired (e.g. Carter, 1998) is as follows: individual experiences are initially registered as a mass of activity in the cortical areas that register sensory information and perceptual experiences. They are then 'fed' as episodic memories to the hippocampus, which plays an active role in 'replaying' them to the temporal cortex until they are established there as composite semantic memories, stripped of their original contextual features. It is believed that this activity takes two to three years and that much of it occurs during dreaming sleep.

However, Vargha-Khadem *et al.* (1997) challenged this model: two of the three children reported in their study sustained hippocampal brain damage at, or shortly after birth. The fact that they were still able to acquire enough semantic memory to hold their own in a mainstream school suggests that the parts of memories containing the semantic information were being laid down without the hippocampus playing a role in 'inputting' episodes. So far the difference between these views has not been resolved.

Is it possible that both Conway's and Vargha-Khadem's claims are correct? Think back to the discussion of 'compensatory' mechanisms in the Featured Method Box 8.6.

Declarative and procedural memory

The potential for episodic memories to play a role in 'laying down' semantic memory exists because both are concerned with knowledge about events, objects etc. – what has been termed 'knowing that'. Thus we know that we saw a friend yesterday (an episodic memory) or that the sky is blue and the earth round (examples of semantic memories). There are logical and empirical grounds for distinguishing these from another type of long-term memory that involves 'knowing how'. This sort of knowledge relates to complex skills such as riding a bike, typing on a keyboard or driving a car. Tulving (1985) has termed this type of memory **procedural memory**. Procedural memories are typically inaccessible to conscious examination and difficult to describe verbally – we find it difficult to describe how to ride a bicycle, for instance, or to explain the rules of grammar even though we speak grammatically most of the time. In contrast both episodic and semantic knowledge are consciously accessible and can be described in words. For this reason they are often referred to collectively as **declarative memory**.

Neuropsychological evidence suggesting that procedural memory may be a separate subsystem comes from the curious case of Clive Wearing, an Oxford musician. After sustaining substantial brain damage from a severe bout of encephalitis, he was unable to retrieve old memories or to form new ones: trapped forever in the present, he greeted his wife each day as

Procedural memory
A subsystem of memory concerned with *knowing how* to do something, e.g. riding a bike, this knowledge being difficult to describe using words.

Declarative memory
A subsystem of memory concerned with *knowing that*, this being either episodic or semantic memory.

if she was a stranger. Yet he was still able to conduct his choir, play the piano and sing. Of course, memory for music involves considerable specialized knowledge and ability, which may even be separately located in the brain. It is unclear how much of this musical memory Wearing retained; what is clear is that procedural elements of his skill were intact even though he suffered marked impairment to both episodic and semantic memory.

Specific impairments of semantic categories

If the memory impairments described so far seem strikingly specific, there are others that are yet more intriguing. A number of researchers have described semantic memory impairments in which patients have selective memory loss for one type of category while their memory for other categories is spared. In the best known example of this, patients fail to recognize living organisms such as lions or elephants, and have difficulty describing their features, but have little difficulty with artefacts such as spoons, saucepans or hammers. A few patients display the opposite pattern of difficulty, indicating a double dissociation. In a very few cases the impairment may concern just vegetables (Hart *et al.*, 1985) or just body parts (Suzuki *et al.*, 1997). While some theorists believe that these findings occur because different categories are stored in *different brain locations*, other researchers argue that they reflect *differences in the content of memory representations* for living and non-living objects (see Forde and Humphreys, 1999, for a discussion). For living things it is mostly perceptual features, such as the presence and shape of body parts, which make them distinctive, whereas for artefacts it is predominantly functional characteristics, e.g. a knife is an object used for cutting and slicing. Either way, the results suggest that the strategy of organizing material into categories (described in Section 2 of this chapter) may be effective in assisting encoding because it maps onto the way that semantic memory is organized in the brain.

Throughout this discussion, we have emphasized the specific nature of memory impairments, and the implications for 'normal' memory as a complex system with many subsystems or components. In the next section we turn our attention to case studies of exceptional memory, and a similar question arises: is exceptional memory a specific skill confined to one area of the memory system or a more global endowment? And what general insights does such atypical functioning provide about the many factors (genetic, biological, social etc.) which may interact to influence memory skills?

4.2 Exceptional memory

Mnemonists
Individuals with
exceptional memory
skills, typically exploited
for performance

Wilding and Valentine (1994) have made an extensive study of **mnemonists**, people who exploit their memory talents for professional performance. To give you an idea of the skills involved, one of their participants, who won the Second World Memory Championships in 1993, memorized 100 digits presented at two second intervals, 1002 randomly generated numbers in half an hour and the order of each card in eight randomly sorted packs of playing cards in one hour.

While being able to remember such meaningless material may only be useful for performance purposes, some types of exceptional memory play a more practical role in people's lives. For instance, Ericsson and Polson (1988) studied an experienced waiter, JC, who had the useful skill of retaining up to 17 different orders in memory without writing anything down. When tested experimentally, he remembered eight orders, each consisting of a main course (eight alternatives with directions about how cooked), a starch (three alternatives) and a salad with a dressing (five alternatives).

Strategies and other components of exceptional memory

Wilding and Valentine developed a battery of tasks and questions designed to map the skills of their participants. Their study is described in Box 8.7.

8.7 Memory expertise: general or specific; strategic or 'natural'?

Wilding and Valentine (1994) presented 10 memory experts with memory tests designed to tap a wide range of memory skills including story recall, recall of words and digits, recognition of faces, early autobiographical memory, and recognition of previously seen pictures of snow crystals. Wilding and Valentine reasoned that very different types of skill are required to excel in these different tasks. Therefore evidence for different performance 'peaks' among the participants would provide support for specificity. They also asked each participant the following questions designed to elucidate the nature and origins of their memory skills:

Do you have a good natural memory?

Were you aware of your memory skills at an early age?

Do you use special techniques to aid memory?

Do you practise regularly?

Do you use your memory skills in your job?

Do you have vivid imagery?

Do you have a near relative with exceptional memory skills?

The results, consisting of an individual profile of task scores for each of the participants, suggested a complex mix of specific and more generalized skills across different participants. For instance, one participant only did well on the test of story recall, and a test of recall of the names of British Prime Ministers; another excelled at the numerical tests; a couple of participants produced very good performance on all the tests.

Wilding and Valentine concluded that their participants fell into different groups: so-called 'memory strategists' were people who had harnessed an everyday memory technique or strategy with exceptional efficiency to enhance one type of performance (e.g. memory for digits). Some of these strategists had generalized their strategies to enhance their performance in a range of tasks. Another group of participants appeared not to be using strategies, but to have a 'natural' memory talent in one specific domain. Yet another group appeared to have started out life with a natural memory talent, but to have enhanced it further by combining it with strategies.

Activity 8.6

Which of the questions in Wilding and Valentine's study are designed to identify strategic components of memory skill and which are designed to identify 'natural' components? Look back at Box 8.7 to help you work out the answers.

The Russian neuropsychologist Alexander Romanovich Luria carried out a remarkable case study that provided unique insights into how skilful use of memory strategies may work together with an innate endowment to produce exceptional memory.

8.8 The Case of 'S' (Luria, 1969)

Alexander Romanovich Luria was one of the few soviet psychologists to become widely known outside his country before the collapse of the USSR. He made valuable contributions to the development of modern neuropsychology and, in the breadth and variety of his methods and theoretical perspective, was ahead of his time. He started his thirty-year, single-case study of a man whom he called S in the 1920s and combined extensive laboratory-type tests with records based on S's introspections about his methods. Luria's study was additionally enriched by his clinical interest, which led him to relate the odd functioning of S's memory to his problems with everyday functioning. Here is an extract from the study:

> *In December 1937, S, who had no knowledge of Italian, was read the first four lines of the Divine Comedy:*
>
> Nel mezzo del cammin di nostra vita
>
> Mi ritrovai per un selva oscura
>
> Che la diritta via era smarrita
>
> Ah quanto a dir qual era e cosa dura ...
>
> *As always, S asked that the words in each line be pronounced distinctly, with slight pauses between words – his one requirement for converting meaningless sound combinations into comprehensible images. And, of course, he was able to use his technique and reproduce several stanzas of The Divine Comedy, not only with perfect accuracy of recall, but with the exact stress and pronunciation. Moreover, the test session took place fifteen years after he had memorized these stanzas; and, as usual, he was not forewarned about it ...*

(Luria, 1969, p.45)

Alexander R. Luria,

S's account of how he remembered passages such as the one above highlights the use of several different strategies:

Semanticisation: converting meaningless information into something that is meaningful for the individual. In S's case, this meant attaching a personal (Russian) meaning to the Italian words: for the Italian word 'Nel', S said: "I was paying my membership dues when there, in the corridor, I caught sight of the ballerina Nel'skaya".

Association: forming associations between the presented information and something which is memorable for the individual. In S's case this relies on a third process – imagery.

Imagery: forming an image which somehow reinforces the information to be remembered. S created visual images representing objects or concepts named by Russian words which had been substituted for the meaningless Italian sounds. He then associated these images with one another. For example, to remember 'Nel mezzo del cammin', S explained that he created a composite image involving two people, Nel'Skaya (for 'Nel'), *together with* another person (the Russian word for together is 'vmeste', which is linked to the Italian word 'mezzo'). He then expanded this image of two people to include "a pack of Deli cigarettes near them" (the brandname 'Deli' is close to the Italian word 'del') and "a fireplace close by" (the Russian word for fireplace 'kamin' is close to the Italian word 'cammin').

Though strategies similar to those described by Luria are used by other mnemonists, and indeed can be employed by anyone wishing to enhance their memory (see Section 2 of this chapter), what is particularly striking about the many feats described in Luria's book is the apparently limitless quality of S's memory. Most of us probably feel that we could never attain such accurate recall, let alone over such long periods, however much we practised. In this sense S's memory seems to work in a qualitatively different way from our own, and to involve a 'natural', innate or even genetic endowment.

Biological contributions to exceptional memory

Aspects of exceptional memory that might suggest an innate component include very early onset, other family members with exceptional memory, and features of memory performance (such as vivid imagery), which are unlikely to have arisen from practice (and which you may have noted in your answer to Activity 8.6). Several of Wilding and Valentine's participants met all of these criteria.

The memory of Luria's participant, S, also had early origins, as well as some unusual features such as **synaesthesia**, the capacity for stimuli

Synaesthesia
The capacity for stimuli presented in one sensory modality to evoke spontaneously experiences in another modality. For example to 'hear' colours

presented in one modality, such as vision, to evoke spontaneous experiences in another modality. Thus for S, sounds had a particular colour and colours had a particular texture. S famously remarked to the psychologist Vygotsky: "What a crumbly yellow voice you have". Synaesthetic and other images, which arose spontaneously whenever S was trying to remember something, gave his memory associations a very vivid and powerful quality. So it seems that S used strategies to build on what was almost certainly a 'natural' talent for imagery and association. His early upbringing, in a small Russian Jewish community, may also have exposed him to a cultural tradition which prized learning from memory, providing both motivation and opportunities for him to practise his skills. Thus the development of exceptional memory implies a complex interaction of biology, learning, culture and motivation.

The discussion in this section raises some complex questions, as yet to be fully answered by researchers. For instance: What exactly do we mean by the claims that exceptional memory has natural/genetic/biological components? Does this mean that the brain mechanisms of people with a naturally exceptional memory operate in a different or especially efficient way? And for those individuals who have acquired their exceptional memory through experience, are there effects on the brain too?

A startling illustration of how learning and practice may have an influence on brain mechanisms is provided by recent studies of London taxi drivers, who undergo an intensive three year training in which they traverse every highway and byway, learning, and being tested on names and locations of streets and the routes through them. Maguire *et al.* (1997) used PET to brain-scan taxi drivers while they imagined the routes they would take to get to and from various familiar locations. The scans indicated intense activity in the right hippocampus, something that did not occur when, for instance, they were simply recalling familiar landmarks. In an earlier section, we saw that the hippocampus may play a role in replaying episodic memories to the cortex, but it seems that spatial memories remain stored in the hippocampus. A follow up study (Maguire *et al.*, 2000) found that the posterior hippocampal area is significantly enlarged (with a compensatory loss in the anterior hippocampus) in taxi drivers, in comparison to control participants, perhaps because of an increase in the number of connections between nerve cells. This is a remarkable demonstration of plasticity in which the structures and mechanisms of the brain adapt to accommodate new experiences, and arguably our own brains also undergo adaptation as we acquire new knowledge and skills.

4.3 Atypical memory and everyday life

This section has documented both impairment and enhancement of human memory. Memory is clearly a complex system made up of separable components, and when one of these goes wrong, other components may continue to operate relatively normally. Yet even a specific impairment usually has profound effects on the individuals' everyday lives: the children with impaired episodic memory, in the Vargha-Khaden study, could take in factual information about the world around them, but were incapable of the routine behaviour necessary for getting to school on time, remembering lessons etc. Depending on which memory subsystem is affected, there may be an impact on identity and sense of self. Carter gives the following poignant description of HM (mentioned in Section 4.1 of this chapter) who is now an old man:

> He is permanently trapped in a single frozen moment. The stream of his life stopped running when he was twenty-five, so for him, his identity is suspended there with it. When asked he tells people he is a young man. He talks about his brother and friends, long dead, as though they were still alive. When given a mirror to look in his face registers horror as he sees an old man look back at him. The cruelty of inviting him to look at his reflection is mitigated only by the fact that within minutes he has clearly forgotten what he saw...
>
> (Carter, 1998, p.282)

Some of the most devastating and global memory loss occurs in Alzheimer's disease. While there has been steady progress in understanding the degenerative biological processes that accompany Alzheimer's (Roth, 1998), most researchers believe that there is, as yet, no way of reversing these processes. Episodic memory is especially vulnerable, since the disease damages hippocampal structures. Working, autobiographical and semantic memory may all suffer. Yet Clare *et al.* (1999) have demonstrated that there is some potential, at least in the earlier stages of Alzheimer's, for memory rehabilitation. For instance, one patient, who experienced the humiliation of being unable to name fellow club members, received training that restored this skill for a considerable period. Even if the scope for re-training is small, the psychological benefit to the person and his/her carers may be considerable.

By comparison, individuals who can exploit their memory talents in everyday roles such as waiters or taxi drivers seem exceptionally lucky. Yet exceptional memory skills may also act as an impairment in everyday life. Those of us with 'normal' memory have to select and encode the information necessary to guide future actions and decisions so as to avoid overloading our minds. If presented with a story, we do not attempt to memorize it verbatim; just storing the central meaning components is sufficient to reconstruct the essential gist on a future occasion. For Luria's man S, each element of an experience or thought evoked a fresh series of vivid images, which impaired his ability to extract overall generalizations or common elements. (This is oddly reminiscent of memory impairments in which episodic experiences fail to 'mature' into semantic memories, see Section 4.1 of this chapter.) S was once presented with the following kind of matrix:

1	2	3	4
2	3	4	5
3	4	5	6
4	5	6	7 etc.

As Luria put it "with an intense effort of concentration, he proceeded to recall the entire series of numbers through his customary devices of visual recall, unaware that the numbers in the series progressed in a simple logical sequence" (Luria, 1969, p.59). Luria describes S as living in an inner world of images so powerful that they frequently blocked him from taking effective action in the real world. To others he appeared a *"dull, awkward, somewhat absent-minded fellow"*, once again underlining the way memory pervades other elements of human experience.

4.4 Conclusion

Section 4 has dealt with the idea that memory varies across individuals. We have considered the basis of claims that people (including ourselves) may have a 'good' or 'bad' memory. But, the chapter as a whole has shown that notions of 'good' or 'bad' memory are complex. Memories are typically reconstructive, rather than straightforward representations of events, even though some memories can be surprisingly accurate and durable. Many factors may influence the efficiency with which we construct and reconstruct memories, including past experience, strategies, knowledge, intentions and context. Individual endowments and underlying brain processes also play a role in constraining or enhancing memory functioning. Altogether, memory is a complex system with many components that, though to some extent separable, operate in close coordination and pervade all areas of our lives.

Summary Section 4

- Case studies of both memory impairment and exceptional memory illustrate diversity in the way memory functions across individuals.
- Neuropsychological case studies support the division of the memory system into functional components subserved by different brain areas.
- Exceptional memory skills are highly specific for some individuals and more global in others.
- There is evidence for both learned strategies and 'natural' talent among memory experts, with an interaction of the two in some cases.
- Some areas of the brain, notably the hippocampus, demonstrate the capacity for plasticity in accommodating complex new information.
- Memory impairments and exceptional skills both have a profound impact on the lives of individuals, underlining the complexity of the memory system and its involvement in all our activities.

Further reading

Carter, R. (1998) *Mapping the Mind*, London, Weidenfield & Nicholson.

An interesting, accessible and well-illustrated account of how the brain works. It is written for a non-specialist audience and highlights the use of recent brain imaging technology.

Fara, P. and Patterson, K. (eds) (1998) *Memory*, Cambridge, Cambridge University Press.

An interdisciplinary approach to memory and includes essays by leading experts across the arts and sciences as well as from psychology.

Luria, A. (1969) *Mind of the Mnemonist*, London, Jonathon Cape.

Luria's fascinating account of thirty years studying the mnemonist 'S'.

Neisser, U. and Hyman, I.E. jr. (eds) (2000) *Memory Observed: Remembering in Natural Contexts*,(2nd edn) New York, Worth Publishers.

This text includes a carefully chosen selection of papers describing widely cited research findings from studies of memory in natural contexts.

Sacks, O. (1985) *The Man who Mistook his Wife for a Hat*, London, Picador.

This is a collection of essays by the neurologist Oliver Sacks, who specializes in case studies of the bizarre consequences of brain disorders and lesions.

Wilding, J. and Valentine, E. (1997) *Superior Memory*, Hove, Psychology Press.

The full account of Wilding and Valentine's in-depth study of memory specialists.

 # References

Baddeley, A.D. and Hitch, G. (1974) 'Working memory', in Bower, G.D. (ed.) *Recent Advances in Learning and Motivation*, vol.8, New York, Academic Press.

Bahrick, H.P., Bahrick, P.O. and Wittlinger, R.P. (1975) 'Fifty years of memory for names and faces: a cross-sectional approach', *Journal of Experimental Psychology: General*, vol.104, pp.54–75.

Bartlett, F.C. (1932) *Remembering: A Study in Experimental and Social Psychology*, Cambridge, Cambridge University Press.

Bousfield, W.A. (1953) 'The occurrence of clustering in recall of randomly arranged associates', *Journal of General Psychology*, vol.49, pp.229–40.

Bower, G.H., Clark, M.C., Lesgold, A.M. and Winzenz, D. (1969) 'Hierarchical retrieval schemes in recall of categorized word lists', *Journal of Verbal Learning and Verbal Behaviour*, vol.8, pp.323–43.

Bozeat, S., Lambon-Ralph, M.A., Patterson, K., Garrard, P., and Hodges, J.R. (2000) 'Non-verbal semantic impairment in semantic dementia', *Neuropsychologia*, vol.38, pp.1207–15.

Brewer, W.F. (2000) 'Bartlett's concept of the schema and its impact on theories of knowledge representation in contemporary cognitive psychology', in Saito, A. (ed.) *Bartlett, Culture and Cognition*, Psychology Press, pp.69–89.

Brown, R. and Kulik, J. (1977) 'Flashbulb memories', *Cognition*, vol.5, pp.73–99.

Brown, R. and McNeill, D. (1966) 'The "tip of the tongue" phenomenon', *Journal of Verbal Learning and Verbal Behavior*, vol.5, pp.325–37.

Carter, R. (1998) *Mapping the Mind*, London, Weidenfield & Nicholson.

Clare, L., Wilson, B.A., Breen, K. and Hodges, J.R. (1999) 'Errorless learning of face-name associations in early Alzheimer's disease', *Neurocase*, vol.5, pp.37–46.

Conway, M.A. (1996) 'Autobiographical memory', in Bjork E.L. and Bjork R.A. (eds) *'Handbook of Perception and Cognition: Memory'*, pp.165–94, Orlando, Fl, Academic Press.

Conway, M.A. (2001) *Episodic Memory and Autobiographical Memory*. Paper presented at the Royal Society Discussion Meeting on Episodic Memory, 24–25 January, London.

Conway, M.A., Cohen, G.M. and Stanhope, N. (1991) 'On the very long-term retention of knowledge acquired through formal education: twelve years of cognitive psychology', *Journal of Experimental Psychology: General*, vol.120, pp.395–409.

Conway, M.A., Anderson, S.J., Larsen, S.F., Donnelly, C.M., McDaniel, M.A., McClelland, A.G.R., Rawles, R.E. and Logie, R.H. (1994) 'The formation of flashbulb memories', *Memory & Cognition*, vol.22, pp.326–43.

Conway, M.A., Gardiner, J.M., Perfect, T.J., Anderson, S.J. and Cohen, G.M. (1997) 'Changes in memory awareness during learning: the acquisition of knowledge by psychology undergraduates', *Journal of Experimental Psychology: General*, vol.126, pp.393–413.

Crombag, H.F.M., Wagenaar, W.A. and Van Koppen, P.J. (1996) 'Crashing memories and the problem of "source monitoring"', *Applied Cognitive Psychology*, vol.8, pp.95–104.

Craik, F.I.M. and Lockhart, R.S. (1972) 'Levels of processing: a framework for memory research', *Journal of Verbal Learning and Verbal Behaviour*, vol.11, pp.671–84.

Craik, F.I.M. and Tulving, E. (1975) 'Depth of processing and the retention of words in episodic memory', *Journal of Experimental Psychology, General*, vol.104, pp.268–94.

Ebbinghaus, H. (1913) *Memory* (H.A.Ruger & C.E.Bussenius, Trans.), New York, Teachers College, (Paperback edn., New York, Dover, 1964).

Ericsson, K.A. and Polson, P.G. (1988) 'An experimental analysis of memory skill for dinner-orders', *Journal of Experimental Psychology: Learning, Memory and Cognition*, vol.14, pp.305–16.

Forde, E.M.E. and Humphreys, G.W. (1999) 'Category – specific recognition impairments: a review of important case studies and influential theories', *Aphasiology*, vol.13, pp.169–93.

Geiselman, R.E., Fisher, R.P., Firstenberg, I., Hutton, L.A., Sullivan, S.J., Avetissian, I.V. and Prosk, A.L. (1984) 'Enhancement of eyewitness memory: an empirical evaluation of the cognitive interview', *Journal of Police Science and Administration*, vol.12, pp.74–80.

Gergen, K. (1999) *An Invitation to Social Construction*, London, Sage.

Godden, D. and Baddeley, A.D. (1975) 'Context – dependent memory in two natural environments: on land and under water', *British Journal of Psychology*, vol.66, pp.325–31.

Godden, D. and Baddeley, A.D. (1980) 'When does context influence recognition memory?' *British Journal of Psychology*, vol.71, pp.99–104.

Hart, J., Berndt, R.S. and Caramazza,A.C. (1985) 'Category – specific naming deficit following cerebral infarct', *Nature*, vol.316, pp.439–40.

Hodges, J.R. and Graham, K.S. (1998) 'A reversal of the temporal gradient for famous person knowledge in semantic dementia: implicated for the neural organization of long-term memory', *Neuropsychologia*, Chapters 36–8, pp.803–25.

James, W. (1890) *The principles of psychology*, vol.1, New York, Holt.

Leonard, M. (1997) *Britain^{TM}: Renewing our identity*, London, Demos and Design Council.

Linton, M. (1982) 'Transformations of memory in everyday life', in Neisser, U. (ed.) *Memory Observed. Remembering in Natural Contexts*, San Francisco, Freeman.

Linton, M. (1986) 'Ways of searching and the contents of memory', in Rubin, D.C. (ed.) *Autobiographical Memory*, Cambridge, Cambridge University Press.

Loftus, E.F. and Palmer, J.C. (1974) 'Reconstruction of automobile destruction: an example of the interaction between language and memory', *Journal of Verbal Learning and Verbal Behavior*, vol.13, pp.585–9.

Luria, A. (1969) *Mind of the Mnemonist*, London, Jonathon Cape.

Maguire, E.A., Frackowiak, R.S.J., and Frith, C.D. (1997) 'Recalling routes around London: activation of the right hippocampus in taxi drivers', *Journal of Neuroscience*, vol.17, pp.7103–10.

Maguire, E.A., Gadian, D.G., Johnsrude, I.S., Good, C.D., Ashburner, J., Frackowiack, R.S.J. and Frith, C.D. (2000) Proceedings of the National Academy of Sciences (USA) vol.97, pp.4398–403.

Mayer, R.E. (1983) 'Can you repeat this? Qualitative effects of repetition and advanced organizers on learning from science prose', *Journal of Educational Psychology*, vol.75, pp.40–9.

Miller, R. (2000) *Researching Life Stories and Family Histories*, London, Sage.

Nuttall, S. and Coetzee, C. (eds) (1998) *Negotiating the Past: The Making of memory in South Africa*, Oxford University Press.

Piaget, J. (1960) *Play, Dreams and Imitation in Childhood*, New York, Norton.

Roth, M. (1998) 'Preface', in Growdon, J.H. and Rossor, M.N. (eds) *The Dementias*, (Blue Books of Practical Neurology), Butterworth Heinemann.

Rubin, D.C., Wetzler, S.E. and Nebes, R.D. (1986) 'Autobiographical memory across the adult lifespan', in Rubin, D.C. (ed.) *Autobiographical Memory*, Cambridge, Cambridge University Press.

Scoville, W.B. and Milner, B. (1957) 'Loss of recent memory after bilateral hippocampal lesions', *Journal of Neurology, Neurosurgery and Psychiatry*, vol.20, pp.11–21.

Stevens, J. (1988) 'An activity approach to practical memory', in Gruneberg, M.M., Morris, P.E., and Sykes, R.N. (eds) *Practical Aspects of Memory: Current Research and Issues*, Vol.1: *Memory in Everyday Life*, Chichester, Wiley, pp.335–41.

Suzuki, K., Yamadori, A. and Fujii, T. (1997) 'A category specific comprehension deficit restricted to body part', *Neurocase*, vol.3, pp.193–200.

Tulving, E. (1972) 'Episodic and semantic memory', in Tulving, E. and Donaldson, W. (eds) *The Organization of Memory*, pp.382–403, New York, Academic Press.

Tulving, E. (1975) 'Ecphoric processing in recall and recognition', in Brown, J. (ed.) *Recall and Recognition*, London, Wiley.

Tulving, E. (1983) *Elements of Episodic Memory*, Oxford, Oxford University Press.

Tulving, E. (1985) 'How many memory systems are there?', *American Psychologist*, vol.40, pp.385–98.

Vargha-Khadem, E., Gadian, D.G., Watkins, K.E., Connelly A., Vann Paesschon, W. and Mishkin, M. (1997) 'Differential effects of early hippocampal pathology on episodic and semantic memory', *Science*, vol.277, pp.376–9.

Warrington, E.K. (1975) 'Selective impairment of semantic memory', *Quarterly Journal of Experimental Psychology*, vol.27, pp.635–57.

Warrington, E.K. and Shallice, T. (1969) 'The selective impairment of auditory–visual short-term memory', *Brain*, vol.92, pp.885–96.

Wilding, J. and Valentine, E. (1994) 'Memory champions', *British Journal of Psychology*, vol.85, pp.231–44.

■ Commentary 8: Memory: structures, processes and skills

Now that you have finished Chapter 8, you have almost completed this first book of DSE212 *Exploring Psychology* and, even if it does not seem so yet, you have already learned a great deal of psychology. Chapter 8 rounds off the coverage of cognitive psychology in this book – although you will meet it again throughout this course and it is also featured in other Open University psychology courses. This chapter has covered an issue that is one of the oldest in psychology. Memory has received consistent attention from the beginning of psychology in the nineteenth century, and a great deal of work has been done, incorporating a range of different approaches.

Theory

1 Cognitive research is directed at understanding the structures and processes of the mind. Cognitive psychologists build theories and test hypotheses systematically so as to choose between conflicting theories on the basis of evidence, and accumulate a body of knowledge.

2 Theories of memory structure, of how memories are constructed, and of atypical memory functioning each explain different aspects of memory and, as a result, they are for the most part complementary.

Methods

3 Memory research is largely a study of memory structures and processes. But memory research also makes an important contribution to the understanding of whole people – their personal sense of who they are.

4 The cognitive perspective on memory contributes evidence and explanations at different levels of analysis. Memory research uses a range of methods and different kinds of data, and uses insider as well as outsider viewpoints.

Themes

5 Memories are basic to our personalized minds – providing a sense of ourselves, and others, as continuous over time. But brain structures and functions have some degree of plasticity, some flexibility. Memories are not fixed: i.e. they are not complete records of experiences, but can be elaborated and changed; and new memories are continually added as we learn and adapt throughout our lives.

6 Memory is 'laid down' biologically, but is the outcome of our experiences. Thus memory structures and processes provide a clear illustration of how we are *constituted* by what we experience. Thinking of nature and nurture as a complex process of interaction is not quite enough to capture the spiralling *interdependence* of biology and experience.

■ Thinking about theory

Progressively solving puzzles and building a body of knowledge

One of the exciting things about cognitive psychology is that it allows psychologists to address issues that are enigmatic or for which there are conflicting theories. Cognitive psychologists conduct their research systematically to solve these puzzles and resolve contradictions, rather like working towards the solving of a difficult jigsaw puzzle. For example, the chapter explains how research inspired by models of memory suggesting it is made up of a number of 'stores' allowed psychologists to recognize that the hypothetical, theoretical construct 'short-term memory' needs to be more complex than had at first been recognized. As a result, the construct 'working memory' was introduced, along with the idea that memory is more active and has several components, rather than being just a simple, passive store. So you can see that theory-building allows researchers to see what questions need to be asked, to test out ideas and to compare and evaluate theories on the basis of evidence, and then, where necessary, devise new ones. This progressive theorizing, testing, comparing and re-theorizing promotes the accumulation of a body of knowledge.

Complementary theories

The study of memory has a long history. One advantage of this is that memory researchers have developed a range of theories that, together, contribute to current understandings of memory. For example, the chapter you have just read considered:

- regions of the brain involved in memory
- how memory is divided into systems or components of memory
- the processes by which memory operates (encoding, storing and retrieval)
- the ways in which we construct memories and so sometimes misremember
- how studies of atypical memory functioning (either through brain damage or exceptional memory) can help us to understand how memory usually operates and which parts of the brain are associated with particular memory processes.

Theories from these different areas attempt to explain different aspects of memory, *at different levels of analysis.* And for this reason they are largely complementary. Conflicts between theories are more likely to occur *within* each of these divisions rather than *between* them. Such conflicts may well be temporary since, as research progresses, new possibilities for understanding arise. The fact that memory research has its roots in different traditions (e.g. introspection, experimentation and biological psychology) is not, therefore, detrimental to the development of the area.

■ Thinking about methods

The study of parts and processes contributes to understanding the whole person

Memory is an area of psychology that is central to all areas of human life. Thus, Chapter 1, Section 2 gave an example of how brain damage resulting in memory loss can lead to a loss of identity. Personality (the subject of Chapter 5) and our understanding of people (Chapter 7) would, similarly, be irrelevant if we could not remember how other people generally behaved sufficiently well to ascribe personalities and attribute motives to them. Perception (Chapter 6) would be an entirely instinctual process without memory and, of course, learning (Chapter 3) would be impossible without memory. Whilst the study of memory is a study of specific processes, it makes a crucial contribution to the understanding of the 'whole person' and to areas of psychology that take a holistic approach, such as theories of identity. So although it makes some sense to differentiate approaches according to whether they deal with the person as a whole or concentrate on psychological processes, these should not necessarily be seen as mutually exclusive categories.

Diversity of research methods, data and levels of analysis

Memory research has traditionally been conducted using an outsider viewpoint, relying to a large extent on experimental studies. However, the breadth of issues studied by memory researchers means that insider viewpoints are also used. Diary methods in the study of autobiographical memories depend on an insider account of personal memories, and research on 'flashbulb' memories requires insider accounts, at least as the first step in data collection – although these accounts may later be standardized and compared with other people's memories. It would, however, be inaccurate to suggest that insider viewpoints are new to memory research in psychology: William James, one of the founders of psychology, used introspection in order to inform his writing on memory.

   The fact that memory research uses both insider and outsider viewpoints means that it needs to draw on different research methods. Memory is a long-established area of psychological enquiry that encompasses different strands of the cognitive tradition, and is constantly updated as new pieces of research help to provide new ways of understanding. So it is perhaps not surprising that a variety of methods have proliferated within memory research. That proliferation has occurred within the dominant method used by psychologists doing memory research (i.e. through different types of experimentation) as well as through use of other non-experimental methods. You saw in the chapter that psychologists use a variety of experimental techniques, including controlled laboratory experiments and quasi-experiments. However, they also employ diary studies, cognitive neuroscience (which uses brain-imaging techniques to study brain functioning during memory tasks), and neuropsychological studies (which investigate the memory deficits that arise from brain damage), as well as developing computer models of how memory works. These different methods rely on different kinds of data; and the findings provide explanations at different levels of analysis – both at the biological level and at the level of inferences about how we function cognitively.

This methodological diversity has been very important in keeping memory research vibrant. It has also meant that while some memory research can be 'ecologically valid' (a tradition that can be traced back to the work of Frederick Bartlett early in the twentieth century), other memory research attempts to study memory by using decontextualized tasks, sometimes involving nonsense words. In addition, the development of theories that view memory as constructive and reconstructive and affected by social contexts as well as individual knowledge has promoted links between social constructionist theories (see Chapter 1, Section 5) and cognitive psychology.

■ Thinking about themes

Fixity and change

We have already seen in Chapter 1 ('Identities and diversities') and Chapter 5 ('The individual differences approach to personality') that memory is central to our understanding that we and others are, in many important respects, the 'same' people over time. In Chapter 8 also, by drawing on examples of exceptional memory and specific kinds of brain damage, we have seen that memory is necessary for preserving a sense of self and maintaining a wide range of psychological functioning. We have also seen that particular brain structures, and the general building up of neuronal connections, are implicated in memory functioning. However, this does not mean that memories, once laid down, are fixed. Since memories are central to learning, they are dynamic – always in the process of being created and developed as we learn and adapt throughout our lives. It is this dynamic aspect of memory that means that we can actively employ techniques to help us remember. We have seen how our memories are constructed and reconstructed, how they can be elaborated, how they can fade, and how they can be quite dramatically changed.

Memory is perhaps one of the best illustrations of the potential flexibility of the mind. If parts of the brain are damaged, especially early in life, there is considerable potential for compensation in other undamaged parts of the brain leading to new learning and new memories. And, at a different level, those whose memories are damaged or failing can sometimes arrive at compensatory strategies that provide a degree of 'making sense' and continuity.

Nature and nurture: experiences become memories and memories become structure

In Commentary 1 we pointed out that, in many areas of psychology, it is unhelpful to think in terms of dichotomies such as nature *versus* nurture. And, as you have read the chapters in this book, you will have seen that 'nature *and* nurture' are inextricably mixed in making us what we are. In many of the chapters the idea of nature *and* nurture, as a shorthand phrase, has been used to explore different aspects of the interplay between biological 'givens' (like genes, developing brains, biochemical pathways) and experience in environments. For example, in Chapter 6 ('Perception and attention') you saw the extent of the interplay between biology and experience. What we 'see' is the outcome of the biological structure and functioning of eye and brain *and* our prior knowledge, as well as the more moment-to-moment influences of the environment – such as the danger of an approaching car at a road junction. What you have now learned about memory enables you to take one more step in understanding nature *and* nurture.

What we know of the structure and processes of memory and the plasticity of aspects of brain functioning makes it clear that 'experiences' (or nurture) are represented biologically. Neuropsychological memory research has shown that our experiences, and our ongoing cognitive functioning, can literally be seen affecting our brains at a biological level. Memory (like all psychological processes) is dependent on brain functioning. Experiences in environments are 'laid down biologically' and therefore constitute our biological being. Memory structures and processes provide a clear illustration of how *we are constituted by what we experience*. Thinking of nature and nurture as a complex process of interaction is not quite enough to capture the spiralling *interdependence* of biology and experience.

However, as the authors of Chapter 8 showed, biology provides only part of the story of what affects memory. For example, the chapter indicates that we can use our knowledge of particular contexts to stimulate and cue our memories. As with the processes involved in perception

(Chapter 6, 'Perception and attention'), memory is an active, selective and constructive (rather than passive) process that is influenced by our previous knowledge, our emotional state and the social dynamics of the current situation.

The chapter that follows (Chapter 9, 'Person psychology: psychoanalytic and humanistic perspectives') differs from all the chapters you have read so far, apart from Chapter 1 ('Identities and diversities'), in that it deals with 'the person as a whole'. Unlike the chapter you have just read, and most of the other chapters (apart from Chapter 1), Chapter 9 is concerned with what makes us uniquely ourselves.

Person psychology: psychoanalytic and humanistic perspectives

Richard Stevens

Contents

Aims

This chapter aims to:

* introduce the key ideas of psychoanalysis and humanistic psychology

* compare and contrast their assumptions, methods and approaches to therapy

* discuss the implications of the two perspectives in relation to the goals, methods and kinds of understanding possible in psychology

* consider what insights these perspectives might offer into our experience of being a person and the ways in which we live our lives.

1   Introduction

In the previous chapters of this book, you explored something of the diversity of psychology and its many different approaches and topic areas. This final chapter takes a broader look at how psychology can help us to understand a person as a whole. In effect, this brings us full circle in Book 1. For we are returning to the questions raised in Chapter 1 about 'who am I?' and 'what makes me the way I am?' You will find that some of the ideas discussed there, such as those of Erik Erikson, relate closely to the theories you will be considering in this chapter. We shall be concerned not just with what makes us unique, but also with what we share in common – with what lies at the heart of our experience of being a human person.

Reflecting on what it is to be a person raises profound questions. Why do we act and feel in the ways that we do? To what extent are our experiences and our lives the products of our biological inheritance and childhood experience? How far are we fixed or open to change? And if we can change aspects of who we are, how can we do this? To what extent, for example, can we exert autonomy and choice and play an active part in creating what we are to become? And how can we make sense and find meaning in the subjective worlds in which we exist?

Such questions have been very much the concern of two major perspectives – *psychoanalysis* and *humanistic psychology*. Both are focused firmly on **subjectivity**. In other words, they explore aspects of our 'inner life' – our subjective experience of ourselves and the world

Subjectivity
The inner world of subjective experience, thoughts and feelings.

around us. In particular, they deal with subtleties of feeling and meaning which are difficult to encapsulate in precise observation and measurement. So, these perspectives differ from those featured in many of the chapters of this book, especially the preceding three. There the emphasis has been primarily on psychology as a science, with investigations which are both precise and open to replication by others. Both these criteria are difficult to attain when dealing with personal, subjective experience.

There is a paradox which psychoanalytic and humanistic perspectives share. Both have exerted profound influence, not only on psychology and psychotherapy but also on the ways in which people in Western culture think about themselves. In a poll by the American Psychological Association, the psychoanalyst Freud received by far the highest rating as the theorist whose ideas have most influenced contemporary psychology. Close behind was Carl Rogers – the major humanistic psychologist. Yet both psychoanalytic and humanistic psychologies have been largely neglected in most psychology departments in the UK and US, and are not even taught in some except in terms of their historical interest. As Billig (1999) has pointed out, a student in literary studies is more likely to read about Freud than is a student of psychology.

In most university psychology departments, the prevailing view, traditionally and still to a large extent today, is that psychology should conform to the methodological approach of natural science. As we noted above, it is not easy to study subjective worlds in this way, and it is this that has led to the relative neglect of psychoanalytic and humanistic perspectives in academic psychology. But for a contemporary psychologist concerned with understanding this subjectivity, they have much to say.

Although there are similarities, there are also key differences between the two perspectives. Humanistic psychology, in fact, began in the 1950s specifically in reaction to the psychoanalytic approach. The core difference, as we shall see, is the emphasis placed by psychoanalysts on unconscious experience and their assumption that people are rarely aware of the underlying motivations which govern their actions and experience. The humanistic position, in contrast, places far greater emphasis on conscious awareness and the potential of people to consciously initiate change in their lives. The different models of the person that the two perspectives present and the different implications these have for methods and therapy make it useful to consider them side by side.

Because these perspectives focus both on subjectivity and the possibility of personal change, they stimulate further thought about some interesting and important questions you have already encountered. What are the aims of psychology? What kinds of data and what methods are legitimate and appropriate? What does it mean to be a person? In this sense, they should help you to reflect on many of the issues raised in Book 1 of this course.

We will look in turn at the core features of each perspective. Then, in the concluding section, we will both contrast and compare their approaches and reflect on what light they may throw on some of the kinds of issues about being a person such as those raised above.

Activities

Included in the text are activities designed to help you relate the ideas presented here to your own life experience. Read these through first and only do them if you feel comfortable about doing so. Note also that some of them may be best done after reading the chapter when you may have more time.

Summary Section 1

- This chapter presents and contrasts psychoanalysis and humanistic psychology.
- Both perspectives focus on understanding the subjectivity of a person and developing ways of facilitating personal change.
- Consideration of the perspectives raises important questions about the aims and methodology of psychology.
- There are key differences between the two perspectives, including the emphasis placed on conscious and unconscious experience.

2 Psychoanalysis

Both psychoanalysis and humanistic psychology consist of a cluster of theories and therapeutic procedures. The classic contributions and the core themes of each perspective are indispensable to any understanding of what these have to offer. In considering psychoanalysis we will focus on the work of Freud since, even though Freud died in 1939, his theories still provide the basis of most psychoanalytic thinking. As Billig puts it, 'Freud is the dominating presence in psychoanalysis. Subsequent writings are either an argument with him or a self-conscious tidying up of loose ends' (Billig, 1999, p.5). However, while classic contributions form the core of each section, they are also supplemented by some indication of the different ways in which they have been developed in more contemporary work. You will also get further opportunity in other Open University courses to read about ways in which later psychoanalysts have developed and modified Freud's ideas.

No theory emerges from a vacuum. Ideas reflect the social and intellectual context of the time. They are likely also to reflect the experience, interests and personality of the people who generate them. So, to understand Freud's ideas, it is helpful to consider them in the context of his life and personality (see the biography box below).

BIOGRAPHY *Sigmund Freud* *(1856–1939)*

Sigmund Freud had a broad education. At school he was good at classics, literature, modern languages and philosophy. At the University of Vienna, after researching in physiology for six years, he took a medical degree. Then, at the age of 29, with the aid of a scholarship, he spent a formative five months in Paris working with the French psychiatrist Jean-Martin Charcot who was using hypnosis to treat his patients.

Freud married at 30 and started his own private practice treating patients with neurotic symptoms. In the closing years of the nineteenth century, after his father died, came a period of intense self-analysis, which generated the groundwork for much of his later theory. In 1900 he published the first major work of psychoanalysis, *The Interpretation of Dreams.* In this, Freud set out his theory of the unconscious and repression and attempted to show how mental phenomena such as dreams as well as neurosis are a product of conflict between different mental systems. In his *Three Essays on the Theory of Sexuality*, he went on to postulate a relationship between the development of sexual drive in early childhood and sexual perversion, neurosis and personality in later adult life.

In 1910 the International Psychoanalytic Society was formed and in the immediately ensuing years Freud generated a steady stream of publications on psychoanalytic technique. Soon, though, growing dissension in the close-knit psychoanalytic circle culminated in the secession of several key figures such as Jung and Adler to form their own 'schools'. Freud's work in the 1920s largely centred on the different ways in which the *ego* is able to defend itself against anxiety. There is then a decided shift in his later writings such as *Civilization and its Discontents* to an analysis of the relationship between the individual and society.

When the Nazis invaded Austria in 1938, Freud, who was Jewish, moved with his family to London where he died in September 1939.

Sigmund Freud (1856–1939) in his study: his collection of archaeological objects can be seen on the shelves behind him

Activity 9.1

If you are in London, you may wish to visit Freud's house in Maresfield Gardens, Hampstead. Alternatively, you could follow the link on the course website to the website about Freud's house and museum. You can see the desk where he worked, his books, the many ancient artifacts that he enjoyed collecting and his famous couch. His apartment in Bergasse, Vienna, in which he spent most of his life, is also open to visitors.

Three broad themes emerged as Freud developed his ideas:

- the importance of *unconscious* feelings and motivations
- the origin of these in the experiences of *early childhood*
- the significance of unconscious anxiety and inner conflict (*psychodynamics*).

Although these three themes have been developed in different ways by subsequent analysts, they still form the core of psychoanalytic theorizing. The following sections examine each of these themes in turn.

2.1 The unconscious

One of Freud's first realizations was that much of the motivation for our behaviour is unconscious and not accessible to us. Early in his career he had been present at the dramatic demonstrations (in Paris) when Charcot used hypnosis to remove (or re-induce) symptoms in his patients, such as paralyses or loss of feeling in the limbs of his patients. Further evidence of unconscious processes came from Freud's work with Josef Breuer which resulted in their joint publication *Studies in Hysteria* (Breuer and Freud, 1895), the first articulation of psychoanalytic ideas. One of Breuer's patients, Bertha Pappenheim (referred to in the *Studies in Hysteria* as Anna 0), had suffered from a difficulty in drinking. Under hypnosis, Anna recounted how she had come across her governess encouraging her pet dog to drink from a glass. Anna vehemently expressed her disgust as she recounted this and apparently was then able to drink without difficulty. Freud and Breuer were convinced that the origins of Anna's phobia lay in associations between the act of drinking and feelings of disgust (and perhaps also dislike of her governess) which she not only had been unable to express at the time but had blocked or repressed from her own awareness.

In a later paper, *The Ego and the Id*, Freud made the distinction between the *preconscious* ideas and memories that an individual can bring to consciousness almost at will, and *unconscious* thoughts which, because of their disturbing nature, are not easily made conscious even though they may still indirectly influence behaviour. Freud's earlier work was directed at developing methods to find out about unconscious thoughts and feelings.

Freud found that many of his patients could not be hypnotized, and he gradually abandoned hypnosis in favour of **free association** or *freier Einfall* (perhaps best translated as 'free coming to mind'). The idea is that this will lead to themes emerging which have unconscious significance for the patient.

For Freud, though, the 'royal road', as he called it, to the unconscious was dream analysis (see Box 9.1) and he regarded *The Interpretation of Dreams*, published relatively early in his career in 1900, as his most significant book. In it he illustrated his ideas with extensive examples of dreams from his

Free association
A technique in psychoanalysis in which patients are encouraged to express freely everything that comes into mind.

patients and colleagues as well as his own. He argued that dreams essentially represent wish-fulfilments. Sometimes, as in the case of children's dreams of sweets and toys, the wish is portrayed directly in the content of the dream. The motivations underlying the dreams of adults are more likely to be unconscious, usually originating in repressed experiences of childhood. Although the unconscious censoring mechanisms of the mind are relaxed during sleep, they are still operative to some extent. Unconscious wish fulfilment is therefore represented in distorted forms. Such disguise prevents the repressed feelings from disturbing sleep. The underlying motivation will be fused with experiences and thoughts from the previous day or even events during the night such as covers slipping off or indigestion.

9.1 Freudian dream analysis

In **dream analysis** the task of the analyst is to interpret the *latent* content of the dream (that is, its underlying meaning) from the *manifest* content, as reported by the dreamer where the unconscious meanings are disguised. This is done using free association and interpretation to unravel the distortions that have occurred.

One key distorting process is *displacement* where the intention or feeling underlying the dream is transferred onto a different person or object. Thus, one patient dreamt of strangling a little white dog. Free association suggested that the dog represented her sister-in-law, who not only was of a notably pale complexion but also had previously been accused by the dreamer of being 'a dog who bites'. To express her hostility directly in the form of a dream in which she killed her sister-in-law would be too disturbing. So the underlying wish was displaced onto a disguised representation of the sister-in-law – the little white dog.

In dreams, according to Freud, unconscious feelings often express themselves in *dramatized* or *pictorial* form. The links between image and feeling are often personal to the dreamer and can be uncovered only with the help of other information about the patient and free association. Some images, however, are commonly found to represent significant objects, events or emotions. These are what Freud means by *symbols*. So he considered, for example, that objects that resemble the penis in shape (e.g. elongated things like snakes, sticks, neckties, trains or trees) or in function (e.g. intrusive things like guns or daggers or erectile things like planes or umbrellas) may symbolically represent it. Likewise, 'small boxes, chests, cupboards and ovens correspond to the female organ; also cavities, ships and all kinds of vessels' (Freud, 1900, p. 242). The actions of climbing ladders, stairs, inclines or flying may be used to symbolize sexual intercourse; having a haircut, a tooth pulled or being beheaded, may symbolize castration.

Dream analysis
Interpreting the latent content from the manifest content of a dream (e.g. by 'working through' the distortions created by condensation, displacement, dramatization/ symbolization and secondary elaboration).

How do contemporary analysts view dream interpretation? Marcus endorses *The Interpretation of Dreams* as 'the most comprehensive account of the psychoanalytic conception of the mind' (Marcus, 1999, p.2). But views are divided over the place of dream interpretation itself. Greenson (1970) agrees with Freud that dream interpretation, used with free association, has the potential to offer the richest insights into the world of the unconscious. Other analysts, however, regard dreams as being just one among many ways in which unconscious themes may express themselves (Brenner, 1969). De Monchaux (1978), though, makes the point that dream interpretation can serve other functions: patients can, for example, use dreams to bring up material in the therapy session which they might otherwise feel reticent about. Dream interpretation is still central to psychoanalytic theory and therapy, but dreams are no longer seen as essentially concerned with wish-fulfilment.

A number of research studies using content analysis have attempted to find evidence for Freud's ideas about the nature and function of dreams (e.g. Hall and Van de Castle, 1966; Brenneis, 1970). It is not easy to draw unequivocal conclusions from these because of the role that interpretation inevitably plays. For example, Hall and Van de Castle (1965) found that men are more likely than women to dream of physical injury or defect. This is consistent with greater unconscious concern with castration anxiety – as predicted by Freud's Oedipal theory (see Section 2.2). But this finding could be due to cultural factors.

These research studies do indicate that dream content is often meaningful and related to life experiences. However, they provide no confirmation that it largely represents *unconscious* desires. Rather, dreams seem to express many kinds of preoccupation and concern. Thus in the example above, men may dream of physical injury more often because they are more likely to be in situations which could lead to it. And evidence of distortions occurring to defend the dreamer against anxiety is also equivocal; for example, patients awaiting surgery report, if anything, higher levels of anxiety in their dreams (Breger *et al.*, 1971). This has led some experienced investigators (e.g. Hall and Van de Castle, 1966; Fisher and Greenberg, 1977) to reject the usefulness of Freud's distinction between manifest and latent content. Solms (2000) however, claims that recent neurophysiological studies do support Freud's ideas. Dreaming appears to depend both on brain structures concerned with cognition and perception, and also on those concerned with initiating actions in response to instinctual and emotional needs (Panksepp, 1999). While such evidence is indirect and limited, it is at least consistent with Freud's basic idea.

Soon after *The Interpretation of Dreams* Freud wrote *The Psychopathology of Everyday Life* (1901), exploring how our unconscious motivations may

express themselves through accidental actions or slips of the tongue
(**Freudian slip**). So a patient's continual late arrival for the analytic session
might be taken to indicate hostility towards the analyst. Or a sequence of
'accidental' mishaps might be interpreted as expressions of unconscious
aggression against the self.

For all psychoanalysts, the primary goal is to identify and interpret
unconscious meanings and motivations, a process Reik (1948) has called
'listening with the third ear'. Initial interpretations, be they based on
dreams, free associations or what patients say or do, are inevitably
tentative, no more than working hypotheses to be matched against further
evidence. But gradually, consistencies and insights may begin to appear.

*Some experimental psychologists place emphasis on the automaticity of
much of our cognition, that is, its implicit or unconscious nature
(e.g. Underwood, 1996). However, they assume a fluid interplay between
conscious and unconscious processes rather than conflict between them.
And they do not conceptualize unconscious processes in the same kind
of motivational or dynamic way as psychoanalysts do. Thus cognitive
psychologists explain most accidental slips as errors of unconscious
processing resulting from cognitive habits or confusions with related
words, rather than as being due to unconscious motivations. Reason (2000)
has re-analyzed several of Freud's examples in these terms. For example,
Freud cites an example from his colleague Stekel who had reported the
embarrassing experience of accidentally untying the bow which held
together the dressing gown of a patient while giving her his hand to say
goodbye. Freud interprets this as a manifestation of underlying erotic
desire. Reason, on the other hand, suggests that Stekel would have often
have found himself in a situation where he was required to undo the
bed-jackets of an indisposed patient to palpate the chest or abdomen. A
momentary distraction could have been sufficient for this habitual action
to have been triggered.*

Freudian slip
An accidental action
or utterance which
expresses unconscious
motivation (in Freud's
original German
fehlleistung, literally
'faulty achievement', but
translated as 'parapraxis'
in the standard edition
of Freud).

Activity 9.2

Try reflecting on your own actions in everyday life. Could any of your own behaviours
or mistakes be attributable to unconscious motivations? What other interpretations
might you give them?

If you can remember them, try recording your dreams as soon as you awake. Free
associate (i.e. follow whatever train of thought comes into your mind) in response to
key images from the dream and note these down. Once you have recorded a few

dreams in this way, look through them. What insights, if any, do they offer you in thinking about yourself?

2.2 The significance of childhood experience

Freud considered that the psychic energy of the unconscious has its source in biological drives. He was an admirer of Darwin (whose *Origin of Species* had been published in 1859 when Freud was three years old). Freud initially classified drives into two basic types rather as Darwin had done – those concerned with survival of the individual (such as hunger and thirst), and those concerned with the survival of the group (i.e. sexuality). It is sexuality or **libido** that Freud considers of greatest significance psychologically and in 1905 Freud published his *Three Essays on the Theory of Sexuality,* perhaps the most important of his books after *The Interpretation of Dreams.*

Libido
Psychosexual energy.

Freud uses the term 'sexual' in its broadest sense to refer to any kind of body stimulation that produces pleasure. During the first five years of life, he argues, the source and nature of such stimulation changes as a result of biological development. For the very young infant, the mouth is the source, and pleasure is derived initially from sucking and later, as teeth develop, from biting (the **oral stage**). (You may have noticed how, once children begin to be able to handle objects, everything is held to the mouth.)

At some time, usually in the second year, excretion is likely to become the focus of attention, pleasurable stimulation being derived from the retention and elimination of faeces (the **anal stage**). Still later, in about the fourth year, the focus of interest shifts to the genitals. This is reflected in curiosity about sex differences and pleasure in touching the genitals and physical stimulation from rough play (the **phallic stage**). From about the age of five until adolescence, there is a 'latency period', during which attention shifts to the world of school, to learning skills and developing peer relationships. According to Freud, at adolescence sexuality becomes directed outwards and instead of the child's own body being the primary source of gratification, the focus (if only in fantasy) shifts onto another person. The pre-genital modes of childhood sexuality will be incorporated into this. Thus, oral stimulation, for example in the form of kissing, is usually involved in sexual relations.

Oral stage
First stage of psychosexual development where the focus is on the mouth and pleasure from sucking and/or biting.

Anal stage
Second main stage of psychosexual development where the focus is on the anal area and the primary source of pleasure is the retention and elimination of faeces.

Phallic stage
Third stage of psychosexual development where the focus is on the genitals and pleasure from stimulating the genital area.

Each developmental stage involves not only a particular *body zone* but also a *mode of activity.* For the oral phase it is sucking and biting. They also each involve a characteristic *psychological quality,* reflecting the nature of the predominant relationship at that time (which is why it is described as a theory of *psychosexual* development). The oral stage, for example, comes when the child is entirely dependent on others for the satisfaction of his or her needs. Psychoanalysts such as Erikson (1950), whom you met in Chapter 1 of this book, have argued that if these needs are met, the result is a general optimism, a sense of the world as a positive place; if they are not, this lays the basis for a generally pessimistic emotional orientation. The anal phase, in contrast, is the prototype for relationships with authority. Perhaps for the first time, children may be required to control their body functions: impulses and desires have to be geared to the demands of others.

Freud associates the phallic phase in boys with **Oedipal conflict** (named after the Greek story of Oedipus who unknowingly killed his father and married his own mother). Because the erogenous zone of stimulation at this stage is the penis, the close affection a boy is likely to feel for his mother becomes 'sexualized'. With his growing awareness of his parents' relationship, the boy comes to see his father as a rival for his mother's affections. This can result in increased hostility towards his father and perhaps also fear of him. According to Freud, the usual way this conflict is resolved is through increased identification with the father, taking on his role and characteristics, and 'introjecting' or assimilating his perceived values and attributes. In this way the basis for conscience or *superego* is established.

Some critics have suggested that, instead of it being universal as Freud supposed, the Oedipus complex may be peculiar to a particular kind of family structure where the father remains dominant and aloof – as in the patriarchal Jewish family in which Freud himself was brought up. The idea of the Oedipus complex almost certainly had a personal foundation. In his self-analysis and through interpreting his own dreams, Freud had been surprised at the hostility and guilt he had discovered in relation to his father and the almost erotic nature of his feelings for his much younger and adoring mother.

It is interesting, in view of the fact that the majority of his patients were women, that Freud has relatively little to say about the development of girls. Perhaps this again reflects his dependence on his own self-analysis as a source of ideas. He believed that for the little girl the crucial issue equivalent to the Oedipal conflict in boys is the realization that she has no penis. This is experienced as a sense of loss which leads her to devalue women and turns her towards her father. Later she will come to identify with her mother because she is in the same position as herself, but her underlying emotional desire to possess a penis will remain. Freud considered that fantasies of being pregnant or even a desire to possess or rival men may represent, unconsciously and symbolically, attempts to acquire the 'missing' part.

Oedipal conflict
Oedipal conflict arises during the phallic phase when a boy comes unconsciously to regard his father as rival for his mother's affection.

Freud's account of female development has been both criticized and extended by analysts such as Irigaray (1985). They reject the notion of **penis envy** *and argue that the key to understanding the development of girls (and boys as well) can be found in cultural practices rather than in anatomical concerns. Chodorow (1978) points out that girls may resent their mothers and love their fathers not because of their sense of loss and desire for a penis but to achieve separation and freedom from a close maternal relationship. Mothers may also unwittingly support cultural norms by building up and idealizing the father, and encouraging belief in a 'paternal universe' (Chasseguet-Smirgel, 1985).*

Penis envy
Freud's controversial and contested notion that the crucial issue in the psychosexual development of a girl is the realization that she has no penis.

How, according to psychoanalysts, does childhood experience impact on adult personality and behaviour? A key concept here, developed from Freud's work, is the general notion of **transference**. This is the idea that the emotional feelings aroused in our early relationships may stay with us and be unconsciously 'transferred' into relationships in adult life. If the response to parental pressure at the anal phase, for example, was overly submissive or rebellious, this may carry over into later relationships with authority. Or, to take another example, one way a young boy may resolve Oedipal conflict may be by over-idealizing his mother and repressing the sexual feelings she arouses in him. This may result in an adult man who has difficulty in integrating sexuality and affection: who uses one woman as a sexual partner but who puts another on a pedestal as a potential wife. In modern psychoanalytic theory and practice, transferences from patient to analyst are considered to be of crucial importance and there is a substantial body of clinical evidence on this subject.

Transference
The psychoanalytic idea that the emotional feelings aroused in our early relationships can be unconsciously 'transferred' into relationships in adult life.

Researchers have recently found some evidence that emotional responses generated in childhood relationships may influence how we respond to new people (e.g. Chen and Andersen, 1999; Andersen and Miranda, 2000). Their experiments suggest that similar emotional reactions to those previously experienced in childhood in relations with parents (or other significant figures) may be triggered if new acquaintances are in some way like the parents (e.g. if they have the same interests or physical characteristics).

Fixation
Refers to an overemphasis in later life on the characteristics or satisfactions associated with a particular phase of psychosexual development.

Another key notion in psychoanalytic theory is **fixation**, which can occur if a child is either over gratified or deprived at one or other of the developmental stages. This may result in an overemphasis in later life on the characteristics or satisfactions associated with the corresponding phase. For example, fixation at the oral stage is likely to result in an adult who is overly concerned with oral gratification. This may take the form of sucking or chewing sweets, smoking, drinking or even excessive talking. Or fixation may express itself in over-use of the mode of relating associated with this stage – dependency. In a later paper, Freud (1908) explored in some detail the various characteristics that can result from fixation at the anal stage. If the pleasure a child takes in playing with his or her faeces is severely constrained by parents, he claimed, the child may develop defences against such forbidden pleasures which may express themselves later as obsessive orderliness and cleanliness. If parents reinforce a child's production on the potty, this may lay the foundation for later pleasure in creating. And miserliness may result from a child developing an unwillingness to 'let go'.

Freud initially believed that, with practically all his patients, the analytic trail led eventually to a repressed conflict centred on some kind of sexual experience or 'seduction' as a child. By the time of the *Three Essays on Sexuality* he had revised this **seduction theory**, attributing the accounts of his patients to *childhood fantasy* rather than actual abuse of them as children. This became a significant trigger for Freud to realize the importance of fantasy in the inner world of both children and adults.

Seduction theory
Freud's initial belief (later changed) that the origins of repressed conflict lay in early sexual experiences.

It has been suggested (e.g. Masson, 1984) that Freud revised his original seduction theory because of the opposition it might arouse; current evidence about the prevalence of the sexual abuse of children may make Freud's earlier view of the occurrence of actual abuse now seem more plausible.

The theme for Freud's psychosexual theory, then, is that the child is the 'parent of the person'. For not only later sexual proclivities and neurosis but also personality have their origins in fixation at infantile phases of psychosexual development. Bear in mind though, when thinking about Freud's notions of the ways in which young children experience their worlds, that their thinking is not based on principles of logic and causality like that of most adults, but is much more a world of fantasy and imagination. Freud believed, for example, that because of the boy's focus on his penis at the time of Oedipal conflict, the fear of his father is likely to be experienced as anxiety over losing it (castration anxiety). If this idea seems odd, it is worth considering the popularity through the ages of fairy stories such as those of the Brothers Grimm. Psychoanalysts such as Bettleheim (1976) have argued that many of these can be interpreted as relating to fantasies focused on different psychosexual stages and that this explains their powerful appeal to children. Unless they are regarded in this way, they certainly involve themes that are strange, to say the least. For example, there are frequent accounts of being eaten or the fear of being eaten (e.g. Little Red Riding Hood, The Three Little Pigs). Could these represent unconscious oral aggression? Note also how older figures are often polarized (e.g. the wicked witch and good fairy godmother, the evil ogre and benevolent king). Could these be expressions of a 'splitting' of ambivalent feelings towards parents? In Jack and the Beanstalk, a plant soars phallic-like into the sky. Jack is chased by a giant (unconscious fantasies of a threatening father?) and triumphs in the end by hacking down the beanstalk while the giant is descending and then cutting off his head (symbolic castration?).

Activity 9.3

Look at one or two fairy stories – a good choice would be those by (or based on) the Brothers Grimm – in the light of the discussion in this section of early psychosexual development. If you feel interpretations such as those above are implausible, how else could you account for the strange themes that fairy stories often contain?

2.3 Psychodynamics

Id
The aspect of the psyche Freud called the 'It' (*das Es*) focused on pleasure from the satisfaction (in reality or fantasy) of biological needs.

Ego
The reality-testing, perceptual aspect of the self which Freud called the 'I' (*das Ich*) which is also focused on integrating the different aspects of self.

Superego (or conscience)
This is based on the introjection of 'moral' attitudes through identification with significant others (especially the father). Designated by Freud the 'Above-I' (*das Uber-Ich*).

In *The Ego and the Id* (1923) Freud drew together his earlier ideas and presented a conceptualization of the psyche or mind as an energy system involving potentially conflicting forces. Freud suggested these were of three types. First, there is the drive for the satisfaction of biological needs. Gratification through actions or fantasy results in *pleasure,* and frustration in tension. Because it is rooted in the body, Freud described this aspect as *das Es,* literally the 'It' but usually translated as the **id**. As the child grows older, perceptual and logical capacities develop, bringing increasing understanding of the world and the goal of *pleasure* becomes tempered by the demands of *reality*. This reality-testing aspect of the self Freud designated the 'I' (or **ego**), denoting that it includes consciousness and is concerned with integrating the different aspects of self. As noted in the discussion of the Oedipus conflict, children, as they grow older, introject or assimilate values and attitudes through identification with adults. This is the basis for the development of the third aspect, the 'Above–I' (or **superego**) as Freud called it to indicate its moral, regulatory power.

These different aspects of the psyche may come into conflict with one another. Sexual desire (the drive for pleasure of the *id*), may be countered either by a fear of punishment (the concern of the *ego* for the consequences of reality) or by guilt that it is wrong (the introjected inhibitions of the *superego*). **Psychodynamics** refers to the conflict between these different aspects of the psyche and the different ways in which this may be played out.

In his later formulations, Freud considered that one consequence of intrapsychic conflict is the experience of **angst**. While this is translated as 'anxiety', *angst* perhaps conveys a more pervasive sense of fear and anguish. Anxiety may be alleviated by reducing conflict through defensive devices. Freud distinguished nine of these, but the list has been expanded by other analysts, including his daughter Anna (Freud, 1936).

The most significant defence mechanism is **repression**. Impulses that in some way are disturbing are shut out of consciousness; thus if sexual feelings have been repressed a person will just not be aware of them. With **displacement**, the impulse is redirected towards a less threatening target (see also the discussion of dreams in Section 2.1). For example, a child's feelings of resentment towards a parent over a particular incident may conflict with usual feelings of affection. Such conflict might be alleviated by displacing the aggression onto a parent substitute such as a teacher or a relative. One kind of displacement which psychoanalysts consider to be of fundamental significance, both for personal adjustment and the development of civilization, is **sublimation**. This is the displacement of libido to non-sexual goals in a way that produces not only the alleviation of inner conflict but a valued outcome, such as creative work or caring for others.

Projection is where repressed feelings (of say aggression or sexuality) are projected onto other persons so that *they* are seen as aggressive or sexually motivated. This process may underlie some forms of prejudice (Adorno *et al.*, 1950). In **reaction formation**, a repressed impulse is held in check by exaggerating the opposite tendency. Thus, being unassertive may be a way of coping with strong aggressive feelings which arouse unconscious fear of retaliation or which conflict with moral ideals. Other defensive processes mentioned by Freud include denial, isolation, regression, rationalization and identification.

Recent experimental work supports the idea that people are capable of 'intentional forgetting' and can block unwanted material from awareness (e.g. Brewin and Andrews, 2000). Some people are particularly good at forgetting negative information. There is also evidence that people who often resort to this ('repressive copers') are more likely to have had troubled relationships in childhood (Myers and Brewin, 1994).

Psychodynamics
Internal psychic conflict between different forces or aspects of the self and the defences and distortions this may involve.

Angst
Anxiety and anguish resulting from inner conflict.

Repression
A much-used defence mechanism where disturbing feelings are shut out of consciousness.

Displacement
A defence mechanism whereby an unconscious motivation is redirected towards a more acceptable or less threatening target.

Sublimation
A form of displacement of libido to non-sexual and personally or culturally valued goals.

Projection
A defence mechanism whereby repressed feelings such as aggression or sexuality are projected onto (and are thus seen as characteristics of) other persons.

Reaction formation
A defence whereby a repressed impulse is held in check by exaggerating the opposite tendency.

Defence mechanisms
Largely unconscious
processes for avoiding
inner conflict and the
anxiety this creates.

It should not be assumed that **defence mechanisms** are necessarily pathological. In some form, they pervade the fabric of our everyday lives – we may forget to pay that annoying bill or be over-polite to a person we dislike. But what particularly interests psychoanalysts are those defences that are rooted in the character and past of an individual. Freud believed that different defence mechanisms tend to assume prominence at different stages of development. For example, the use of projection is quite natural for very young children. Desires to do forbidden acts may be projected onto pets or dolls who may then be criticized and chastised accordingly. Where fixation has occurred at an early stage of development and a particular defence has been used a lot, this may become the characteristic way in which the later adult attempts to reduce anxiety. For the psychoanalyst, personality emerges, in part, from the typical defences we come to employ.

Activity 9.4

Make a list of the defence mechanisms discussed above. For each one, try to think of situations, either actual or imaginary, which would illustrate it in operation.

Can you think of an example of a defensive strategy of this kind that you have engaged in? Try to be alert to such possibilities in the future.

9.2 FEATURED METHOD

Psychoanalytic therapy and the nature of clinical evidence

Psychoanalytic therapy essentially aims at bringing unconscious material into conscious awareness. It uses a variety of means to do this. Like his theory, Freud's *therapeutic technique* developed over his lifetime. Initially, psychoanalytic therapy was aimed at *catharsis* – releasing repressed feelings. Later, emphasis was placed on *interpreting* unconscious motivations. What the patient said and did, including reports of dreams and actions, were analysed using methods such as free association. The *resistances* of the patient to interpretations offered, and hesitations when recounting memories or experiences were regarded as indicative of sensitive areas and typical defensive strategies.

Eventually the most important procedure for Freud became the analysis of *transference*. Unconscious desires and feelings (towards parents in particular) were thought to be transferred by the patient onto the therapist, and an analysis of the relationship between patient and analyst considered to be an important source of insights.

Interpretation and the analysis of transference remain the staple approach of most contemporary analysts though there is considerable variation in technique depending on orientation and approach. Psychoanalysis typically involves several sessions a week over several years. So repeated observations can be made of verbal and non-verbal behaviours, reports on current life and past experiences and of transferences. The analyst is in a position to make private conjectures about meanings and motivations that 'emerge' from the patient's unconscious and seek validation from further instances over long periods of time. Sometimes the analyst's interpretations can themselves be used as a way of testing conjectures by observing the patient's reactions both immediately and in terms of changes over time. Finally, a patient's transferences can have an effect on the analyst. Trained psychoanalysts have all undergone psychoanalysis themselves. This is designed to enable them to use their own reactions as an aid to understanding the patient's unconscious motives and conflicts.

Since these methods are difficult to describe, an example from clinical practice might be useful. Patrick Casement describes a patient who spoke so quietly that he could hardly hear her. Rather than just ask her to speak more loudly or try to work with the little he could hear, he 'began to sense that there might be an important communication in the softness of her asking. As I could not hear her words, it was almost like having to listen to a preverbal child' (Casement, 1990, p.166).

Casement interpreted this to his patient: 'I think that there is something important about the way in which you are talking to me - talking so that I can hardly hear. I could again have asked you to speak louder. Instead I have realized that I will only pick up what you are trying to get across to me if I listen very carefully, as a mother might with her infant who does not have any words. And what I am sensing is that you are feeling that I am not in touch with you. I believe that this is what you need me to understand, that I am not at this moment understanding you' (Casement, 1990, p.166).

The patient began to cry. Casement reports that once she could speak again she told him: 'but you understood that you did not understand. That is what makes the difference' (Casement, 1990, p.166). He takes her emotional reaction and response to his interpretation to be an expression of her realization that her parents had often assumed that they understood her when in fact they had not.

This brief example demonstrates several features of the psychoanalytic method for gaining access to the inner world and subjectivity and for bringing about change. It shows, for example, the interplay between the present interaction and past experiences, the process of transference, and the process of reconstruction. It also illustrates the therapeutic role of interpretation and the way that an interpretation follows from a conjecture and how the patient's response to the interpretation is used to provide further evidence to validate the conjecture.

2.4 Variations in psychoanalytic theory

The three ideas outlined in the preceding sections – the notion of a dynamic *unconscious*, the significance of *childhood experience* and the idea of *psychodynamics* or defensive processes, form the core of the psychoanalytic approach: all psychoanalytic schools work with some version of these. There are, however, many variations on these themes. During Freud's lifetime, several of his colleagues such as Jung and Adler broke away to form their own schools. Later, under the impact of Nazism, other analysts moved both to Britain (e.g. Melanie Klein and Anna Freud) and to the USA (e.g. Erik Erikson, Erich Fromm and Karen Horney), each developing their own version of psychoanalytic ideas and influencing those of others around them. Yet another school arose in France, stimulated by the study of linguistics (e.g. Jacques Lacan). These different schools have extended and varied psychoanalytic ideas which continue to develop today, largely rooted in the clinical work of practising analysts. While it is not always easy to classify the differences between these schools, four ways in which they might be distinguished are briefly discussed below.

(1) One major point of difference is what is regarded as the *major driving force in psychological life*. For Freud, as we have seen, it was instinct – specifically sexuality. In contrast, for Alfred Adler, Freud's first colleague to break away, it was striving to overcome feelings of inferiority. In Britain a very different approach called **object relations** emerged in the 1950s, and is still influential today. (The term 'object' is used here in the grammatical sense of subject–object and refers to the other people who are the objects of our feelings). This group (who originally included John Bowlby, W. Ronald Fairbairn and Donald Winnicott) believe that our primary psychological need is to connect with other people (i.e. we are 'people-seeking' rather than 'pleasure-seeking'). As Gomez puts it, we are 'essentially social, our need for contact with others is primary and cannot be explained in terms of other needs' (Gomez, 1997, p.2). Bowlby (1971, 1979) has been particularly influential in demonstrating the importance of emotional attachment and the damaging effects of relationship deprivation in early childhood.

Object relations
A British approach to psychoanalysis which emphasizes the need for contact with others rather than instinctual needs as the driving force in human behaviour.

Alfred Adler (1870–1937), the first to break away

John Bowlby (1907–90) and Donald Winnicott (1896–1971), prominent members of the British 'object relations' school

(2) We also find in psychoanalysis varied conceptions of the *nature and development of early childhood experience*. Melanie Klein was one of the first analysts to work directly with children, pioneering the close observation and interpretation of children's play. The world of early experience which she portrays is very different from that of Freud (see Klein, 1975). For her the critical phases come in the first year of life. During that time she believed that even Oedipal conflict can be experienced and the vestiges of ego and superego functioning are already apparent. Klein's focus is not so much on sexuality as on the child's handling of aggression and rage.

Melanie Klein (1882–1960), who focused on very early life including the turbulent rage and aggression experienced by young infants

(3) Another point of difference amongst psychoanalytic theories is the *role assigned to society*. In Freud's later work society was seen in opposition to biological drives, forcing the individual to repress feelings and come to terms with its constraints. The group of analysts who emigrated to the USA, and are collectively known as the **neo-Freudians**, developed a very different view. Fromm, who had been influenced by Marxist as well as existential ideas (see Section 3), regarded the social context both as shaping personality and as a supportive medium through which individuals can express and satisfy their needs. As you saw in Chapter 1,

Neo-Freudians
A group of analysts who emigrated from Europe to the USA and who emphasize the significance of social-cultural contexts in understanding the individual.

Neo-Freudians Erich Fromm (1900–80) and Erik Erikson (1902–94) who moved from Germany to the USA in the 1930s

Carl Jung (1875–1961), who broke away to form his own school called 'analytical psychology'

Erikson's ideas take a similar 'psychosocial' stance and he uses both anthropological and psychobiographical studies to demonstrate how personal subjectivity and historical and cultural contexts are closely intertwined (see Erikson on Native American tribes (1950), on Luther (1959) and Gandhi (1969)). Neo-Freudians typically place more emphasis on personality development throughout life rather than just its foundations in early childhood.

(4) In psychoanalysis we also find different ways of thinking about *key concepts*. For example, one point of difference between Jung and Freud is in their concept of the unconscious. Jung was impressed with the parallels he found between the symbols contained in the myths and art of widely disparate cultures and noted that they sometimes resembled the paintings and the dream images recalled by his patients. Whilst accepting the idea of the personal

unconscious, he also formulated the idea of a 'collective unconscious' constituted by predispositions representing the residue of core universal experiences of modern man's remote ancestors and manifested as archetypes.

Even such a brief account demonstrates how psychoanalytic theories offer a varied and stimulating set of tools for thinking about inner worlds and subjectivity and the implications of childhood experience, relationships and culture.

Summary Section 2

- Three core themes underpin psychoanalysis: (1) a dynamic unconscious, (2) the significance of early childhood experience and (3) inner conflict and defensive processes (psychodynamics).
- Methods for uncovering unconscious meanings include free association, the analysis of neurotic symptoms, dreams, slips and mistakes, transferences and behaviour in general.
- Freud argued that dreams are unconscious wish-fulfilments. Latent desires are disguised in the manifest content of the dream through distortions such as displacement and dramatization.
- Freud postulated developmental stages (oral, anal and phallic) in the first five years of life, each related to a body zone, mode of activity and a psychological modality. Childhood experiences have consequences for adult personality, neurosis and sexual style.
- Other key notions in Freud's psychosexual theory are the Oedipus conflict, transference, fixation, and childhood fantasies of being seduced.
- Psychodynamics refer to inner conflicts (especially between the different aspects of the psyche – id, ego and superego) and the defensive processes used unconsciously to defend against the anxiety such conflict creates. These include repression, sublimation, projection and reaction formation.
- The aim of psychoanalytic psychotherapy is to release repressed unconscious material by bringing it into consciousness. Freud used analysis of dreams, and interpretation of resistances and transferences.
- Psychoanalytic theories vary in terms of (1) what is the primary motivational force, (2) the nature and significance of childhood experience, (3) the role of society and (4) conceptualizations of key concepts.

3 Humanistic psychology

We turn now to our second perspective. This started as an explicit movement in the late 1950s when a group of American psychologists (who included Abraham Maslow, George Kelly, Carl Rogers and Gordon Allport) set up the Association for Humanistic Psychology. At the time the dominant perspective in academic psychology was behaviourism, and in psychotherapy it was psychoanalysis. They felt that neither perspective captured core aspects of human experience. Behaviourism, for example, disregarded subjective experience, and psychoanalysis questioned the validity of self-awareness and our assumption that we have the power of conscious choice. They wanted a perspective that did justice to people's capacity to be self-aware and to be responsible for directing their own lives. Because it originated as a reaction to two other dominant traditions, humanistic psychology has sometimes been called 'the third force'.

As noted earlier, any perspective needs to be seen in the context of its time. Humanistic psychology took root and flowered in the 1960s when the cultural emphasis was on emancipation from tradition and exploration of new ideas and attitudes, both personal and political. Humanistic psychologists did not entirely discard the ideas of scientific psychology and of psychoanalysis, but they wanted to go beyond them. In doing this, they drew inspiration from a variety of sources including European existential philosophy and the Buddhist tradition of Asia.

There is no one dominating figure in humanistic psychology (although Carl Rogers perhaps comes nearest to this role). It encompasses a variety of psychologists and psychotherapists who share a set of assumptions about the nature of people, the aims of psychology and the best methods to achieve these. Like psychoanalysts, their focus and starting point is human subjectivity, but the way that this is conceptualized is quite different. Instead of a focus on unconscious meanings, the concern of humanistic psychologists is on *conscious awareness* of ourselves and the world about us. This is called an *experiential* approach because its concern is how people *experience* their worlds. It is also a *phenomenological* approach (in the broad sense of that term) because it focuses on phenomena – i.e. things as they appear to us. (You may remember that reference was made to the phenomenological approach in Chapter 6.)

Psychic determinism
The notion that our actions and experiences are determined by unconscious residues of early experience.

As we have seen, psychoanalysis assumes **psychic determinism** – that our actions and experiences are powerfully influenced by unconscious residues of early experience over which we have little control and of which we may be largely unaware. In contrast, humanistic psychology emphasizes our ability to become aware of our feelings and our power to initiate change and development in our own lives. This position is what might be termed **existential**, referring to the way that each of us is intrinsically involved in the process of existence. Each of us is aware of being a distinct individual, immersed in a flow of experience and moving through life towards old age and eventual death. And in most situations we are aware of having some **autonomy**, i.e. some power to choose what we do. If you choose, you can put down this chapter now and do something else, like make a cup of tea. Life's bigger choices may not be so easy, and there are likely to be many constraints on our behaviour. But in many situations, we experience the sense of having some potential for choice. Humanistic psychology works from the assumption that this power of choice and action allows each of us to play a part in creating the kind of person we become – a process referred to as **personal growth**.

Like psychoanalysts, most humanistic psychologists are concerned with helping people to change. While they are sceptical of the value of interpretation, various methods are used to help people become more alert to their own feelings and to explore different directions for change. They generally take a holistic or 'whole person' approach, sometimes working with the body (e.g. by using massage) as well as with the experiences and imagination of the client.

In summary, humanistic psychology is characterized by:

- a phenomenological emphasis on *conscious experience*;
- the existential assumption that people have the potential to develop themselves and their lives: in part to *create themselves*;
- a *holistic approach*, i.e. one which encompasses the whole person – mind, feelings and body;
- a *wide range of methods* for facilitating personal growth.

Each of these features will be explored in turn in the sections that follow.

Existential
Relating to the experience of being and existing and all that this implies (e.g. being conscious, finite and having the capacity for choice).

Autonomy
A person's power to initiate the thoughts and actions they choose.

Personal growth
Psychological development, particularly where a person him or herself takes responsibility and an active role in the process.

3.1 Conscious experience

At the core of our experience of being is the flow of conscious awareness. Moving inexorably through time, sometimes lagging, sometimes so fleeting that we are aware of awareness only in retrospect, the ever-changing kaleidoscope of consciousness is marked by changes in quality – from drowsiness to the freshness of waking, from the grey mists of depression to the excitement of expectation.

Our conscious experience is structured into meaningful patterns. We are aware that dusk is falling; we are feeling angry; our team has won by two goals; our daughter has had a child. We are embedded in a reality which for most of us has, in fair measure, coherence, interconnectedness and predictability. Occasional reflections though (at times of deaths or births, for example) may alert us to how much about our existence is puzzling and unknown. And moments of tragedy or even drunkenness may radically change our conscious state.

How far we are conscious of our 'self' at any time will vary. Sometimes we are only too aware of an 'I' who is doing and experiencing; at other times our sense of self is immersed in the experience of the moment.

Activity 9.5

While we all experience conscious awareness, we tend to take it for granted. We don't often deliberately reflect on what it is like. You might like to try the activity below, which tries to help you to become more explicitly aware of what you are experiencing *here* and *now*.

1 Make yourself comfortable and relax for a while, breathing slowly, steadily and deeply, but without effort.

2 Let your mind focus on whatever you can see, hear, smell and taste. Try to be aware both of what you are experiencing and also of what that feels like.

3 After a while, close your eyes and shift your attention to bodily sensations and feelings.

4 Then turn your focus to what you are experiencing at any particular moment. What is this like?

5 Finally, let your mind free, following whatever fantasies or images that emerge.

Afterwards, spend a few moments quietly reflecting on the different phases of your experience. How easy was it to be 'aware of being aware'?

Reflecting on one's own subjectivity is not easy. For example, the act of trying to be consciously aware of what is going on tends to change the nature of your experience. So introspection is, inevitably, in effect retrospection – remembering what an experience was like rather than reflecting on it while it is happening. It becomes even more difficult if you try to express what you are experiencing to somebody else. We may just not have the words to do this. Moreover, conscious experience is not only ever-changing but in a sense is not fixed or given. For example, how you experience something may be affected or 'constructed' by the way you or other people talk or think about it.

These problems make investigating the nature of subjective experience problematic. Psychologists have nevertheless tried to develop a particular kind of 'phenomenological' qualitative method for documenting different kinds of subjective experience. A typical procedure is to collect individual accounts of specific kinds of experience (e.g. 'anger' or 'being at home'). These are then analysed to find out what features they have in common. The studies specify the nature and kinds of feeling involved in the experience, what other kinds of experience it can be distinguished from, and what kinds of situation tend to elicit it. Examples of experiences studied in this way include close friendship (Becker, 1987), being burgled (Fischer and Wertz, 1979), feeling left out (Aanstoos, 1987), feeling guilty (Yoder, 1990), longing (Palaian, 1993), and the experience of having coronary artery by-pass surgery (Trumbull, 1993). A good account of this method can be found in Becker (1992).

Peak experiences

One particular type of conscious awareness is what the influential humanistic psychologist Abraham Maslow (1973) has called the **peak experience**. He claims that peak experiences are characterized by:

- A sudden shift in consciousness, so that what is being experienced is flooded with delight and fullness. Attention is completely focused and filled by the experience.
- The experience of the moment seems complete in itself, having its own intrinsic meaning and wholeness. There is a sense of fusion with life, and anxiety is completely absent.
- There is a sense of plentiful and available energy; almost anything seems possible.

Peak experience
A specific state of consciousness characterized by a sense of delight, wholeness, meaningfulness and abundant energy.

Maslow's research indicated that peak experiences can be sparked off in a variety of situations. These include listening to music, looking at a landscape or the sun setting, making love and the tranquillity which can follow this, meditating or listening to poetry. Or it may be generated by events in the flow of everyday life, such as simply sitting with your family having a meal, or walking home after having studied intensely for several hours. Maslow believed that peak experiences are not just enjoyable but that they serve to release vital psychological energies and stimulate a sense of purpose.

   As we have noted, precise description of experiential states is always difficult, especially when, like peak experiences, these only occur spontaneously and relatively rarely. In effect, we can only take Maslow's claims here on trust or use our own life experience to support (or otherwise) the conclusions he draws. Their particular value, however, is not so much as 'established facts', but their potential to stimulate us to reflect on our own experience and the possibilities that may be open to us.

Note here that this is a different way of thinking about psychology than you may have explicitly encountered so far. The purpose of psychology is seen by humanistic psychologists as not just to establish facts on the basis of evidence but to stimulate our thinking about the experience of being human, and to provide ideas which may be used by people in the process of their own personal growth.

Activity 9.6

1   Make a list of a few occasions in your life which seemed like peak experiences. In what kinds of situation did they occur?

2   Although peak experiences occur spontaneously, spend a few minutes thinking about whether there is anything you can do to make them more likely to happen. Might it help, for example, to put yourself deliberately more often into the kinds of situation when they occurred before, and/or to be more open and alert to them?

One problem here lies in distinguishing and describing different kinds of experience. For example, Csikszentmihalyi (1992) set out to find what kind of experience people find most enjoyable. His findings from many different countries suggest that this is to be in 'flow'. **Flow experience** is total involvement in an activity or experience we enjoy for its own sake. Examples he gives include dancing, rock climbing, looking after a child and playing chess. But how can we label experiences? How can one determine, for example, whether a particular experience is a peak experience or being in flow (or indeed both)? How far also is what you experience influenced (or 'constructed') by reading accounts of this kind and descriptions of other people's experiences?

Flow experience
Term used by Csikszentmihalyi to refer to the experience of total involvement in an activity enjoyed for its own sake.

Personal construct theory

A different kind of approach to understanding conscious experience comes from the influential work of George Kelly. Like Maslow, Kelly was both an academic psychologist and a psychotherapist. Listening to his clients, he became aware of how crucial their ideas and beliefs about themselves and others are. From his own work, he was also aware of the

George Kelly (1905–66), originator of Personal Construct Theory

way a scientist goes about research, developing theories by formulating hypotheses and then testing these to support or disprove them. Kelly (1955a) argues that this essentially is the way that all of us operate in our everyday lives. We derive our beliefs and feelings about ourselves and the social world through our experiences and interactions, and then modify and extend these by testing them out.

The core notion in Kelly's theory is that of **personal constructs**. These relate to the discriminations which underpin our ways of experiencing the world. Constructs are bipolar (i.e. with two poles or ends) dimensions such as *friendly–cold*, or *stimulating–dull*. Constructs are personal in that they are part of the way a particular person makes sense of the world.

The method Kelly primarily used to uncover a person's construct pattern was the **repertory grid** (see Box 9.3).

Personal constructs
Term used by Kelly to refer to the bipolar discriminations underlying the ways in which a person makes sense of his/her world.

Repertory grid
A method devised by Kelly for eliciting and plotting the relationships between the constructs used by a person.

9.3 FEATURED METHOD

Repertory grid

This requires a person to think first of specific people who occupy roles in his/her personal life (e.g. father, mother, best friend, partner). These are what Kelly called the *elements* of the grid. In turn, different combinations of triads of these elements (e.g. sister, boss, neighbour) are selected from the set and the client is asked in what way two of the three are alike and the third one different. (Although this example uses people, elements could of course refer to any aspect of a person's world – different kinds of food, cars, etc.). Thus I might say that my sister and my best friend are both lively but a colleague is different because she is reserved. In this case, the distinction being made is the bipolar construct *lively–reserved*.

Working with a client, Kelly would first elicit a number of personal constructs in this way. He would then ask the client to go through the list of elements and indicate for each one which end of each construct fitted them best. In this way a grid could be established showing the elements that the client had selected and the ratings the client had given each of these on each construct. The inter-relationships between these can then be analysed and the patterning of the way this client uses her/his constructs becomes evident. For example, if a client tends to use the dimension *happy–sad* in a similar way to *lively–reserved*, this may tell us something about how the client experiences other people (see Table 9.1). The repertory grid method is not only helpful as a way of understanding how a particular client experiences their subjective world, it has also proved very fruitful for research comparing the subjective experiences of different individuals or groups.

Table 9.1　An example of a repertory grid

Constructs		Elements							
		1	2	3	4	5	6	7	8
		Father	Mother	Best friend	Partner	Sister	Boss	Neighbour	Colleague
1	happy — sad	3	2	(5)	4	(1)	7	3	[1]
2	intelligent — stupid	(4)	4	(5)	4	3	3	[1]	3
3	generous — mean	2	(5)	4	(5)	2	[1]	2	3
4	lively — reserved	3	2	(5)	4	(4)	3	3	[1]
5	religious — not religious	[1]	3	2	3	(4)	1	(4)	3
6	warm — cold	2	(5)	(4)	4	2	[1]	1	3
7	altruistic — egoistic	3	(5)	3	(5)	2	1	3	2

Notes:

The numbers and names along the top horizontal axis indicate the 'elements' (in this case people the construer knows).

The list of numbers and bipolar names in the columns on the far left indicate the constructs. Seven are listed here. In practice, there may be considerably more than this.

In the grid to the right of these columns, the numbers indicate the ratings of 'fit' from 1 (low) to 5 (high) given by the client of each element (i.e. name) on the construct indicated.

The three elements or people used to elicit each construct are indicated by the circles or a square around the numbers in the grid in bold type: the two alike are circled, the one who is different has a square surround.

You can see that analysing the way ratings of elements on each construct interrelate on a grid of this kind can tell you about the way this person construes people. For example, this client gives almost identical ratings to her elements (i.e. people related to) on the constructs happy–sad (1) and lively–reserved (4). This suggests the two constructs are being used in a very similar way.

Source: based on Kelly, 1955b

One particular way in which people's constructs vary is how rigid or 'impermeable' they are. If construct patterns are too fixed (if a person always believes for example that people who are intelligent are always cold) this may lead to unhappiness or difficulties in relationships. A core part of psychotherapy, as well as education and life experience in general, is developing new ways of construing and making sense of the world. One technique that Kelly devised is *fixed role therapy*. Together with the client, Kelly would write a characterization of a person who differed in significant ways from the way the client normally construes the world. The client would then be asked to act out being this character for a few weeks as a way of experimenting with new ways of experiencing and construing.

Kelly emphasizes then how subjective experience is potentially always open to change. Any event or experience, he asserts, can be construed in an infinity of ways (what he calls **constructive alternativism**). Changing the ways in which we construe our worlds offers us the potential to change ourselves.

Constructive alternativism
Term used by Kelly to signify that any event or experience can be construed in an infinite variety of ways.

3.2 Creating yourself

An existential perspective

A significant part of conscious awareness is a sense of ourselves as existing persons. The implications and meaning of this are the province of existentialism. For an existentialist, the awareness of being is particularly brought home to us by consciousness of the possibility of non-being – that one day we shall cease to be. This is not necessarily a depressing idea: being fully aware of one's own finiteness can actually intensify your 'here-and-now' experience of being.

Also central to the existentialist approach is the sense that we are free to choose and create what we are. This is not to deny the many constraints on our lives – many of the conditions of our existence are clearly outside our control, such as the fact that we will die, who our parents are, our first language and cultural context. However, within these constraints, existentialists argue that we have freedom to choose and to create our actions and experiences (this is known as **situated freedom**). They argue that it is important (or, as they term it, **authentic)** to acknowledge this freedom, accepting it and taking responsibility for our decisions, experiences and actions – for who we are to become. As Shaffer expresses it:

Situated freedom
The idea that we have freedom but that it is constrained by factors (both physical and social) not of our choosing.

Authentic
Existentialist term for conscious awareness of the reality of our existence (e.g. that existence is impermanent and individuals have both responsibility and freedom to choose).

> *Human beings realize that their relationship to the world is contingent and finite, and that the world, as experienced by them, will die with them. The more they face this ultimate aloneness, epitomized in the inevitability of their death, the more they sense that the meaningfulness of life, which might appear to be validated by the collective, and seemingly purposeful, activity ceaselessly taking place around them, can only be confirmed or refuted on the most personal level.*

(Shaffer, 1978, p.20)

The search for meaning

Viktor Frankl, an Austrian existential psychiatrist, has emphasized the importance for people of the **will to meaning**, or finding a sense of purpose and a direction in life. He quotes Friedrich Nietzsche's line: 'he who has a why to live can bear with any how'. When we are in severe danger, our ability to survive may be all the point and purpose we need. The existentialist philosopher Jean-Paul Sartre describes, for example, how members of the French Resistance, under continual threat of being discovered and shot, felt a sense of freedom and excitement they rarely experienced before the war. If you have been in a situation of great danger you also may remember how good it was afterwards simply to be alive. When continued survival is not immediately at risk, though, we seek purpose and meaning elsewhere. In some societies and historical periods, religion serves this need. In the contemporary Western world, Frankl considers, most people live in an existential vacuum. They have few accepted religious or cultural values to guide them. Each person's 'why', he argues, must therefore be constructed by him or herself.

Frankl distinguishes four ways in which personal meaning may be sought. One way is through *actions*, in particular creative activity. By building a machine, creating a garden, a poem or a painting we give value and meaning to our life. A second way is through *experience* – of beauty, nature or music, for example. A third way is through *love*, 'encountering another unique being in the very uniqueness of this human being' (Frankl, 1959, p.69). Finally, in situations of inescapable difficulty, we may find meaning through *fortitude*. For example, Frankl himself spent several years incarcerated in Auschwitz and Dachau. He found that one way in which some prisoners were able to give meaning to their lives, even in these awful circumstances, was by the strength of spirit with which they bore their suffering.

The Austrian therapist Viktor Frankl
(1905–97) who emphasized our need for
meaning

Activity 9.7

List three ways in which meaning is given to your life. One way of distinguishing these is to think of aspects of your life (such as a relationship or activity) which, if they were no longer possible, would significantly detract from the meaning which life has for you. Do these come within one or other of the categories which Frankl suggests? Are there other categories you would want to add (e.g. spiritual meaning, religious belief, having children)?

Existential ideas were imported into American psychology by writers such as Rollo May (1958). The emphasis then became placed firmly on our power to initiate and bring about events as we choose; in other words, on personal agency. This is a central theme in Maslow's idea of self-actualization and (as we shall see later) in the work of the most influential humanistic psychologist – Carl Rogers.

Self-actualization: the ideas of Abraham Maslow

In his theory of motivation, originally published in 1954, Maslow argues that human needs form a hierarchy which reflects their emergence in both evolution and the life of an individual (Maslow, 1987). First come the *physiological needs* necessary for human survival (both as individuals and as a species): the needs for food, drink, sleep and basic sexuality. Next come *safety needs*: people require a protected, reasonably predictable environment, a level of physical or economic security. Then comes the need for *love and belonging*: we need acceptance by other people and contact with them (both physical and social). The fourth level in Maslow's hierarchy is about *esteem* – that others should recognize our qualities and abilities and that we should also respect ourselves. These four kinds of need are termed *deficiency needs* in that they represent a drive to attain a state of satisfaction. For a while, at least, they can be satisfied.

Maslow distinguishes deficiency needs from the fifth and highest level in the hierarchy, the need for **self-actualization**. This is a term originated by Goldstein (1939) and used by Maslow to refer to the human desire for self-fulfilment, 'to become everything that one is capable of becoming' (Maslow, 1987, p.22). This may take as many forms as there are individuals. For some, self-actualization may be in creativity, for others in discovery and understanding. It may be expressed athletically or in the desire to be an ideal mother. Unlike the other needs, self-actualization is not a

Self-actualization
The human desire for self-fulfilment and developing one's potential.

drive to attain an end-state where the need is assuaged. Rather, expression of the need is an end in itself. Maslow has called it a *being need* (see Figure 9.1).

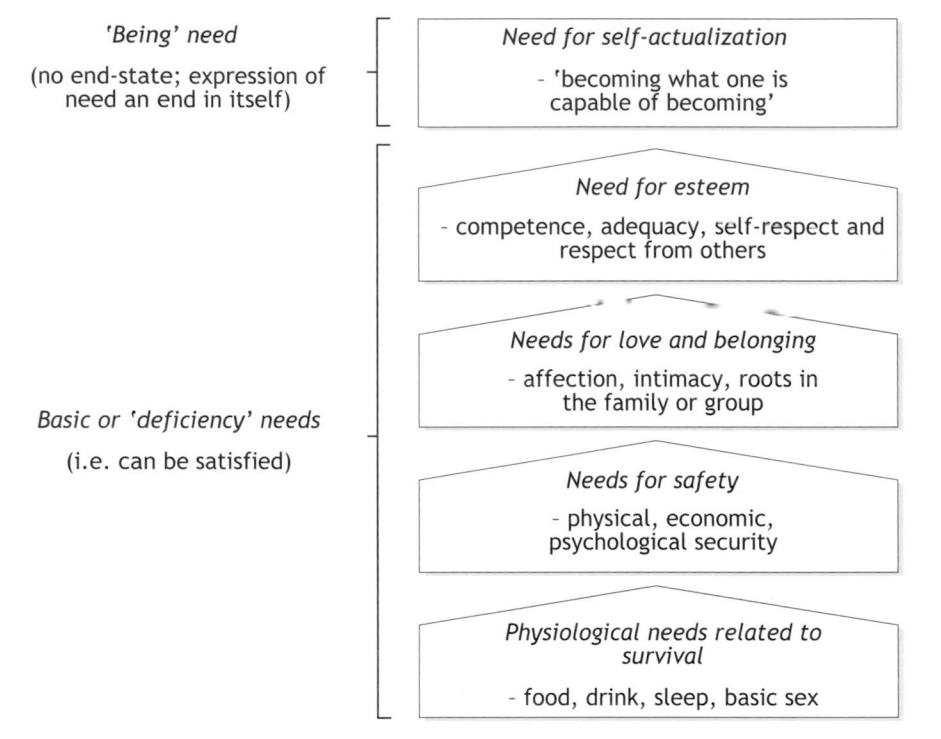

'Being' need

(no end-state; expression of need an end in itself)

Need for self-actualization
- 'becoming what one is capable of becoming'

Need for esteem
- competence, adequacy, self-respect and respect from others

Needs for love and belonging
- affection, intimacy, roots in the family or group

Basic or 'deficiency' needs

(i.e. can be satisfied)

Needs for safety
- physical, economic, psychological security

Physiological needs related to survival
- food, drink, sleep, basic sex

Figure 9.1 Maslow's hierarchy of needs (Source: Roth, 1990, p.436)

Maslow selected about thirty 'probable' self-actualizers, including Thomas Jefferson, William James, Albert Einstein and Albert Schweitzer. On the basis of biographical material in the case of the historical figures, and impressionistic analysis of the conversation and behaviour of those he knew, Maslow listed what he regarded as the typical features of a self-actualizer: 'The most significant of these is being involved in a cause outside of themselves. They are working at something which they love, so that the work-joy dichotomy in them disappears' (Maslow, 1973, p.45).

According to Maslow's analysis, self-actualizers are also creative, natural, spontaneous, prefer simplicity and see the world in non-stereotyped and often original ways. Although not necessarily unconventional, they are not bound by convention. They tend to be non-evaluative and accepting, both of themselves and of others. They are capable of deep and intimate relationships if they choose and have concern for others, but they are also people who can be quite happy alone. They are able to wonder at and enjoy life and they are likely to report having had peak experiences. Most of Maslow's sample were aged over 60 years and he concludes that self-actualization is a characteristic of maturity.

Maslow did not intend to imply that self-actualizers necessarily display these characteristics all the time. Neither were all their traits positive. They were often seen as impersonal and a little cold, and sometimes stubborn or ruthless. They could show personal vanity, guilt and anxiety (Maslow, 1987). Maslow also made the interesting point that what are often considered to be antithetical or opposite characteristics are likely to be merged in self actualizing people.

Maslow's sample of self-actualizers was informal and limited, selected almost entirely from personal acquaintances and public figures. His selection criteria were (1) full use made of talents and capacities, (2) no evidence of neurosis (though it is hard to see how some of his sample meet this criterion), and (3) satisfaction of deficiency needs.

Abraham Maslow (1908–70), pioneer of research into the 'healthy' personality

All three of Maslow's selection criteria could be regarded as dependent on the value judgements of the researcher and none of them is easy to assess. You may also feel that at least some of the features of the self-actualizers he lists are circular in that they merely reflect the nature of the individuals selected for in the first place. Is it surprising, for example, that people selected for making full use of their talents have devoted themselves to work that they love?

While open to the kinds of criticisms indicated above, Maslow's research is an interesting, albeit rudimentary, attempt to explore the idea of a 'healthy' personality which an individual can become, and it was undertaken at a time when the more usual focus was on neurosis. (For more recent research on psychological well-being see the discussion of positive psychology in Section 3.4).

Personal growth: the work of Carl Rogers

Carl Rogers is regarded as the major figure in humanistic psychology and his ideas have had a radical influence on psychotherapeutic practice as well as on academic psychology. Like Maslow and Kelly, Rogers had a varied background in both academic psychology and as a psychotherapist. His training was not only in clinical psychology but in science and theology as well.

Three key concepts underlie Rogers' work: (1) subjective experience, (2) self-actualization and (3) the self.

Carl Rogers (1902–87), the leading humanistic psychologist, who developed person-centred counselling

(1) Rogers asserts the 'fundamental predominance of the subjective', that each person lives essentially in her/his own particular personal and subjective world. While he accepts that a person will not be conscious of *all* aspects of their subjective world, like Kelly he believes that the conscious awareness of a person is the most important source of knowledge about her/him.

(2) Like psychoanalysts, Rogers emphasizes the dynamic, goal-directed character of our behaviour. However, in place of Freud's *libido* (or the 'people-seeking' of the Object Relations school – see Section 2.4), he postulates a basic tendency towards *self-actualization* or personal growth, in other words towards developing our potential and enriching experience.

(3) Rogers argues that our **sense of self** rests on two primary sources. One is our own *experience* – of what we find enjoyable, painful and exciting, of what we can and cannot do. The other is *evaluations of self by others* – definitions of our self which have been imposed by our parents and other significant people in our world. Problems can arise, particularly in childhood, when these evaluations are *conditional*. If you tell me 'I love you because you never get angry' I may believe this but then keeping your love is conditional on me never becoming angry. But what happens if I do feel angry? The result is an incongruence between my self-concept based on your conditional regard and my self-concept based on experience. The danger here, Rogers believes, is that fear of losing your love, and the self's need for consistency, may result in me either misperceiving my feelings of anger or blocking them from awareness. To help clients deal with this, Rogers developed his technique of **person-centred counselling** (see Box 9.4).

Sense of self
Our self concept which, in Rogers' view, originates in both our own actual experiences and evaluations of the self by others.

Person-centred counselling
A psychotherapeutic approach, originated by Rogers, involving unconditional regard but no interpretations, aimed at encouraging clients to explore and become aware of their feelings.

9.4 Person-centred counselling

The aim of person-centred counselling is to help clients restore their ability to become aware of what they really feel. To facilitate this, Rogerian therapists attempt to provide an atmosphere of non-evaluative, **unconditional regard** – a warmth and respect for clients regardless of what they think or do. They encourage their clients in a *non-directive* way to explore and express whatever feelings they have. In other words, they listen carefully and, without interpretation, try to reflect back what they hear their clients to be saying. The aim is to allow clients both to become more aware of their feelings and to feel they can express these without censure. Once clients realize that they can do this and still be accepted, they can begin to open themselves up to what they really feel. Out of this may emerge a more consistent sense of self. There is no longer the same need to shut off feelings because they are incongruent. The hope is that clients will now be able to open themselves up to relationships and situations which before would have been experienced as threatening.

Unconditional regard
A non-judgemental attitude of warmth and respect.

For Rogers, psychological maturity is when a person, by being able to integrate significant experiences into a developing self, becomes capable of self-enhancement and growth. He sees this process of 'becoming a person' (the title of one of Rogers' books published in 1961) as continuous and lifelong. In line with the assumption of personal agency, clients are responsible for their own personal growth – the counsellor can only facilitate by providing the *conditions* for it to occur.

With his background in academic psychology, Rogers considered that therapy, theory construction and research best go hand-in-hand to form a developing mode of enquiry. Therapy provides a rich source of hypotheses. These can then be tested by more formal research methods. Research results lead in turn to modification of the theory and therapeutic procedures in a continuous, on-going interaction. Rogers himself was very active in researching outcomes. By analysing the content of psychotherapeutic interviews, for example, he and his colleagues have shown that the number of negative self references tends to decrease and positive ones increase during the course of counselling. Using a variety of measures, Rogers has also demonstrated that counselling generally results in greater congruence between perceived self and ideal self, and in a sense of greater freedom and autonomy.

The nature of personal autonomy

But what does this notion of freedom and autonomy mean? Much of what you have read in this course so far has looked at how we are shaped by our social context, biology and evolution. Can we *really* be the agents of our own actions?

The idea of personal autonomy (sometimes called personal agency), as used in humanistic psychology, should not be thought of as contradicting the idea that social context and biology shape what we are. Rather, personal autonomy emerges from the nature of our cognitive abilities. The idea of 'emergent properties', which you encountered in Chapter 4, is very relevant here. In this case, our capacities for self-awareness, monitoring our own feelings and imagining future scenarios, which are themselves made possible by our biology, socialization and development, provide the basis for our capacity to generate novel thoughts and actions. There is no assumption of a 'free will' which is somehow exclusive of the biological and social influences which shape us. For this reason, our capacity to create ourselves is better referred to as 'personal autonomy'. A useful analogy is the human capacity for language. While our capacity to speak depends on biologically determined physiological processes as well as on social learning, any one of us has the ability, nevertheless, to make statements that we have never heard before.

Both Maslow and Rogers believe that, given the right preconditions, self-actualization will occur spontaneously. Growth-enhancing alternatives will be spontaneously chosen through 'the discovery of meaning from within oneself, meaning which comes from listening sensitively and openly to the complexities of what one is experiencing' (Rogers and Stevens, 1973, p.52). It might be argued though that the existential problems of choice and of creating direction and meaning in one's life are not so readily soluble. Even in optimum conditions, it is just not possible to become 'all that one is capable of becoming', which is what Maslow suggests that self-actualizers do. People are not just faced with having to choose between defensive strategies or opening themselves up to growth. They may also be confronted with alternatives (for example, in careers or relationships) which offer equal potential for enhancing their lives but which are mutually incompatible.

Activity 9.8

Exercising personal autonomy.

- Think of something which you would like to do and are capable of doing, but would not ordinarily do.

- Imagine yourself doing this.

- Do it.

- Reflect on what you have done.

The point of this exercise is to heighten your awareness of your capacity to create actions.

3.3 A holistic approach

A key assumption of the humanistic approach is that a person is a whole. We exist as a body, mind and possibly spirit. We inhabit both personal and social worlds. Humanistic psychology tries to encompass, both in its ideas and methods, these varied aspects of being: in other words it takes a *holistic approach*.

Humanistic psychotherapy

In keeping with its holistic emphasis and the idea that personal development involves several aspects of being, humanistic psychotherapy contains a wide variety of methods.

Encounter groups

In an encounter group about a dozen people, usually with a 'facilitator' or leader, meet either regularly or for one long intensive session, perhaps lasting over a weekend. Most are run along the lines of Rogers' person-centred approach (he was one of the originators of encounter groups). Acceptance and non-evaluation are emphasized. Explanations and judgements are discouraged. The focus is on what is happening *here-and-now* and not on events or people not present. The leader or facilitator's task is to encourage an atmosphere of trust so that members feel free to express what they really feel, though some facilitators may intervene to question and even challenge. Participants engage at an emotional and physical level rather than just through words. Touching, for example, may be a more powerful way to show care and to give support. Members are free to act out their feelings – shouting, crying, caressing and holding each other. A fundamental rule, though, is that they should only do what feels right for them.

Gestalt therapy

The term *gestalt* means configuration or whole. The primary aim of Fritz Perls, the originator of gestalt therapy, was to stimulate clients into greater awareness and integration of their feelings. The focus is on what the client is feeling 'here and now'. Perls was totally against asking *why*. He distrusted reasons and interpretations of psychological states, seeing these as a way of avoiding feelings by intellectualizing. In keeping with his famous motto of 'lose your mind and come to your senses', Perls encouraged his clients to become aware of and 'own' the actual bodily and perceptual sensations they were experiencing at the time rather than talk about what was troubling them. In a gestalt workshop, there is a lot of dramatization. The posture and voice tone of a member may be mirrored by the therapist. Clients may role-play the therapist (for example, to voice the criticisms that they think may be being made of them). They are encouraged to explore inner conflict by expressing the different sides within them as separate 'voices', sometimes initiating dialogue between these. They may also be encouraged to act out their blocked emotions by shouting, crying, beating a pillow or screaming at the therapist. His techniques, Perls believed, help clients to understand and accept themselves, release blocked emotions and stimulate vitality and spontaneity. (Note that gestalt therapy is quite different from gestalt psychology which you encountered in Chapter 6. They have in common only a concern with the property of wholeness.)

Psychosynthesis

Psychosynthesis, originated by Roberto Assagioli, focuses on the existential search for meaning and 'higher values' such as compassion, love, wisdom and joy. In particular, it aims to increase the balance or synthesis between different aspects of the person – intellectual, emotional and spiritual. As the rational mode is dominant in Western culture, psychosynthesis tends to focus on the development of intuition. Assagioli was particularly interested in encouraging development of the **transpersonal** self, in other words, spiritual awareness. Practitioners of psychosynthesis see themselves as guides rather than therapists. They draw on a variety of methods, particularly meditation and techniques for directing and focusing consciousness. For example, clients learn to create vivid images in their minds so that they can visualize desired actions or specific states that they wish to attain.

Transpersonal
A study of experiences in which the sense of identity of self extends beyond the individual or personal to encompass spiritual aspects of being.

While humanistic methods take varied forms, they do share a number of principles in common:

- A focus on the here and now.

- The attempt to empathize with and understand the client's experience but not to interpret it.

- Engaging in an authentic manner (i.e. while the therapist is there to facilitate the client, he or she tries to respond genuinely as a person during the therapeutic encounter).

- Allowing and encouraging clients to express their feelings overtly (e.g. in crying or movement).

- A focus on growth and development rather than dealing with past events.

- Encouraging clients to take the responsibility for change and their own feelings and actions.

The goal of humanistic psychotherapy is to encourage clients to open themselves up to as full awareness of their feelings as possible. The assumption is that if clients feel safe enough to explore these, they can find their own direction and power to change. The process of opening up may involve reflecting back (as in Rogerian person-centred, non-directive counselling) so clients become more fully aware of what they are expressing, or even pushing or challenging a client where they are resistant to doing this. It means being there for the client in an authentic and responsive way and, where necessary, providing a stable reference for their experiential world. For example, a client (M) in existential therapy spoke about an inner destructive force which was taking her over (Davidson, 2001). She felt lost and that there were big black holes around her which were 'dark and deep and could swallow her up'. She was afraid of the negative force within her and that it might destroy her therapist as well. Davidson did not query or try to interpret her client's statements. Instead she acknowledged how terrifying M's experiential reality must be while at the same time assuring her that she as therapist did not feel engulfed by this or left with something destructive. When M came back the following week, she spoke of how valuable the session had been for her. By not denying or attempting to interpret her experienced reality, her therapist had allowed her to work through the experience and to see that her perceived threat of her therapist's annihilation was unfounded. Her experience was hers alone. She could be supported and understood without drawing others into her terrifying world. As can be seen, the kinds of psychotherapy described above work from a set of basic principles rather than rest on specific theoretical propositions. Their application will thus be dependent on the skills and styles of specific individual therapists (and on the particular techniques they use such as gestalt or psychosynthesis).

Like psychoanalytic theories, the concepts and methods of humanistic psychology permeate Euro-American culture. This influence can be seen in the emergence of consciousness-raising groups, assertiveness training, self-help books and the 'new age' movement. Humanistic principles have been applied in many areas of everyday life, in the workplace, in schools, and to facilitate more effective communication in relationships. Rogers himself applied his person-centred approach to such diverse areas as the problems that can arise in marriage (1973), education (1983) and to international relations (1977). Humanistic principles have even been related to the experience of dying. Thus Elizabeth Kubler-Ross (1970) and others have encouraged friends, helpers and relatives of dying persons to adopt a greater openness. Dying people are helped to prepare for and experience their fate ('the final stage of growth', as she calls it) in a more 'authentic' way (in that they can be more genuine and open about what they are experiencing).

Another integral feature of humanistic psychology is an active concern with fostering joy. This may come from the deep and close community of the group and sharing painful and intimate feelings with other members, through heightening sensuous awareness, through the experience of communal celebration, or by quietly promoting a conscious appreciation of life in all its rich and varied forms.

3.4 Current work in the humanistic tradition

In keeping with its key tenet of personal growth, the major impact of humanistic psychology has been on the field of psychotherapy and counselling. Both Rogerian non-directive counselling and also existential psychotherapy, which aims to understand an individual's world view and explore other possible ways of being, are used widely in both Europe and the USA.

The concern with the varied aspects of being a person is evident in the continuing research and theoretical developments in the field. To give a brief taste of the range of these, phenomenologists have been concerned to refine their procedures for exploring and conceptualizing different aspects of a person's subjective experience of the world (Valle, 1998). Existentially-oriented psychotherapists are also exploring further the issue that concerned Frankl – the ways in which we seek existential meaning in life (Wong and Fry, 1998; Reker and Chamberlain, 2000) and how these change as we progress through life (Dittman-Kohli and Westerhof, 2000). Spinelli (1999) has explored the phenomenon of evil. And, in the field of 'transpersonal psychology', Wilber (1995) has theorized about spiritual aspects of being.

One of the most interesting recent exemplars of the humanistic tradition is what is known as **positive psychology**. Although they make no specific acknowledgement of Maslow, positive psychologists take up his emphasis on ways in which psychology might contribute to psychological health. Seligman and Csikszentmihalyi (2000) make clear that the aims of this approach are to use psychology to enhance 'well-being' both at personal and community levels.

As exemplified by Csikszentmihalyi's work on flow mentioned earlier in Section 3.2, the core issue that is being explored in positive psychology is what conditions and experiences make for well-being and happiness.

Positive psychology
An approach to psychology (initiated by Csikszentmihalyi and Seligman) which aims to use psychology to enhance the well-being of both persons and communities.

Mihaly Csikszentmihalyi (pronounced 'chikshentmeehai') researched 'flow' experience and is helping to develop positive psychology

Beyond a certain minimum level, for example, economic growth and personal income do not seem to matter much (Argyle, 1986). Factors that do really seem to make a difference include *temperament* (Diener, 2000), having *good friends* with whom we can express our feelings (Perkins, 1991) and having some form of *religious faith* (Myers, 2001). Other topics being explored by 'positive psychologists' are what constitutes *optimism* and how we can cultivate it (Peterson, 2000) and what is *wisdom* and how it is attained (Baltes and Staudinger, 1998).

The aim of positive psychology, which is to enable people to use psychology themselves to create more fulfilling lives, is very much within the humanistic spirit. However, some of its assumptions rest on a problematic base. One problem is who is to decide what 'well-being' consists of? What people assume well-being to be and the descriptions of it given by participants in the studies may merely reflect prevailing cultural values. The danger here is that, because they have been elicited by research and/or are put forward by psychologists, what are essentially culture-bound beliefs about well-being may come to be regarded as universally applicable without regard for individual and cultural variations.

Summary Section 3

- Core tenets of humanistic psychology are: (1) the significance of conscious subjective experience, (2) that people are capable of autonomy and personal growth and (3) the importance of taking a holistic approach.
- Maslow discusses 'peak experiences' and emphasizes their importance. (An analogous notion is Csikszentmihalyi's description of being in 'flow'.)
- Kelly has provided a way of exploring the *personal constructs* underlying our experience of the world in his repertory grid.
- The *existential perspective* heightens our awareness of our finiteness and capacity for choice.
- Frankl emphasized the human *search for meaning* in life.
- Maslow was interested in the healthy personality and studied those whom he considered to be *self-actualizers.*
- Three key concepts in Rogers' theory of the person are subjective experience, self-actualization and the self.
- By providing non-conditional regard, the aim of *person-centred counselling* is to re-establish congruence in the client's concept of self.
- *Personal autonomy* is best regarded as an emergent process, rather than as a nebulous 'free-will' which is in opposition to determinism.
- The ideas and assumptions of the humanistic tradition underpin a variety of current approaches in psychotherapy and counselling. They have stimulated a range of research on aspects of personal awareness, well-being and personal growth.
- *Positive psychology* has taken up Maslow's challenge of finding ways in which psychology can enhance well-being.

Activity 9.9

Before reading the final section:

1   Go back over the chapter and list:

- Three ways in which the psychoanalytic and humanistic perspectives are similar.

- Three ways in which they are different.

2   Make a note of the different kinds of therapy methods you have encountered in this chapter so far.

These topics are discussed in the next section.

4   On being a person: comparing and contrasting psychoanalysis and humanistic psychology

Now we have examined each perspective, what comparisons and contrasts can we draw between them? One problem in doing this is that they make rather different kinds of contribution so we are not comparing like with like. Psychoanalysis, for example, has a long history and a developed and organized system of psychotherapeutic practice. It offers detailed theories of childhood socialization and of the nature of the psyche. In contrast, humanistic psychology offers a set of broad assumptions and a way of thinking about being a person, and provides an 'umbrella' for a variety of techniques and approaches for achieving personal growth. Also, it is worth bearing in mind that in clinical practice the difference between psychoanalysis and humanistic psychology is often not clear-cut and psychotherapists are quite likely to draw on ideas and techniques from both perspectives.

However, both perspectives offer different models of the person and different ways of bringing about personal change, so they do present some interesting contrasts. In particular, these relate to the questions highlighted in the Introduction about the nature of subjectivity, how far we are autonomous, and whether and how we can change. So these questions will be used as headings to frame brief reviews of the relative positions of the two perspectives. The section will conclude with an evaluation of their contributions and their implications for the study of psychology.

4.1 How can we gain access to subjective experience?

As we have seen, both perspectives focus on subjectivity and the inner world of lived experience but they do this in very different ways. Psychoanalysts focus on the impact of the *unconscious* mind on meanings, motivations, behaviours and conscious experiences. Humanistic psychologists, while not entirely rejecting the relevance of unconscious feelings (see, for example, Rogers' notion of incongruent sources of the sense of self discussed in Section 3.2), primarily focus on the significance of a person's *conscious* feelings and thoughts.

Given this different emphasis, it is not surprising that they use very different kinds of methods to understand the subjective world of their clients. Some of these are used for research but most are applied in the framework of the psychotherapeutic encounter. As we have seen, psychoanalytic techniques include dream analysis, free association, and the analysis of transference and resistance. Another method underpinning psychoanalytic theorizing is what we might call 'imaginative reconstruction'. Thus the experiential world of childhood may be inferred on the basis of adult recollections, behaviour and feelings in the transference relationship with the analyst, or the intrinsic nature of the child's situation.

Humanistic techniques for accessing subjectivity (i.e. unpacking the meanings and feelings that constitute subjective experience) include collecting and analysing accounts (e.g. of peak or flow experiences), analysing lives (e.g. Maslow's study of self-actualizers) and repertory grid analysis. Because of their emphasis on accessing unconscious meanings and the use of clinical evidence, psychoanalytic methods clearly involve interpretation. However, even another person's conscious experience is not out there to 'see'. Accessing it also depends on some (albeit lesser) degree of reconstruction and interpretation.

4.2 Are we determined or autonomous?

Psychoanalysts, as we have seen, start from a position of *psychic determinism* in that they believe that our actions and experiences are governed by unconscious meanings largely laid down in childhood, over which we have little control. In contrast, humanistic psychologists emphasize *autonomy*, the potential for personal growth, and our capacity, at least in part, to create ourselves.

One critical issue here is – what does the idea of autonomy actually mean? It was argued earlier that it does not necessarily imply a notion of 'free-will' which is in opposition to determinism, but can be seen as a function of self-awareness and the capacity to generate new ideas and actions. The debate between the perspectives centres around whether or not self-awareness is something that is directly accessible and unproblematic. How far can we really be aware of the motivations underlying our own actions and consciously direct them? As we have seen, the positions of the two perspectives are quite distinct here. Humanistic psychologists emphasize that, with self-awareness, we can change our lives and ourselves if we choose to do so. Psychoanalysts, in contrast, suggest that what we think of as self-awareness may well be an illusion and they point to how often, when we think we are consciously directing our lives, we return to the same repetitive patterns.

4.3 How can we change? And to what extent can we achieve this?

To help their patients change and develop, psychoanalysts focus on interpretation on the basis of clinical evidence. They then work with the understanding produced by this to try to give patients greater insight into their own unconscious motivations. Their assumption is that doing this will create a climate which will lead to positive change. Techniques used for this process include working through resistances and the analysis of transference. Thus, in psychoanalysis, the analyst plays a crucial role in bringing about change in patients; for the aim of psychoanalytic therapy – to bring unconscious material into conscious awareness – requires the help and skill of the analyst.

In contrast, underpinning the humanistic approach is the central idea that clients, not the therapist, are the primary agents of their own development. As we have seen, humanistic-type methods for facilitating personal change are varied and include encounter groups, gestalt therapy, body-work and psychosynthesis. Other examples are Kelly's fixed role therapy, Roger's person-centred counselling, and existential psychotherapy which is designed to help people consciously explore their ways of being and the meaningfulness of their lives. What they all have in common is a focus on the 'here-and-now', encouraging full awareness of senses and feelings, freedom to use bodily expressions as well as words, and discouraging both interpretation and evaluation. Interventions may be used, but the emphasis is on encouraging clients to make their own choices and to work by themselves at heightening awareness of their feelings. Humanistic methods tend to focus more on current experience of the client in contrast to the psychoanalytic emphasis on the experiences of childhood. In particular, humanistic psychologists deliberately avoid interpretations and explanations for they are likely to be sceptical not only of their validity but also of the idea that providing interpretations to a client, even if they are valid, in itself can produce change.

The psychoanalyst's rejoinder is that humanistic-type psychotherapy is likely to be superficial and changes are short-term; that without full awareness of unconscious motivations and the influence of unconscious residues from childhood, clients may be in no position to make effective choices and change themselves.

As we can see then, the respective therapy methods of the two perspectives reflect the theoretical differences between them. The debate centres on their respective models of the person and their different assumptions about the origins and nature of our actions and feelings, in particular the role of the unconscious and the validity of psychoanalytic interpretations. The humanistic use of the word 'client' in preference to the psychoanalyst's 'patient' (with its connotations of the expertise of medical practice) reflects such different assumptions and approaches.

But to what extent is any form of psychotherapy able to bring about personal change? One problem in assessing this is that, on the whole, both psychoanalysts and humanistic psychologists have been more concerned to develop ideas and methods than formally to evaluate how and to what degree they can produce change. Assessing the efficacy of any psychotherapy is not an easy task. It is not easy, for example, to measure the kind of changes in subjectivity that psychotherapy might be expected to produce. Even clients' own evaluations of this are not necessarily a reliable guide as they will have made a considerable investment of time and money and therefore will want to believe that the psychotherapy has worked. For such reasons, it is difficult for evaluation studies to produce definitive evidence of change (see Fonagy, 2000), which is not to say, of course, that no change takes place.

Spinelli (1994) has also pointed to the fact that there is no empirical evidence that one method of psychotherapy is superior to any other. Drawing on an analysis by Howe (1993), Spinelli argues that the most potent aspect of psychotherapy is not the particular form that it takes, but instead it is having a therapist (or group) who accepts, understands and enables clients to talk about their most intimate feelings. Yalom (1998) agrees, but adds that the open expression of emotion is also vital.

4.4 Psychoanalysis and humanistic psychology: contributions and implications for psychology

Psychoanalysis claims to make two quite distinct contributions to psychology. It offers (1) a detailed theory of the human condition and (2) a clinical method – a set of concepts and methods for penetrating to the unconscious meanings underlying subjective experience. Such claims have attracted considerably more attention to psychoanalysis compared with humanistic psychology for the latter does not attempt to provide, as psychoanalysis does, a comprehensive theory of why we are as we are. Rather it focuses largely on providing ideas (e.g. peak experience, personal growth) and methods (e.g. non-directive counselling) which are intended to heighten our awareness of what it regards as key aspects of the human condition and of our potentialities. The value of these largely rests on appeal to experience and whether or not they help people in living their lives. For such reasons, while humanistic ideas and assumptions have also been assimilated in both psychotherapeutic practice and in everyday life, they have not been exposed to the same rigorous critique.

Psychoanalysis has attracted both ardent adherents and vociferous critics. On the one hand, there are assertions of its intrinsic value in illuminating aspects of life and culture (see Elliott, 1998) and creative attempts to reconceptualize its ideas in the light of other perspectives (see Billig, 1999). On the other, there have been attacks on the validity of its central ideas (Webster, 1995; MacMillan, 1997), its 'pseudoscientific nature' (Cioffi, 1998; Crews, 1998), and the institutional control over what ideas are deemed acceptable (Malcolm, 1997).

There is quite a bit of empirical support from experiments, observational and cross-cultural studies in support of several psychoanalytic ideas (for a brief review of these see Stevens, 1983), and we saw some examples of these in Section 2. Nevertheless, it is perhaps psychoanalysis' status as a set of theoretical propositions that has been most vulnerable to attack. Thus Eysenck (1985) has criticized the unscientific nature of psychoanalysis, in particular because psychoanalytic propositions are difficult to convert into an operational and testable form. A concept like repression, for example, can really be defined only by reference to unobservable things such as *id*, *ego*, and *superego* and the idea of the unconscious. However such criticisms, whether directed at psychoanalysis or at humanistic psychology, do not take into account the nature of the subject matter with which they both deal – subjectivity. By their very nature, neither conscious experience nor unconscious meanings are easily open to external test for they can only be accessed through *some* form of interpretation.

To understand the subjectivity of another human, it might be argued, is a different kind of enterprise from the scientific study of the natural world and requires a different form of epistemology. Both psychoanalysis and humanistic psychology offer opportunities for personal exploration and ways of understanding ourselves. It may be argued that it is best to regard psychoanalytic practice as an art, and much of humanistic psychology as a form of personal philosophy. But to reject them because they are not strictly speaking 'scientific' would be to exclude subjectivity and the core of personal existence from the remit of psychology.

Both psychoanalytic and humanistic perspectives stimulate our thinking about what it is to be a person. They emphasize the role of meanings in constituting what we are. They offer us tools for personal change and increasing self-understanding. The existential position of humanistic psychology also raises the question of the openness of existence and the part we ourselves play in creating what we are. In such ways, these perspectives pose important questions for the goals of psychology. They move psychology beyond a determinist form of science and causal explanations of behaviour to encompass subjectivity and the philosophical and moral implications of what we might become.

Summary Section 4

- Psychoanalysis and humanistic psychology differ in terms of their respective emphases on unconscious motivation and on conscious awareness and choice, and on their views of the value of interpretation.
- The perspectives also differ in terms of the methods used for both accessing subjectivity and facilitating personal change, and how they see the role of therapist and patients.
- Both psychoanalysis and humanistic psychology offer a means of exploring subjectivity and personal change, and stimulate our thinking about what it is to be a person and how to live our lives.

Further reading

Psychoanalysis

Casement, P. (1990) *Further Learning From the Patient*, London, Routledge. By a practising analyst, this book gives an excellent sense of the process of psychoanalytic therapy.

Frosh, S. (1997) *For and Against Psychoanalysis*, London, Routledge. Not always easy reading, but provides a good evaluation of psychoanalysis (both theory and therapy) from a sympathetic but relatively detached viewpoint.

Masson, J. (1992) *Final Analysis*, London, Fontana. Very readable and personal (if controversial) account of what it is like to train as and become a psychoanalyst.

Stevens, R. (1983) *Freud and Psychoanalysis: An Exposition and Evaluation*, Buckingham, Open University Press.
A readable introduction to Freud and psychoanalytic theory with a good evaluation which includes a comprehensive review of scientific tests of psychoanalytic hypotheses.

Humanistic psychology
Rogers, C. (1973) *Encounter Groups,* Harmondsworth, Penguin.
A readable, classic description and evaluation of encounter groups and more generally of Rogers' approach.

Rowan, J. (2001) *Ordinary Ecstasy: The Dialectics of Humanistic Psychology* (3rd edn), London, Brunner-Routledge.
A personal view of humanistic psychology but with much interesting and relevant material.

Spinelli, E. (1997*) Tales of Unknowing: Therapeutic Encounters from an Existential Perspective*, London, Duckworth.
Very readable and gives excellent insights into the process of existential therapy.

References

Aanstoos, C.M. (1987) 'A descriptive phenomenology of the experience of being left out', in van Zuuren, F.J., Wertz, F.J. and Mook, B. (eds) *Advances in Qualitative Psychology: Themes and Variations*, Berwyn, PA, Swets North America.

Adorno, T.W., Frenkel-Brunswik, E., Levinson D.J. and Nevitt Sanford, R. (1950) *The Authoritarian Personality*, New York, Harper and Row.

Andersen, S.M. and Miranda, R. (2000) 'Transference: how past relationships emerge in the present', *The Psychologist*, vol. 13, no.12, pp.608–9.

Argyle, M. (1986) *The Psychology of Happiness*, London, Methuen.

Baltes, P.B. and Staudinger, U.M. (1998) 'Wisdom', in Friedman, H. (ed.) *Encyclopedia of Mental Health, Volume 3*, San Diego, CA, Academic Press.

Becker, C.S. (1987) 'Friendship between women: a phenomenological study of best friends', *Journal of Phenomenological Psychology*, vol.18, no.1, pp.59–72.

Becker, C.S. (1992) *Living and Relating: An Introduction to Phenomenology,* London, Sage.

Bettleheim, B. (1976) *The Uses of Enchantment: The Meaning and Importance of Fairy Tales*, London, Thames and Hudson.

Billig, M. (1999) *Freudian Repression: Conversation Creating the Unconscious*, Cambridge, Cambridge University Press.

Bowlby, J. (1971) *Attachment*, Harmondsworth, Penguin.

Bowlby, J. (1979) *Making and Breaking of Affectional Bonds*, London, Tavistock.

Breger, L., Hunter, I. and Lane, R.W. (1971) 'The effect of stress on dreams', *Psychological Issues,* vol.7, Monograph 27.

Brenneis, C.B. (1970) 'Male and female ego modalities in manifest dream content', *Journal of Abnormal Psychology*, vol.76, pp.434–42.

Brenner, C. (1969) 'Dreams in clinical psychoanalytic practice', *Journal of Nervous and Mental Diseases*, vol.149, pp.122–32.

Breuer, J. and Freud, S. (1895/1991) *Studies in Hysteria*, London, Penguin.

Brewin, C. and Andrews, B. (2000) 'Psychological defence mechanisms: the example of repression', *The Psychologist*, vol.13, no.12, pp.615–7.

Casement, P. (1990) *Further Learning from the Patient*, London, Routledge.

Chasseguet-Smirgel, J. (1985) *Creativity and Perversion*, London, Free Association Books.

Chen, S. and Andersen, S.M. (1999) 'Relationships form the past in the present: significant-other representations and transference in interpersonal life', in Zanna, M.P. (ed.) *Advances in Experimental Social Psychology, Volume 30*, San Diego, CA, Academic Press.

Chodorow, N. (1978) *The Reproduction of Mothering: Psychoanalysis and the Sociology of Gender*, Berkeley, CA, University of California Press.

Cioffi, F. (1998) *Freud and the Question of Pseudoscience*, Chicago, Open Court.

Crews, F. (1998) *Unauthorized Freud*, New York, Viking.

Csikszentmihalyi, M. (1992) *Flow: The Psychology of Happiness*, London, Rider Press.

de Monchaux, C. (1978) 'Dreaming and the organizing function of the ego', *International Journal of Psychoanalysis*, vol.59, pp.443–53.

Darwin, C. (1859) *On the Origin of Species*, London, Murray.

Davidson, S. (2001) 'An existential approach to working with a client labelled as schizophrenic' (unpublished personal communication).

Diener, E. (2000) 'Subjective well-being: the science of happiness and a proposal for a national index', *American Psychologist,* vol.55, pp.34–43.

Dittman-Kohli and Westerhof, G.J. (2000) 'The personal meaning system in a life-span perspective', in Reker, G.T. and Chamberlain, K. (eds).

Elliott, A. (ed.) (1998) *Freud 2000,* Oxford, Polity.

Erikson, E.H. (1950) *Childhood and Society*, New York, Norton.

Erikson, E.H. (1959) *Young Man Luther: A Study in Psychoanalysis and History*, London, Faber.

Erikson, E.H. (1969) *Gandhi's Truth*, London, Faber.

Eysenck, H.J. (1985) *Decline and Fall of the Freudian Empire*, Harmondsworth, Viking.

Fischer, C.T. and Wertz, F. (1979) 'Empirical phenomenological analyses of being criminally victimized', in Giorgi, A., Knowles, R. and Smith, D.L. (eds) *Duquesne Studies in Phenomenological Psychology*, Pittsburgh, Duquesne University Press.

Fisher, S. and Greenberg, R.P. (1977) *The Scientific Credibility of Freud's Theories and Therapy*, Hassocks, Harvester Press.

Fonagy, P. (2000) 'The outcome of psychoanalysis: the hope of a future', *The Psychologist*, vol.13, no.12, pp.620–3.

Frankl, V.E. (1959) *Man's Search for Meaning: An Introduction to Logotherapy*, Boston, Beacon Press.

Freud, A. (1936) *The Ego and the Mechanisms of Defence*, London, Hogarth Press.

Freud, S. (1900/1991) *The Interpretation of Dreams*, Penguin Freud Library, Volume 4, London, Penguin.

Freud, S. (1901/1991) *The Psychopathology of Everyday Life*, Penguin Freud Library, Volume 5, London, Penguin.

Freud, S. (1905/1991) 'Three Essays on the Theory of Sexuality', in *On Sexuality*, Penguin Freud Library, Volume 7, London, Penguin.

Freud, S. (1908/1991) 'Character and anal erotism', in *On Sexuality*, Penguin Freud Library, Volume 7, London, Penguin.

Freud, S. (1923/1991) 'The ego and the id', in Freud, S. *On Metapsychology: The Theory of Psycholoanalysis*, Penguin Freud Library, Volume 11, London, Penguin.

Freud, S. (1930/1991) 'Civilization and its discontents', in Freud, S. *Civilization, Society and Religion*, Penguin Freud Library, Volume 12, London, Penguin.

Goldstein, K. (1939) *The Organism*, New York, Van Nostrand.

Gomez, L. (1997) *An Introduction to Object Relations*, London, Free Association Books.

Greenson, R.R. (1970) 'The exceptional position of the dream in psychoanalytic practice', *The Psychoanalytic Quarterly*, vol.3, pp.519–49.

Grimm, J. and Grimm, W. (1968) *Fairy Tales*, London, Hamlyn.

Hall, C.S. and Van de Castle, R.L. (1965) 'An empirical investigation of the castration complex in dreams', *Journal of Personality*, vol.33, pp.20–9.

Hall, C.S. and Van de Castle, R.L. (1966) *The Content Analysis of Dreams*, New York, Appleton-Century-Crofts.

Howe, D. (1993) *On Being a Client: Understanding the Processes of Counselling and Psychotherapy*, London, Sage.

Irigaray, L. (1985) *This Sex Which is Not One*, Ithaca, NY, Cornell University Press

Kelly, G.A. (1955a) *The Psychology of Personal Constructs, Volume 1*, New York, Norton.

Kelly, G.A. (1955b) *The Psychology of Personal Constructs, Volume 2*, New York, Norton.

Klein, M. (1975) *Love, Guilt and Reparation*, London, Hogarth Press.

Kubler-Ross, E. (1970) *On Death and Dying*, London, Tavistock

MacMillan, M. (1997) *Freud Evaluated*, Cambridge, MA, MIT Press.

Malcolm, J. (1997) *In the Freud Archives* (2nd edn), New York, Knopf.

Marcus, L. (ed) (1999) *Sigmund Freud's The Interpretation of Dreams: New Interdisciplinary Essays*, Manchester, Manchester University Press.

Maslow, A.H. (1973) *The Farther Reaches of Human Nature*, Harmondsworth, Penguin.

Maslow, A.H. (1987) *Motivation and Personality* (3rd edn), New York, Harper and Row.

Masson, J. M. (1984) *The Assault on Truth: Freud's Suppression of the Seduction Theory*, London, Faber and Faber.

May, R. (1958) 'Contributions of existential psychotherapy', in May, R. Angel, E. and Ellenberger, H.F. (eds) *Existence*, New York, Basic Books.

Myers, D.G. (2001) *The American Paradox: Spiritual Hunger in an Age of Plenty*, New Haven, CT, Yale University Press.

Myers, L.B. and Brewin, C.R. (1994) 'Recall of early experience and the repressive coping style', *Journal of Abnormal Psychology,* vol.107, pp.14–48.

Palaian, S. (1993) 'The experience of longing: a phenomenological investigation', *Dissertation Abstracts International*, 54, 1678B.

Panksepp, J. (1999) *Affective Neuroscience: The Foundations of Human and Animal Emotions*, Oxford, Oxford University Press.

Perkins, H.W. (1991) 'Religious commitment, yuppie values, and well-being in post-collegiate life', *Review of Religious Research*, vol.32, pp.244–51.

Peterson C. (2000) 'The future of optimism', *American Psychologist,* vol.55, pp.44–55.

Reason, J. (2000) 'The Freudian slip revisited', *The Psychologist*, vol.13, no.12, pp.610–11.

Reik, T. (1948) *Listening with the Third Ear*, New York, Farrar, Straus and Co.

Reker, G.T. and Chamberlain, K. (2000) (eds) *Exploring Existential Meaning: Optimizing Human Development Across the Life Span*, Thousand Oaks, CA, Sage.

Rogers, C.R. (1961) *On Becoming a Person: A Therapist's View of Psychotherapy*, London, Constable.

Rogers, C.R. (1970) *Encounter Groups*, Harmondsworth, Penguin.

Rogers, C.R. (1973) *Becoming Partners: Marriage and its Alternatives*, London, Constable.

Rogers, C.R. (1977) *On Personal Power: Inner Strength and its Revolutionary Impact*, New York, Delacorte Press.

Rogers, C.R. (1983) *Freedom to Learn for the 80's*, Columbus, Merrill.

Rogers, C.R. and Stevens, B. (1973) *Person to Person*, London, Souvenir Press.

Roth, I. (ed.) (1990) *Introduction to Psychology, Volume 1*, East Sussex, Lawrence Erlbaum Associates/The Open University.

Seligman, M.P. and Csikszentmihalyi, M. (2000) 'Positive psychology: an introduction', *American Psychologist,* vol.55, no.1, pp.5–14.

Shaffer, J.B.P. (1978) *Humanistic Psychology*, Englewood Cliffs, NJ, Prentice Hall.

Solms, M. (2000) 'Freudian dream theory today', *The Psychologist*, vol.13, no.12, pp.615–7.

Spinelli, E. (1994) *Demystifying Therapy*, London, Constable.

Spinelli, E. (1999) 'Everything is broken', Inaugural professorial lecture, London, Regent's College.

Stevens, R. (1983) *Freud and Psychoanalysis: An Exposition and Appraisal*, Milton Keynes, The Open University Press.

Trumbull, M. (1993) 'The experience of undergoing coronary artery bypass surgery: a phenomenological investigation', *Dissertation Abstracts International*, 54, 1115B.

Underwood, G. (1996) (ed.) *Implicit Cognition*, Oxford, Oxford University Press.

Valle, R.S. (1998) (ed.) *Phenomenological Inquiry in Psychology: Existential and Transpersonal Dimensions*, New York, Plenum Press.

Webster, R. (1995) *Why Freud Was Wrong: Sin, Science and Psychoanalysis*, London, HarperCollins.

Wilber, K. (1995) *Sex, Ecology and Spirituality: The Spirit of Evolution*, London, Shambhala.

Wong, P.T.P. and Fry, P.S. (1998) *The Human Quest For Meaning*, Mahway, NJ, Erlbaum.

Yalom, I.D. (1998) *The Yalom Reader: Selections from the Work of a Master Therapist and Storyteller*, New York, Basic Books.

Yoder, P. (1990) 'Guilt, the feeling and the force: a phenomenological study of the experience of feeling guilty', *Dissertation Abstracts International*, 50, 5341B.

■ Commentary 9: Person psychology: psychoanalytic and humanistic perspectives

This final chapter brings us back to the questions 'Who am I?' and 'What is it that makes us unique individuals?' with which we started the book (in Chapter 1, 'Identities and diversities'). However, you will understand by now that different psychologists approach issues in very different ways, and the chapter you have just read introduces two further perspectives that psychologists use to address questions of what makes us who we are.

Theory

1 Both psychoanalytic and humanistic perspectives have influenced how we think about ourselves in Western cultures. These perspectives have, to some extent, been marginalized within academic psychology, although they each have an active following within their communities outside mainstream psychology.

2 Psychoanalytic and humanistic psychology are conflicting perspectives. Although they have some similarities, their basic assumptions cannot be reconciled.

Methods

3 Both perspectives involve methods that were unusual in psychology when they were introduced, and hence were criticized. Now their methods are more widely used.

4 Both psychoanalytic and humanistic psychology have a holistic approach focusing on individuals and their experience of their lives and who they are. Each, therefore, makes central the analysis of inner experience using people's own accounts.

5 The humanistic perspective privileges the insider viewpoint, believing people's own accounts of their subjectivity to be unproblematic. The psychoanalytic perspective moves between an insider viewpoint and the outsider viewpoint of the interpreting psychoanalyst.

Themes

6 Because psychoanalytic and humanistic psychology have different models of what it is to be a person, they take different positions on fixity and the possibility of change; and they produce different ideas about what forms of therapy are most appropriate.

■ Thinking about theory

Popular culture is influenced by psychoanalytic and humanistic ideas
Both psychoanalytic and humanistic perspectives have had major influences beyond psychology, so that terms like 'the unconscious' (Sigmund Freud) and 'personal growth' (Carl Rogers) are commonly used in everyday talk. This influence is more profound than just the introduction of new words, for in Western cultures it is widely accepted that we all have complex, conflicted, partially unconscious psychological lives that, with help, we may be able to change in order to improve our psychological functioning. Such ideas, and others that take for granted the importance of early experience, such as relationships with carers and developing sexuality, are not simply 'facts' about psychological life. Instead, they have entered popular culture from the theories developed by psychoanalysts. This takes us back to one of the ideas presented in the introductory chapter – that psychological ideas enter popular culture, although often the origins of the ideas have become obscured and forgotten.

Given the ubiquity and influence in popular culture of ideas that originate in psychoanalysis and also, to some extent, humanistic psychology, it is paradoxical that these perspectives have been largely neglected in most psychology departments in the UK and the USA. However, some of the basic ideas of psychoanalysis can be seen in slightly different forms in well-established areas of psychology. For example, in Chapter 7 ('Perceiving and understanding in the social world'), you saw evidence of the automaticity of everyday life – that much of our information processing and decision making (our choosing what to do) takes place below conscious awareness and is influenced by our motivations. Also, you may remember from Chapter 8 ('Memory: structures, processes and skills'), the term 'procedural memory' – used for memories that are difficult to describe because they are not accessible to conscious examination. It was also suggested in that chapter that the memory strategies used by people with exceptional memories may simply not be accessible to them. It would certainly not be accurate to suggest that researchers in social cognition and memory who use such ideas would see themselves as influenced by psychoanalytic psychology. But these ideas about processes 'below conscious awareness', and yet often affected by motivations and meanings, can certainly be seen as complementary with the psychoanalytic perspective.

Conflicting perspectives
In Commentary 3 we alerted you to the possibility of different relationships existing between perspectives and suggested three ways of thinking about this. Perspectives can be complementary, conflicting or coexisting.

Although the two perspectives described in this chapter, psychoanalysis and humanistic psychology, have some areas of overlap, they are fundamentally in conflict. It is not possible to espouse both of them because they have different underlying premises. Humanistic psychology began as a conscious reaction against behaviourism because the latter disregarded subjective experience, but it was also a reaction against psychoanalysis because psychoanalysis questions the validity of self-awareness and what appear to be conscious choices. Humanistic psychologists question the validity of psychoanalytic interpretations and believe that this therapeutic process takes away control from the client and gives too much power to the therapist.

The nub of the conflict between the two perspectives lies in their views of the unconscious and conscious awareness. For humanistic psychologists, access to subjectivity – via what is consciously experienced and can be reported on – is relatively unproblematic. And what is experienced consciously is assumed to be available for rational choices and personal agency. For psychoanalysts, conscious experience is always partial at best and often distorted. Furthermore, the unconscious is seen as the source of motivation – most of what drives us is located in the unconscious and most of the choices we make are driven by needs of which we are unaware, rather than being the result of informed and conscious deliberation. With this level of difference, it is not possible to reconcile the two perspectives.

Applying psychological knowledge

Both psychoanalysis and humanistic psychology have the explicit aim of improving people's psychological functioning and changing their lives for the better through therapy. However, the chapter you have just read clearly shows that different theories can lead to different ways of effecting change. Humanistic psychologists consider that conscious awareness is central to people's ability to achieve personal growth, whilst psychoanalysts focus on bringing aspects of the unconscious into consciousness so as to reach some understanding of unconscious processes and their influence on our lives.

It is sometimes possible to evaluate conflicting perspectives by comparing the usefulness of their applications. So can we evaluate psychoanalysis and humanistic psychology through the efficacy of their therapies? Unfortunately this is not possible. The evaluation of therapies – outcome research – is extremely difficult to carry out. One reason is that it is hard to define successful outcomes. Another is that, in many respects, different therapies are not comparable. For example, they attract different kinds of patients. And what actually happens in therapy is often not accessible to scrutiny. This is not to say that there is no evidence for the efficacy of the therapies – outcome research has demonstrated gains in psychological well-being but, in the main, these do not differentiate between therapies.

■ Thinking about methods

Unusual and contested methodology

As we saw in Chapter 9, psychoanalytic and humanistic ideas have been less influential within psychology than might be expected given their influence on culture in general. This is partly because the account-based methods they use are very different from the experimental methods that have been most influential within psychology. For this reason the two perspectives have been subjected to much methodological criticism. However, as we have seen, the range of psychological methods has proliferated in recent years and, for example, there are now psychologists outside psychoanalysis who use psychoanalytic ideas and methods in their research. And the same holds for humanistic psychology. This eclecticism and cross-fertilization has helped to maintain psychology's social relevance and its cutting edge as a discipline.

Insider and outsider viewpoints

Both psychoanalytic and humanistic psychology are concerned with 'whole people', rather than with studying psychological 'processes'. The only other place in the book where this approach has been central is in Chapter 1 ('Identities and diversities'). The holistic approach of both psychoanalytic and humanistic psychology focuses on 'subjectivity', which is concerned with exploring reflexivity – the ways in which we reflect on, and experience ourselves, our relationships, our lives and our worlds. These insider viewpoints of participants in research or patients/clients in therapy are, therefore, central to psychoanalytic and humanistic psychology. However, both perspectives use these insider viewpoints as a means of gaining insights that can then be analysed by researchers or therapists. The use of insights from outsider viewpoints is, therefore, also important to both humanistic and psychoanalytic psychology.

As far as therapy is concerned, however, there is a difference in emphasis between the two perspectives on insider versus outsider viewpoints. Humanistic therapists use clients' verbal accounts of their inner experiences to focus on understanding their subjectivity – 'privileging' what the client says and the client's reported versions of the world. For the most part, this insider viewpoint is maintained. Humanistic therapists do not step back into the outsider viewpoint, making their own interpretations, as they would distrust the relevance and validity of this. Instead, they encourage their clients to make their own choices and to work towards becoming more aware of their own feelings. Psychoanalysts, on the other hand, use a variety of data as well as insider accounts, as the chapter has shown. They listen to accounts of their patients' inner experiences, such as memories of childhood experiences, and of the 'here and now'. But they also use (often incomplete) verbal reports such as free associations; dreams; neurotic symptoms and slips of action; behaviour in the consulting room; transferences and countertransferences (the effects patients have on them as the therapist). Whilst psychoanalysts do take an insider viewpoint on all of these data, trying to understand from the point of view of the patient, they *also* stand back and take an outsider position. It is from this outsider, 'expert' position that they offer interpretations to help the patients understand their unconscious motivations.

■ Thinking about themes

Fixity and change

As we have seen, both psychoanalytic and humanistic psychology use therapy and/or self-reflection and personal agency to foster change in order to make people more psychologically healthy. Neither theory, therefore, sees people as fixed or determined. Humanistic psychology views biology as influencing (rather than determining) human psychology, and previous experience as also helping to shape behaviour. Whilst accepting such influences, humanistic psychologists place great emphasis on our capacity as humans to change ourselves, and our circumstances, as a result of conscious reflection and autonomous choice. For psychoanalytic psychology, biological drives and early childhood experiences are particularly important in producing what we become. And because these forces exert their influence at the unconscious level they are all the more difficult to change or moderate. However, psychoanalytic therapy is about bringing unconscious motivations and conflicts into consciousness with the help of another person – the analyst. Once this happens, reflection by the patient, and reflection and interpretation by the analyst, can help to promote change. This is a rather different position on fixity and change. Change is seen as more problematic. The assumption is that much of what we do is determined by unconscious forces and most of our choices are made without awareness. Change is possible but is won with difficulty and requires the help of another person.

■ Epilogue

Now that you have read all the chapters and commentaries in Book 1, you have encountered many perspectives, theories, methods and themes. This final reflection aims to bring together some of these ideas. It will highlight material you have already met that shows how psychology is a plural discipline where progress depends, in part, on engaging in internal debate. The epilogue makes three main points:

Theory

1   Psychology is characterized by multiple perspectives. Some of these are complementary, some conflict with each other and others coexist (the three Cs).

Methods

2   Psychology is a multi-method enterprise into which new methods continue to be incorporated.

Themes

3   Three pervasive psychological themes emerge from the chapters in this book: What makes us distinctively ourselves in relation to other humans and what makes us, as humans, different from other animals? To what extent are our characteristics fixed or capable of flexibility, being able to adapt and change in response to our environments? In what ways are we the products of nature *and* nurture? The commentaries have all indicated that it is too simplistic to view such questions in terms of dichotomies. Rather than seeing these as 'either/or' choices, the commentaries have argued for the value of a 'both ... and' approach that recognizes complex interactions.

■ Thinking about theory

Beginning to map the discipline of psychology

In this book you have met a variety of psychological perspectives, each with its own assumptions about its subject matter, about legitimate data and about methods. Each perspective produces many theories. It is clear, therefore, that psychology is a multifaceted discipline. What are these perspectives you have met already? We would like to identify 11, some of which cut across the chapters of the book (see Table 1). These perspectives have been developed to different extents in this introductory book.

Table I   The perspectives and the chapters that include them

Social constructionist (Chapter 1)

Experimental social psychology (Chapter 1; Chapter 7)

Psychoanalytic (Chapter 1; Chapter 9)

Evolutionary psychology (Chapter 2)

Biological psychology (Chapter 2; Chapter 4; Chapter 5; Chapter 6)

Behaviourism (Chapter 3)

Sociocultural psychology (Chapter 3)

Cognitive psychology (Chapter 3; Chapter 6; Chapter 7; Chapter 8)

Neuropsychology (Chapter 4; Chapter 6; Chapter 8)

Psychometrics and individual differences (Chapter 5)

Humanistic psychology (Chapter 9)

Note: Developmental psychology has not been covered yet, but is discussed in Book 2 and, more comprehensively, in other Open University courses.

Together, these perspectives comprise most of the major features on the map of psychology that you have begun to draw. Our map of psychology is different from what you might find in many other courses where perspectives are grouped together into broad categories, frequently reflecting the history of psychology or the topic of study. For example, you will often find that experimental social psychology, social constructionist and sociocultural approaches are grouped together into a superordinate category of 'social psychology'. And you might well find parts of evolutionary psychology grouped with some comparative and neuropsychological approaches under the heading 'biological psychology'. Research on perception, attention, and memory (including neuropsychological approaches to studying these) are often grouped together as 'cognitive psychology'. Psychometrics and individual differences might be referred to as 'individual differences' or as 'personality'. And often a grouping called 'personality' or 'person psychology' places psychometric trait theories alongside humanistic psychology and psychoanalytic psychology.

We have chosen to disrupt these common groupings and instead to interleave chapters from different traditions. We have done this because, as we identified earlier in this book, the way in which we organize issues affects how we view them. Arranging chapters into the different groupings of biological, cognitive, social, etc. often masks similarities of approach (e.g. the use of the experimental method) and of the questions asked across these different groupings. The more commonly found psychological *topics* also often give a false sense that psychological issues arising from the same traditions necessarily share the same methodological approaches. For example, as you have seen, while all the areas included under the umbrella of cognitive psychology have common roots, they use methods ranging from introspection, through diary studies to experiments – the most favoured cognitive psychological method (e.g. see Chapter 8). Similarly, some social psychology focuses on naturally occurring language, while some uses experiments. Experimental social psychology thus uses some of the methodology developed within cognitive psychology, whilst social constructionist approaches use very different methods.

As we explained in the introductory chapter, the organization of the book is designed to introduce psychological traditions while making visible both similarities and differences in current approaches to psychology. We have placed side by side perspectives that use very different methods (as, for example, in Chapters 1 and 2); and we have also placed side by side chapters where similar methods are used for different purposes (as in Chapters 6 and 7). We hope that this has helped you to begin to map the range of methods in psychology and to gain a sense of how particular methods are designed so as to address specific types of question. We also hope that it helps you to see some ways in which methods are not confined to the perspectives in which they are most commonly used.

Complementary, conflicting and coexisting theories: the three Cs
These three ways of relating (complementary, conflicting and coexisting) apply at the level of perspectives and also at the level of theories within perspectives. For example, the individual differences view of personality presented in Chapter 5 is a perspective unified by its methodological approach, its belief in the consistency and stability of personality, and by debates about the structure of personality and the extent to which it is inherited or environmentally determined. But, for example, there is not just one trait theory of the structure of personality. You saw that the individual differences perspective has given rise to four theories – aspects of which are coexisting and aspects of which conflict. Where theories within perspectives conflict, it is a matter of doing further research to clarify which, if any, gain support.

We have seen that often there are quite different ways of looking at a topic, of explaining it and even applying its findings, and that these differences seem just to *coexist*. As in many other areas of study, there is a tendency for psychologists to remain within their perspective(s) and fail to communicate with those who work in other perspectives. One example of this is the sidelining of psychoanalysis for decades. Even now, whilst it is possible to see the potential cross-fertilization and even complementarity between this perspective and – say – aspects of cognitive psychology, ther is very little contact between the two. Another example is the coexistence of the three different approaches to learning you saw in Chapter 3 (behaviourist, cognitive and sociocultural) that offered very different kinds of insights into the processes of learning.

Another useful way to think about some instances of complementary and coexisting relationships between perspectives is in terms of *levels of analysis*. For example, you saw that biological explanations of depression might be seen just to coexist with social accounts of depression. But these descriptions and explanations (biological and social) consider the phenomena of depression at different levels of analysis. The different explanations, at different levels of analysis, can be placed in a complementary relationship that enriches understanding overall. For example, the biological basis of personality and psychometric trait theories of personality structure, which are explanations at different levels of analysis, can be thought of as complementary and mutually enriching.

Perspectives can conflict, as we saw in the final chapter with psychoanalytic and humanistic psychology. It becomes clear from an examination of these two perspectives that they produce different models of 'what people are like' and so have different implications for how people experiencing psychological distress might best be helped. Perspectives can also conflict because of their underlying assumptions about 'how to do psychology' and about 'what data are legitimate'. These conflicts, for example between experimental social psychology and social constructionism, in turn usually depend on assumptions and beliefs about what the subject matter of psychology *should* be. You will meet examples of this kind of conflict in Book 2 of the course (*Challenging Psychological Issues*).

Don't worry if you do not yet feel entirely comfortable with the idea of the 'three Cs'. Book 2 takes forward these ideas by presenting different perspectives and their associated theories on different topics. It thus builds up the notion that psychology is a diverse discipline that seeks progressively to solve puzzles about what it is to be human as well as dilemmas produced by conflicting evidence from psychological research. As you work through Book 2, these ideas will become clearer.

■ Thinking about methods

Psychology as a methodologically informed discipline

As well as having encountered a range of perspectives, you have also encountered a variety of methods. This is not surprising since different perspectives use different methods. Part of what keeps psychology vibrant is its ability to advance by incorporating new ways of thinking and new methodologies and hence to be a multi-method enterprise. For example, neuropsychological techniques involving brain imaging quickly became established within psychology at the end of the twentieth century as technological developments opened exciting new research possibilities.

The mapping of the human genome at the beginning of the twenty-first century is also likely to have a major impact on psychology. The potential for new insights is also opened up in psychology by new ways of thinking about and using old research methods. Thus, psychoanalytic methods of free association (now almost a century old) have become more popular and generated new methods. A renewed focus within psychology on studying everyday life has also generated new approaches. For example, the focus on how we all use language in our everyday interactions (Chapter 1) and the errors we commonly make and accidents we have as we perceive the world (Chapter 6) have all generated fruitful and exciting lines of research. Qualitative methods have been developed and refined so that there are now interesting and rigorous ways of exploring subjectivity. This diversity means that while the experimental hypothetico-deductive method is longstanding and continues to be a major psychological method, other methods now coexist with, or complement it.

■ Thinking about themes

As well as mapping most of the major perspectives in psychology and their associated methods, this book has also mapped three themes that underpin thinking about psychological issues. These have been addressed in the nine commentaries. The first theme concerns what makes us distinctively ourselves in comparison with other humans; and what makes us different from other animals. The second is whether we should see people and non-human animals as relatively fixed or as essentially flexible, with the capacity to adapt to circumstances and to develop and change. The third concerns the ways in which we are the products of both nature *and* nurture.

What makes us distinctively ourselves in comparison with other humans?

In this book you have met two ways of addressing this question. The psychosocial and social constructionist perspectives on the study of identity, and both the psychoanalytic and humanistic perspectives on subjectivity, approach this question holistically and primarily use accounts of inner experiences (mostly from an insider viewpoint) and/or symbolic data as their evidence. In contrast, the theories of personality from within the psychometric perspective focus on aspects of people, rather than taking a holistic approach. This involves a nomothetic stance, from an outsider perspective, that is concerned with generalizations about personality structure and often a search for the causes of personality. Whilst individuals can be placed at different positions on personality dimensions, the underlying intent is to map the dimensions that apply similarly to everybody, rather than to represent the ways in which we are all unique.

What makes us different from other animals?

Within Chapter 3, different views on whether or not we are like other animals are presented. For example, the comparative approach draws parallels between human and non-human animal learning using the behaviourist perspective. This comparative approach also underpins Chapter 2 and Chapter 4. The sociocultural perspective in Chapter 3 emphasises the cultural basis of humanness. The notion of situated learning emphasizes interactions between *people* sharing complex systems of meaning and communications. But the use of primitive tools and the sharing of information about tool use can also be observed in primates (as discussed in Chapter 2). It has gradually come to be recognized that it is more difficult than psychologists at first thought to be certain what differentiates human and non-human primates. This is, therefore, a theme that will continue to exercise psychologists.

Fixity and change

It is important to note here that, whilst psychological debates are often presented as dichotomies (fixity *versus* change, nature *versus* nurture), this kind of oversimplification can be dangerous. Such factors are not independent – they operate in interactive ways and therefore these should be seen as 'both ... and' rather than as 'either/or' choices.

We have also seen that issues concerning fixity and change are relevant virtually across the board in psychology – although they appear in somewhat different forms. For example, change can be thought of as the unfolding developmental sequence that applies to biological growth from the zygote to an adult human, and also as the process of psychological development – as seen in the discussion of psychosexual stages in Chapter 9. These themes are taken forward in Chapter 1 of Book 2, on 'Lifespan development'.

Evolutionary psychology and biological psychology help to illuminate the importance of both flexibility and stability for human survival. For example, animals have to be sufficiently flexible to make the changes necessary to adapt to their environments if they are to survive, and a degree of plasticity allows animals to reconstruct their memories and skills following brain damage (Chapter 8). At the same time, all biological systems also need stability for survival as, for example, in the biological notion of homeostasis (Chapter 4).

The kinds of change that underpin evolutionary psychology are profoundly different from the kind of changeability you read about in Chapter 1 and in the chapter on learning (Chapter 3). In Chapter 1, how to think about changes in identity over the lifespan was an issue for all the perspectives discussed. But there was a sense in which these changes were either developmental – unfolding in response to environments and life events – and/or consciously and actively pursued. Psychologists studying learning are often concerned with deliberately sought changes within a lifetime. Indeed, humans sometimes consciously choose to make substantial changes in themselves and their lives by seeking therapeutic help (Chapter 9). But much change, perhaps most change, happens 'passively' and below awareness as we learn over our lifetimes.

By way of contrast, in evolutionary psychology, changes in species differ in being changes over almost unthinkably longer timescales, but they are in no sense consciously pursued changes or purposive adaptations. There is no purpose, choice or planning to evolution because genetic alteration is a random process.

Nature and nurture - biology and experience

A theme that appears in many areas of psychology, and one that is related to the question about how adaptable humans and non-human animals are, is that of the influence of *nature and nurture*. The behaviour of people and animals cannot be understood without taking account of the importance of their environments *as well as* their biology. You saw, for example in Chapters 1 and 9, that identity and holistic psychological functioning have a basis in biology and the body, but that social and cultural environments, and each person's idiosyncratic experiences in those environments, are also crucial. In contrast to Chapters 1 and 9, Chapters 6 and 8 are not concerned with whole people, but with processes (perception/attention and memory). Both these chapters give more emphasis to fixity and to nature than do Chapters 1 and 9. However, they too take a 'both ... and' approach and draw attention to the importance of experiences in environments for shaping mental structures and influencing cognitive processes.

■ The end of the beginning

As you close this book, we hope that you will take a moment to feel proud of yourself for having successfully completed this part of the course. We also hope that you are feeling enthused about the discipline you have chosen to study. All of us who have contributed to this book believe that psychology is an exciting, stimulating discipline of relevance to everyday life. We wish you well as you build on this foundation in order to take further the ideas and issues you have encountered so far.

Index

Acknowledgements

Book 1 Part 2

Grateful acknowledgement is made to the following sources for permission to reproduce material in this book:

Chapter 6

Figures

Figure 6.2: MacDonald, A. *et al* (2000) 'Dissociating the role of the dorsolateral prefrontal', *Science*, vol.228, 9 June 2000, American Association for the Advancement of Science; Figure 6.3: Halligan, P.W. and Marshall, J.C. (1993) 'The history and clinical presentation of neglect', *Unilateral Neglect: Clinical and Experimental Studies*, Psychology Press Limited. By kind permission of Taylor & Francis Books Limited; Figure 6.4: Gross, R. and McIlveen, R. (1997) 'The Muler-Lyer illusion', *Cognitive Psychology*. Reproduced by permission of Hodder and Stoughton Educational Ltd; Figure 6.6: Over, R. (1997) 'Explanation of geometric illusion', *Cognitive Research*. Reproduced by permission of Hodder and Stoughton Educational Ltd; Figure 6.9: Courtesy of Dr Martin Langham, University of Sussex.

Illustrations

p.10: Simons, D.J. and Levin, D.T. (1998) 'Failure to detect changes to people during real-world interaction', *Psychonomic Bulletin and Review*, vol.5, no.4, Dec 1998. Psychonomic Society Inc.

Chapter 7

Illustrations

p.64: Courtesy of The Guardian Newspapers Limited.

Chapter 8

Figures

Figure 8.3: Craik, F.I.M. and Tulving, E. (1975) 'Depth of processing and the retention of words in episodic memory', *Journal of Experimental Psychology: General*, 1975, vol.104, no.3. American Psychological Association, Inc. Copyright 1975 by the American Psychological Association. Adapted with permission; Figure 8.6: Bahrick, H.P. *et al* (1975) 'Fifty years of memory for names and faces: a cross-sectional approach',

Journal of Experimental Psychology: General, 1975, vol.104, no.1. American Psychological Association, Inc. Copyright 1975 by the American Psychological Association. Adapted with permission; Figure 8.7: Rubin, D.C. *et al* (1986) 'Autobiographical Memory', Cambridge University Press; Figure 8.8: Carter, R. (1998) 'States of mind', *Mapping the Mind*. Moonraker Designs Limited.

Tables

p.133: Loftus, E.F. and Palmer, J.C. (1974) 'Speed estimates for the verbs used in experiment 1', *Journal of Verbal Learning and Verbal Behaviour*, vol.13. Harcourt Brace & Company (Academic). Copyright © 1973 by Academic Press, Inc.

Illustrations

p.122: Copyright © Corbis/Bettman Archives; p.131: Reproduced by permission of the Department of Experimental Psychology, University of Cambridge; p.135: Copyright © EPA/PA Photos Ltd; p.154: Copyright © Novosti Photo Library.

Chapter 9

Figures

Figure 9.1: Maslow, A.H. (1987) 'Maslow's hierarchy of needs', *Motivations and Personality*. Pearson Education, Inc.

Tables

Table 9.1: Kelly, G.A. (1991) 'An example of a completed role construct repertory test', *The Psychology of Personal Constructs*. Routledge/Taylor & Francis Books Ltd.

Illustrations

p.177: Copyright © Sigmund Freud Copyrights/Mary Evans Picture Library: p.190: Copyright © Corbis/Bettman Archives; p.191: (upper left) Lucinda Douglas-Menzies, (upper right) Copyright © Hulton Archives, (lower right) Copyright © Jane Brown/Camera Press Ltd; p.192: (upper left) Courtesy of the Jewish American Archives, (upper right) Copyright © Ted Streshinsky/ Corbis, (lower left) Copyright © Sigmund Freud Copyrights/Mary Evans Picture Library: p.199: Ohio State University; p.202: Copyright © Katharina Ratheiser/Viktor Frankl Institute, Vienna; p.205: Copyright © Ann Kaplan/ Corbis/Bettman Archives; p.206: S. Nozizwe; p.213: Courtesy of Mike Csikszentmihalyi

Every effort has been made to trace all the copyright owners, but if any has been inadvertently overlooked, the publishers will be pleased to make the necessary arrangements at the first opportunity.